Online Communication and Collaboration: A Reader

Communication and collaboration via the Internet has risen to great prominence in recent years, especially with the rise of social networking, Web 2.0 and virtual worlds. Many interesting and worthwhile studies have been conducted on the technology involved and the way it is used and shaped by its user communities. From some of the more popular coverage of these interactions, it might be thought that these are new phenomena. However, they draw on a rich heritage of technologies and interactions.

Online Communication and Collaboration presents a very timely set of articles that cover a range of different perspectives upon these themes, both classic and contemporary. It is unusually broad in the range of technologies it considers – many books on these topics cover only a few forms of collaboration technology – and in considering well-established technologies as well as recent ones. It blends academic and popular articles to combine scholarly rigour with readability.

The book is divided into eight parts, covering the foundations of online communication and collaboration, together with current collaboration technologies such as wikis, instant messaging, virtual worlds and social network sites. These modern communication tools are considered in terms of their interactions but also looking back at lessons to be learnt from their technological 'ancestors'. The book also contains an extended case study of online collaboration, taking open-source software as its example.

Online Communication and Collaboration will be of relevance to a wide range of higher education courses in fields related to soft computing, information systems, cultural and media studies, and communications theory.

Helen Donelan, Karen Kear and Magnus Ramage have long experience in researching and teaching this field, and are all Lecturers or Senior Lecturers in the Communication and Systems Department at the Open University, UK.

This Reader is part of *Communication and Information Technologies* (T215), a course offered by the Open University, UK. The Reader is provided for the third block of the course: *Creating and Collaborating.*

About *Communication and Information Technologies* (T215)

Digital communication and information technologies have become fundamental to the operation of modern societies. New products and services are rapidly transforming our lives, both at work and at play. This course helps students to learn about these new developments, and to develop the understanding and skills needed to continue learning about them in the future. The course teaches the core principles on which the new technologies are built and, through a range of online and offline activities, enables students to investigate new topics and technologies.

About *Online Communication and Collaboration: A Reader*

The theme of this book is online collaboration. The book takes a broad, people-focused view of communication technology and discusses the issues raised in online collaborative environments. Readers of the book will learn about communication tools and technologies, including recent 'Web 2.0' developments such as wikis and social networking sites.

Details of T215 *Communication and Information Technologies* and other Open University courses can be obtained from the Student Registration and Enquiry Service, The Open University, PO Box 197, Milton Keynes, MK7 6BJ, United Kingdom: Telephone +44 (0) 845 300 6090, email general-enquiries@open.ac.uk.

Alternatively, you may wish to visit the Open University website at http://www.open.ac.uk, where you can learn more about the wide range of courses and packs offered at all levels by the Open University.

Online Communication and Collaboration: A Reader

Edited by
Helen Donelan, Karen Kear and
Magnus Ramage

Routledge
Taylor & Francis Group
LONDON AND NEW YORK

The Open University

First published 2010
by Routledge
2 Park Square, Milton Park, Abingdon, Oxon, OX14 4RN

Simultaneously published in the USA and Canada
by Routledge
270 Madison Avenue, New York, NY 10016

Routledge is an imprint of the Taylor & Francis Group, an informa business

Published in association with The Open University,
Walton Hall, Milton Keynes, MK7 6AA, United Kingdom

© 2010 selection and editorial material: Helen Donelan, Karen Kear and
Magnus Ramage

Typeset in Times by
Integra Software Services Pvt. Ltd, Pondicherry, India
Printed and bound in Great Britain by
CPI Antony Rowe, Chippenham, Wiltshire

British Library Cataloguing in Publication Data
A catalogue record for this book is available from the British Library

Library of Congress Cataloging in Publication Data
Online communication and collaboration : a reader / edited by Helen
Donelan, Karen Kear, and Magnus Ramage. — 1st ed.
    p.   cm.
  1. Computer networks—Social aspects.   2. Internet—Social aspects.
3. Interpersonal relations.   4. Interpersonal communication.   I. Donelan, Helen Margaret,
1973–   II. Kear, Karen Lesley, 1957–   III. Ramage, Magnus Alastair, 1970–
  HM1017.O55 2010
  303.48'33—dc22   2009029262

ISBN10: 0-415-56477-8 (hbk)
ISBN10: 0-415-56478-6 (pbk)

ISBN13: 978-0-415-56477-9 (hbk)
ISBN13: 978-0-415-56478-6 (pbk)

Contents

Figures

Tables

Acknowledgements

In conducting this project, we have been helped along the way by many people, and while we can mention only a few of them, we are deeply grateful to everyone who has encouraged us in this undertaking.

The Communication and Systems Department at the Open University was a source of great support to us, particularly members of the T215 Course Team. We would especially like to thank Judith Williams, Course Team Chair, for reading the many drafts and offering valuable advice on making them better, and Richard Smith, Course Manager, for handling copyright issues and compiling the third-party materials.

The production process of the book has been supported by a number of colleagues within the Open University. Again we can mention only a few: David Vince and Giles Clark of the university's Copublishing group; and Deana Plummer of the university's Learning and Teaching Solutions department.

We are also grateful to John Rees, the course's External Assessor, for his valuable comments that helped shape the contents of the Reader.

Editors

Helen Donelan has a background in mobile communications. Her PhD, from the University of Leeds, focused on the design and development of mobile communications systems and resulted in a number of research papers. Her current research interests are in online communication and collaboration for career development and learning. In particular, a recent project investigating women's experiences of using online social networks for career progression has resulted in several publications. She teaches in the area of communication and systems and is currently involved in developing a new undergraduate course in information and communication technologies.

Karen Kear has a background in science and software development. Her PhD, from the Open University, was concerned with design features of online communication systems. She has many years' experience of designing and writing distance learning materials, all in courses which use communication technologies. She is a fellow of the UK's Higher Education Academy, and an active researcher in the field of online communication for learning. She is a reviewer for several journals on educational technology, and has published a number of journal articles and conference papers in this area.

Magnus Ramage has a background in information systems, with a PhD from Lancaster University in the evaluation of computer-supported cooperative work. His research interests include: the lives and work of the key systems thinkers; the nature of information across multiple disciplines; the planned and unplanned evolution of information systems over time. He is co-author of the book *Systems Thinkers*, a guide to the major thinkers in the field of systems thinking, published in 2009 by Springer. He also has several journal and conference papers in the fields of information systems, systems thinking, computer science and organisation theory.

Introduction

Welcome to *Online Communication and Collaboration: A Reader*. This is a book about the way we communicate and interact together, enabled by technology. Communicating and collaborating with other people are important aspects of our working and social lives, and increasingly these activities are carried out online. For example, at work much of our communication is via email, and at home people connect with friends via social network sites such as Facebook. It is therefore important that we understand how to communicate and work well with others online. Skills in online communication and collaboration are particularly important for the modern workplace, where teams may include people in different offices, different sites or even different countries.

Online communication and collaboration has risen to prominence in recent years, especially with the rise of social networking, Web 2.0 and virtual worlds. Many interesting and worthwhile studies have been conducted on the technology involved and the way it is used and shaped by its user communities. From some of the more popular recent coverage, it might be thought that these are new phenomena. However, they draw on a rich heritage of technologies and interactions.

This Reader presents a set of articles covering a range of different perspectives on online communication and collaboration, both classic and up-to-date. It seeks to be broad in the range of technologies it considers, and to cover recent developments, together with well-established technologies. In selecting the contents for the Reader, we have sought to blend academic and more popular articles, combining scholarly rigour with readability. In a few places where we did not find a suitable third-party article, we have written original material for the Reader, grounded in our own areas of expertise.

Some of the concepts and technologies discussed in this Reader have sparked debate, and resulted in published works from both supporters and critics. We have tried to illustrate both sides of these debates, in order to clarify the different issues surrounding online communication and collaboration.

The Reader is divided into eight parts, as described below.

- *Part I: Working in groups* introduces ideas about how people can work together in groups or teams. It starts by discussing face-to-face groups, then moves on to consider groups where members communicate mainly online.
- *Part II: Collaborative technologies* looks more deeply into how collaborative work can be supported by communication technologies. It focuses on how people work together, and how this relates to the technology used.
- *Part III: Wikis and instant messaging* considers some of the technologies that can be used for communication and collaboration. It discusses a range of tools, and then looks at two – wikis and instant messaging – in more depth.
- *Part IV: Online collaboration in action* looks at a case study of online collaboration: the open source operating system Linux. It considers how Linux has been developed and maintained by an online community of volunteer software developers.
- *Part V: Online communities* considers the concept of a 'community' and whether communities can exist online. It introduces some theories of online communication, and relates these to the development of community.
- *Part VI: Virtual worlds* looks at communication within 3D 'virtual worlds'. It starts by discussing the original text-based virtual worlds, called MUDs, then moves on to consider modern virtual worlds such as *Second Life*.
- *Part VII: Web 2.0* explores what is meant by the expression 'Web 2.0'. It considers issues such as mass participation and user-created content, and how these relate to what is on the Web, how it is used and the impact on society.
- *Part VIII: Social networking* discusses social network sites, such as Facebook, MySpace and Twitter. It looks at the evolution of social network sites, and the ways in which they can connect people together.

We believe that the readings we have selected are thought-provoking and informative. We hope that by collecting them in this Reader we can contribute to further understanding and improved practice of online communication and collaboration.

Part 1

Working in groups

Introduction to Part I

In Part I we will consider some of the research and theory of how people work in groups. This encompasses aspects relating to individual group members, the group as a whole, and the task that the group is carrying out. The readings in Part I cover all three of these aspects. We start by looking at how groups work in face-to-face environments (on which most of the research and theory is based) but later move on to consider online environments.

Much of the literature on the individual aspect of group work is about the roles people take on in a team. The word 'role' expresses the idea that different people behave differently in a group situation. The most well-known framework for team roles was developed by Meredith Belbin (Belbin, 1981). Belbin found that a good team has a balance of the different roles. The first reading in Part I explains Belbin's ideas and the different team roles. It is from the book 'Group Communication' (Hartley, 1997). As Hartley points out, researchers other than Belbin have also developed models for the roles that people take on in a team.

In relation to the group as a whole, there has been considerable research on how group interactions change over time. Many researchers claim that groups go through different stages of development, and the most well-known theory of group development is that of Bruce Tuckman (Tuckman, 1965). He claimed that groups move through four stages in sequence: forming, storming, norming and performing. The second reading in Part I (Jaques and Salmon, 2007) discusses these ideas. It begins by considering a range of aspects of group working, such as group maintenance activities, participation and leadership. It then moves on to present several models of how groups progress through different stages. The first model discussed is very like that of Tuckman, but has a further stage at the end. The final model relates to online groups in an educational setting. The reading uses the term 'e-moderator' to mean the facilitator of an online forum, and 'e-tivity', for an online educational activity.

The remainder of Part I focuses on online group work, and how this can be carried out successfully. As Jaques and Salmon (2007) point out, when working on any group task, it is important to actively manage the process. With the additional challenge of collaborating online, it is vital to plan, schedule and monitor the work. The third reading in Part I (Einon, 2010) discusses the issues of planning, scheduling and review within the context of online group work. The article stresses the importance of creating milestones for the work, and monitoring progress towards these milestones.

Using online communication tools, group members can be physically remote from each other but can still interact. Synchronous communication tools, such as chat rooms or instant messaging, require users to be online at the same time. However, members of a group are likely to have different time schedules, so 'asynchronous' tools, such as discussion forums, are usually needed. The distinction between synchronous and asynchronous communication is an important one, and is explored further in Part III, and elsewhere in this Reader. Asynchronous communication tools have significant benefits in allowing people to communicate when it is most convenient for them. However, problems can arise when collaborating asynchronously. These ideas are explored in the final reading in Part I (Kear, 2010) which focuses on issues raised when collaboration is undertaken via discussion forums.

Working as part of a group is rarely easy, and when most or all of the group's communication is online, it is a significant challenge. It is therefore valuable to understand how people work in groups, and to consider how these ideas might apply in an online context. The readings in Part I discuss some of the aspects that need to be considered when working in an online group. If group members have an understanding of these issues, the process of online collaboration should be more effective and more enjoyable.

References

Belbin, R.M. (1981) *Management Teams: Why they Succeed or Fail*, Oxford: Heinemann.

Einon, G. (2010) 'Managing computer-supported collaboration', in Donelan, H., Kear, K. and Ramage, M. (eds.) *Online Communication and Collaboration: A Reader,* London: Routledge, pp. 26–29.

Hartley, P. (1997) *Group Communication*, London: Routledge, pp. 120–127.

Jaques, D. and Salmon, G. (2007) *Learning in Groups*, London: Routledge, pp. 32–44.

Kear, K. (2010) 'Collaboration via online discussion forums: issues and approaches', in Donelan, H., Kear, K. and Ramage, M. (eds.) *Online Communication and Collaboration: A Reader,* London: Routledge, pp. 30–33.

Tuckman, B. (1965) 'Developmental sequence in small groups', *Psychological Bulletin,* 63, pp. 384–399.

Who does what?

Structure and communication

Peter Hartley

[...]

R. M. Belbin and team roles

The foreword to Meredith Belbin's first major text on management teams suggests that it is 'the most important single contribution of the past decade to our understanding of how human organisations work' on the grounds that the management team is critical to the success of every organisation and that our 'knowledge of what makes a successful team is tiny'.[1] Of course, nearly twenty years after this was written, there is now much more research on team dynamics. But Belbin's work still demands special attention as it was derived from many years' systematic observation of groups and still provides one of the most accessible and comprehensive analyses of team roles which can be applied to a range of groups.

Over a period of around ten years, Belbin and colleagues observed several hundred teams of managers engaged in management games and exercises, using an observation scheme which was developed from Bales's IPA [...] They administered questionnaires and personality tests and manipulated the membership of the teams to see how successful different combinations were. The result of this research was a comprehensive model of team-building which is based on the following observations:

- that the behaviours of team members are organised in a limited number of team roles which are independent of the members' technical expertise or formal status
- that managers tend to consistently adopt one or two of these team roles
- that these preferred team roles are linked to personality characteristics
- that the effectiveness of the team depends upon the combination of team roles adopted by the team members

One of the best ways of evaluating Belbin's theory is to try it for yourself. [...][2]

From Hartley, P. (1997) *Group Communication*, London: Routledge, pp. 120–127.

The team roles

Belbin identifies eight team roles and their main contribution to the group is given in Table 1.1. He also links each role strongly to a given personality type which I have not reproduced here as I think it implies too static a picture of team dynamics.

The titles in brackets are the labels used in Belbin's earlier book. He renamed roles mainly because managers using the system felt that the original labels were inappropriate in some ways. For example, chair was considered too sexist and also to imply too high a status. So chair became co-ordinator. Company worker was considered to have rather negative connotations and to be too low in status, and so it became implementer.[3]

Some implications/observations

Perhaps the most fundamental implication of this approach is that all roles are valuable, unlike other approaches which suggest that some roles are destructive or negative. However, my own experience in using the questionnaire is that, even with the revised titles, individuals do feel that some roles are considerably more 'attractive' than others. People feel pleased to be identified as a plant but not so satisfied at being an implementer.

Another major implication is the suggestion that groups can develop strategies to adjust any perceived imbalance. For example, one of the illustrations Belbin uses in his first book is the management team who discovered after doing the questionnaire that they were all strong shapers. They realised that, left to their natural devices, they would all be pushing so hard to support their own points of view that the group would never achieve anything and be locked in perpetual conflict.

Table 1.1 Belbin roles and their main contribution to the group

Role	Main contribution to the group
Co-ordinator (chair)	Organises and co-ordinates
	Keeps team focused on main objectives
	Keeps other members involved
Team leader (shaper)	Initiates and leads from the front
	Challenges complacency or ineffectiveness
	Pushes and drives towards the goal
Innovator (plant)	Provides new and creative ideas
Monitor-evaluator	Provides dispassionate criticism
Team worker	Promotes good team spirit
Completer	Checks things are completed
	Monitors progress against deadlines
Implementer (company worker)	Practical and hard-working
	Focuses on the practical nitty-gritty
Resource investigator	Makes contacts outside the group

As a result, they worked out a number of strategies which they used successfully to make the most of their creative energies and minimise the chances of disruptive conflict. They elected the cleverest person as the plant. He was then allowed to select the chair on the basis that a good, compatible chair/plant combination is often associated with success. The plant was sent off to think at regular intervals which allowed the other members to get on with business. They also adopted very clear decision-making rules which avoided lengthy argument, voting on every issue.

Another important implication is best expressed as a question – using Belbin's role descriptions, who is the leader? Is it the chair or the shaper or is this [a] notion of dual leadership? [...] Belbins's answer to this is that it depends on the situation: 'just as there are horses for courses, so there are leaders for teams'.[4] Where the situation demands both 'skilful use of the reserves of the group with the effective control of team members' then the strong chair is the most effective leader. Where the situation needs someone to instigate action and drag the team along with them then the shaper is more effective. Deciding what the situation requires needs a detailed knowledge of the team members and the job or tasks facing them. Belbin also suggests that a tougher and more intelligent chair can provide effective leadership to the Apollo or think-tank type of group discussed below.

Belbin's recipe for success

Based on his observations of successful teams over the years, Belbin offers a recipe for an effective team which is a combination of the following qualities:

The right person in the chair

This means that the person who is carrying out the functions of chairing the group meetings has the appropriate personality and skills, i.e. they are trusted by the other members and know how to control the discussion without dominating it.

One strong plant in the group

By a strong plant, Belbin means someone who is both creative and clever and who has the right types of creativity and interests for the task in hand.

Fair spread in mental abilities

The good news for us lesser mortals is that a group composed completely of very clever people often if not invariably fails as a team (what Belbin christened the Apollo syndrome). Such a group spends so much time analysing and criticising each other's ideas that they do not achieve much. What is needed is a spread of abilities, including the clever plant and competent chair.

Wide team-role coverage

This increases the range of the team and can also mean that there is no unnecessary friction in which different members 'compete' for the same role.

Good match between attributes and responsibilities

This is where members are given roles and jobs which fit their abilities and personal characteristics.

Adjustment to realisation of imbalance

Like the group of shapers who adjusted a few paragraphs ago, this is where the group can recognise any gaps in its make-up and can adopt strategies to make good these problems.

How far can we generalise Belbin's results?

There are a number of important issues which need to be resolved before we can confidently apply Belbin's results to every group everywhere:

Are the behaviour descriptions valid?

Can we be happy that the descriptions of behaviour used by Belbin accurately capture the essential features of team roles? My conclusion (supported by my own observations of teams and groups) is that he does offer valid summaries of consistent patterns of behaviour in groups. Unfortunately there is not yet enough independent research on Belbin's system to provide categorical support.[5]

Does Belbin's questionnaire give a reliable measure of the roles?

Despite the age and extensive use of the questionnaire, there seems to be surprisingly little work on its reliability and validity, apart from Belbin's own research. Adrian Furnham and colleagues searched the Social Science Citation Index from 1982 to 1992 and found no studies at all. They then conducted their own analysis and suggested that 'there remains some doubt, from a psychometric point of view, whether he has been able to provide a reliable measure of these role preferences'.[6] Unfortunately they did not use the standard method of scoring and were immediately criticised by Belbin who now uses Interplace, a computer-based system which integrates self-reports and observations. This system is only available on a commercial basis.[7] But, of course, this does not allay possible doubts over the original questionnaire.

However, more recently, Victor Dulewicz[8] has done further statistical analysis on managers' scores on both Belbin's role and the associated personality profiles. When these scores were correlated with bosses' ratings of managers' performances, he found that the results were in line with the role descriptions offered by Belbin's ratings which confirms that the role preferences seem to be both valid and reliable measures. Dulewicz's paper also provides a good summary of the roles and how they were developed.

Weren't Belbin's studies done on limited samples and in a limited context?

The immediate answer to this has to be yes. For example, in the research discussed in the first book, Belbin notes that the management teams were predominantly male and from a very limited range of ethnic backgrounds. Similarly, there was a possible limited mix of social and cultural backgrounds. Without much more comprehensive information on different types and compositions of groups we must be wary of over-generalising.

What are the consequences of labelling?

Belbin recommends that groups should complete the questionnaire and then discuss their respective profiles. This means that each member will be 'labelled' with their results. Everyone in the group will know their own profile and everyone else's. But what are the psychological consequences of this process? How does this new self-knowledge affect you and others? This does not seem to have been investigated as yet (and it is also very difficult to investigate). Suppose you do the Belbin questionnaire and come out as a strong plant – what does this do to your self-image and expectations? It could make you over-confident in your own creative abilities. What if the rest of the team come to rely on you to provide all the ideas? Will this more 'pressurised' situation feel the same as before?

What if your perceptions do not match others' perceptions of you?

Belbin discusses this problem in his second book. On the basis of work he has done comparing self and others' perceptions, he suggests that when individuals complete his questionnaire they can end up with one of three profiles:

- coherent, where the individual's profile matches the perceptions of others
- discordant, where there is a mismatch. The individual's perception directly conflicts with the perceptions of others. In this case, individuals need to take action either by reassessing their self-conception or by reconsidering how they project themselves to others
- confused, where there is also a mismatch but it is inconsistent both with self and others' perceptions. In this case, individuals need to reconsider what roles they wish to take on in groups

So can you trust your score?

Given the questions raised above, if you do the Belbin questionnaire, the obvious answer is to check any results by discussing your profile with friends who know how you operate in groups and who you can trust to give an honest summary of your strengths and weaknesses. You may also like to talk to people who see you in very different groups to see if the same picture emerges.

Alternatives to Belbin

This chapter has focused on Belbin as his work is both accessible and widely used. There are other schemes which also suggest that group effectiveness is based upon successful co-ordination of specific member roles.

One well-known system in the UK has been developed by Margerison and McCann.[9] This Team Management System (TMS) offers a range of tools and methods including a questionnaire designed to measure individual work preferences on dimensions such as decision-making and relationships, and an analysis of the functional demands of given work roles. They also define the eight key roles for an effective team in ways which invite comparison with Belbin. At least some of these roles share common attributes: Belbin's 'shaper' seems similar to the TMS role 'thruster organiser', Belbin's 'plant' seems similar to TMS 'creator innovator'. TMS provides managers who complete their questionnaire with a report which identifies their preferred roles. There are also important differences from Belbin – teams must be properly coordinated and they identify a set of skills known as 'linking skills' which can be used by all the team members.

As with Belbin, TMS offer examples and evidence which suggest that organisations have used the scheme effectively. To date, there does not seem to have been an independent comparison of the two systems in terms of their relative usefulness.

[...]

Notes

1 The foreword by Antony Jay introduced Belbin's first major book on team roles: Belbin, R. M. (1981) *Management Teams: Why they succeed or fail*. Oxford: Heinemann.
2 See pages 153–8 at the back of Belbin's book, note 1.
3 These changes and other problems of terminology are discussed in his second book: Belbin, R. M. (1993) *Team Roles at Work*. Oxford: Butterworth Heinemann.
4 See page 62 of Belbin's second book, note 3.
5 Some interesting studies are now emerging, for example: Senior, B. (1995) Team roles and team performance: Is there really a link? Paper presented to the Annual Conference of the Occupational Division and Section, University of Warwick.
6 You will need a fairly sophisticated understanding of statistics to follow the debate between Belbin and his critics. The quote is from page 256 of the Journal: Furnham, A., Steele, H. and Pendleton, D. (1993) A psychometric assessment of the Belbin

Team-Role Self-Perception Inventory. *Journal of Occupational and Organizational Psychology*, 66, 245–57; Belbin, R.M. (1993) A reply to the Belbin Team-Role Self-Perception Inventory by Furnham, Steele and Pendleton. *Journal of Occupational and Organizational Psychology*, 66, 259–60; Furnham, A., Steele, H. and Pendleton, D. (1993) A response to Dr Belbin's reply. *Journal of Occupational and Organizational Psychology*, 66, 261.

7 Interplace is described in: Belbin Associates (1988) Interplace: Matching people to jobs. Cambridge.

8 Again you will need statistical knowledge to follow the detail in Dulewicz's paper: Dulewicz, V. (1995) A validation of Belbin's team roles from 16 PF and OPQ using bosses' ratings of competence. *Journal of Occupational and Organizational Psychology*, 68, 81–99.

9 For details of the TMS approach, see: McCann, R. and Margerison, C. (1989) Managing high-performance teams. *Training and Development Journal*, 11, 53–60.

Studies of group behaviour

David Jaques and Gilly Salmon

[...]

Social and task dimensions

It is easy to assume that groups differ substantially in their nature: informal social groups like coffee circles appear to have few rules or procedures and certainly no specific goals. Their members belong for the emotional satisfaction they get from being with people they like and enjoy. Membership in these groups is voluntary and tends to be fairly homogeneous. The success of the social group is measured in terms of how enjoyable it is.

Other groups, however, such as committees, working parties, staff meetings and discussion groups, usually have goals (though not always as shared and explicit as they might be), and more or less formal rules and procedures. The membership tends to be more heterogeneous – based on whatever is required to do the work – and sometimes brought together out of compulsion or sense of duty more than free choice. The success of the task group is measured in terms of how much work it achieves.

However further study of these apparently different kinds of group indicates that they have more similarities than differences – the social or task dimensions exist for all groups though they may be in different proportions. As Knowles and Knowles (1972) observe:

> [M]ost groups need the social dimension to provide emotional involvement, morale, interest, and loyalty; and the task dimension to provide stability, purpose, direction and a sense of accomplishment. Without the dimension of work, members may become dissatisfied and feel guilty because they are not accomplishing anything; without the dimension of friendship, members may feel that the group is cold, unfriendly, and not pleasant to be with.

From Jaques, D. and Salmon, G. (2007) *Learning in Groups: A handbook for face-to-face and online environments*, London: Routledge, pp. 32–44.

Group maintenance and group task functions

Group functions have been classified thus:

1 *group-building and maintenance roles* – those which contribute to building relationships and cohesiveness among the membership (the social dimension);
2 *group task roles* – those which help the group to do its work (the task dimension).

The first set of functions is required for the group to maintain itself as a group; the second set, for the locomotion of the group toward its goals. For example, some *group-building functions* are:

- *encouraging* – being friendly, warm, responsive to others, praising others and their ideas, agreeing with and accepting the contributions of others.
- *mediating* – harmonising, conciliating differences in points of view, making compromises.
- *gate-keeping* – trying to make it possible for another member to make a contribution by saying, 'We haven't heard from Jim yet', or suggesting limited talking – time for everyone so that all will have a chance to be heard.
- *standard-setting* – expressing standards for the group to use in choosing its subject matter or procedures, rules of conduct, ethical values.
- *following* – going along with the group, somewhat passively accepting the ideas of others, serving as an audience during group discussion, being a good listener.
- *relieving tension* – draining off negative feeling by jesting or throwing oil on troubled waters, diverting attention from unpleasant to pleasant matters.

And the following are some *task functions*:

- *initiating* – suggesting new ideas or a changed way of looking at the group problem or goal, proposing new activities.
- *information-seeking* – asking for relevant facts or authoritative information.
- *information-giving* – providing relevant facts or authoritative information or relating personal experience pertinently to the group task.
- *opinion-giving* – stating a pertinent belief or opinion about something the group is considering.
- *clarifying* – probing for meaning and understanding, restating something the group is considering.
- *elaborating* – building on a previous comment, enlarging on it, giving examples.
- *coordinating* – showing or clarifying the relationships among various ideas, trying to pull ideas and suggestions together.

- *orienting* – defining the progress of the discussion in terms of the group's goals, raising questions about the direction the discussion is taking.
- *testing* – checking with the group to see if it is ready to make a decision or to take some action.
- *summarising* – reviewing the content of past discussion.

(Knowles and Knowles 1972, p. 54)

All the functions are clearly not needed in the same measure all the time and it can happen that any one of them used at the wrong time can interfere with the progress of the group. When a group is not functioning effectively, it will probably be because nobody is performing one or more of the functions listed above that is crucial at that point for the group to progress. It is also typical in any group that some of its members will tend to perform certain functions more readily and effectively than others and there is a risk that they might become typecast in that role, rather than the various functions being shared and performed as and when the group needs them and individual members can recognise the need for them.

Group members may also exhibit behaviour which does not help the group to progress in achieving its goals. This 'non-functional role', as it is commonly called is likely to satisfy only the personal needs of the person in question. Non-functional roles might include:

- *blocking* – interfering with the progress of the group by going off on a tangent, citing personal experiences unrelated to the group's problem, arguing too much on a point the rest of the group has resolved, rejecting ideas without consideration, preventing a vote.
- *aggressing* – criticising or blaming others, showing hostility toward the group or some individual without relation to what has happened in the group, attacking the motives of others, deflating the ego or status of others.
- *seeking recognition* – attempting to call attention to oneself by excessive talking, extreme ideas, boasting, boisterousness.
- *special pleading* – introducing or supporting ideas related to one's own pet concerns or philosophies beyond reason, attempting to speak for 'the grass roots', 'the housewife', 'the common man', and so on.
- *withdrawing* – acting indifferent or passive, resorting to excessive formality, doodling, whispering to others.
- *dominating* – trying to assert authority in manipulating the group or certain members of it by 'pulling rank', giving directions authoritatively, interrupting contributions of others.

(Knowles and Knowles 1972, pp. 55–7)

Other members of the group will probably feel irritated or at least uncomfortable with such behaviours, and react with silence, hostility or rejection. Yet [it] may of course be difficult to pinpoint some of the categories simply, because a non-functional behaviour may be seen in different ways by different members and almost certainly by the person themselves. But [it] is reasonable to assert that any group that is able to recognise these behaviours for what they are and sees them as a symptom of somebody's unmet personal needs, and to constructively deal with them, is going to be able to devote itself more effectively to the group-building functions.

The effects of group size

The tendency for many of the above behaviours to become dominant can increase with group size [...]. Even in small discussion groups participants contribute unequally and there is little doubt that the scope for participation decreases exponentially as numbers increase as the following graphs clearly indicate.

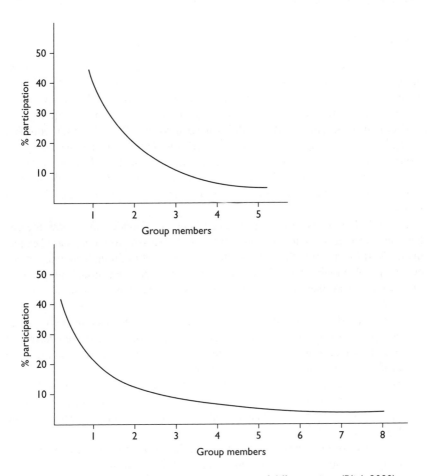

Figure 2.1 Distribution of participation in groups of different sizes (Bligh 2000)

In the first diagram, which shows the percentage of contributions in a group of five, one member – the highest contributor – has made over 40 per cent of the contributions while another – the lowest contributor, has made only 7 per cent. In the second diagram, a group of eight, the difference becomes more marked. The highest contributor has maintained a similar level of contribution but the lowest six have each made only 3–8 per cent of the contributions. The implication of this is that larger groups need more structure organised for them if they are to function effectively within the usual time boundaries; either the leader will have to take a firmer hand and set up sub-groups with specified tasks, or some other form of leadership will emerge.

In online groups, size is a significant interaction variable in achieving discussion to enhance academic learning. Discussion in smaller groups of six to eight creates more evidence and experience of higher levels of knowledge construction compared to larger groups if there are effective task-centred e-tivities and structures in place (Schellens and Valcke 2004).

Leadership

Thus far, in looking at group functions, we have made little distinction between those relating to leaders compared with those of other members. Leadership can happen in different ways: a leader may be designated prior to the group's starting or may assume such a role because of his or her external position; such leaders may lack many of the qualities needed for handling the often complex dynamics of the group. Leaders may also emerge naturally or be elected by the group. What most commonly happens, whether or not the role is allocated is that some form of leadership rotates within the group according to task and personal interest at a particular time and is thus a function of the interaction of such variables.

The style (real or perceived) of leadership can profoundly affect both the climate and the achievement of a group. In a classic series of laboratory-based experiments Kurt Lewin and others studied the influences of different leadership styles on group behaviour. They tested three types of leader behaviour: 'autocratic', 'democratic', and 'laissez-faire'. The effects were clear and dramatic:

- *Autocratically led groups* were more dependent on the leader and less considerate in their peer relationships, engaged in scapegoating, and even destroyed what they had, as a group, constructed. They were however quicker and more productive in the achievement of their task than the other groups.
- *Democratically led groups*, though slower in getting going, showed more initiative, friendliness and responsibility, supported each other, expressed greater satisfaction and continued the work in the absence of the leader.
- *Laissez-faire groups* produced less work than autocratically and democratically led groups, spent more time talking about what they should be doing,

played around and experienced more aggression than the democratic group but less than the authoritarian.

The autocrat was the least liked of the leaders, with the democrat by far the most popular. This study has been substantiated by most of the research conducted over the past 50 years to the effect that, though some situations may require autocratic and others laissez-faire leadership, in most normal situations, groups thrive best when the leadership functions are democratically shared among the members of the group. However, under certain conditions, such as when urgent decisions are needed or when the group is large, autocratic leadership may be more effective. Where the commitment of members to a decision and its implementation is paramount, democratic groups are valued.

Such understandings are firmly substantiated in more recent work by Galanes (2003) who conducted interviews with 23 'effective group leaders' and participants on what they believed was important in leading groups. The following five categories emerged from her research:

1   Establishing the intention for the overall project

- Having vision and making it clear.
- Making sure members know the ultimate goal.
- Motivating members to want to be part of the group at the outset; helping people buy in to the project; inspiring members to support the vision, mission, goals.
- Having a clear sense of purpose, knowing where you want the team to go.

2   Building the team and developing a positive group culture

- Understanding group dynamics and using them to create a warm, supportive, inclusive climate.
- Making sure people know each other; knowing that members need to get something out of the group and working to make sure individual needs are met.
- Valuing people as individuals; selecting the members with the right kinds of skills and attitudes; making sure they feel valued, wanted and respected.
- Creating an atmosphere where people feel safe to contribute, that the leader will support members in expressing themselves and stop behaviours that are counterproductive to this.
- Having a meeting that is fun, light-hearted, enjoyable; having a good sense of humour.
- Allowing a graceful way for non-productive members to leave the team.

3 Monitoring and managing the team's interactions during meetings

- Trusting in the group process and the group's expertise.
- Monitoring to check participation levels, checking in with members between meetings.
- Building consensus.
- Keeping members informed about things that affect them.
- Supporting questioning, disagreement and conflict, but not personal attacks.
- Asking the right kinds of questions.
- Using the right kind of leadership for the situation.
- Using appropriate techniques to achieve goals.

4 Managing the group's task and keeping the group focused

- Agreeing and being committed to the leadership task.
- Reducing any uncertainty in the group about the overall task, having a clear picture of it and communicating it to the group, constantly paying attention to the group's progress towards the goal.
- Keeping the group task-focused and moving towards its goal.
- Paying attention to process and structure.
- Preparing for meetings, getting ready for meetings.
- Organising the group's work, dividing up the tasks, making sure everyone has something to do, delegating, following up.
- Managing the group's time.
- Removing obstacles to the group's work and progress.
- Evaluating the group's process and progress, looking for ways to improve, asking members to do the same.

5 Communication behaviours and personal characteristics

- Modelling the behaviour s/he wants others to show; admitting mistakes, not dominating discussion; being less of a contributor than encourager of others.
- Inspiring confidence in others.
- Personal characteristics: self knowledge, self monitoring, passion, integrity, honesty, work ethic, knowledgeable about the issue.
- Exhibiting 'we' rather than 'I' behaviour, putting the team first.
- Listening and demonstrating the value of listening.
- Exhibiting effective interpersonal communication skills, making it easy for others to talk to her/him.
- Doing things to help themselves, e.g. calming affirmations, introduction.

Groups in motion

Much of what we have been discussing so far has been concerned with the variables that make up a group – its properties and the membership and leadership functions. But groups are thriving and developing organisms which never stand still. Groups move both as a unit, and through the interaction of the various elements within them. A change in structure [...] can affect participation which in turn may affect communication, norms, leadership and so on. Figure 2.2 from Guirdham (1990) shows a useful visual summary of the generic stages with the different emphases on individual, group and task needs indicated by the size of the circles.

Stages of group development

It may be informative nevertheless to look at one approach in more detail. Of the various schema that have been proposed, the following, based on Lawrence in Bligh (1986), probably best fits [...] psychodynamic orientations [...].

Forming

When a number of people come together for the first time to form a group there is an initial concern with the nature of the task: what has to be done and by what

Stage of group development	Individual needs	Group needs	Task needs
Forming	◯	◯	○
Storming	◯	◯	○
Norming	◯	◯	◯
Performing	○	◯	◯
Ending	○	○	◯

Figure 2.2 Relative influence of individual, group and task needs on group members' behaviour at different stages of group development
Based on Guirdham (1990) *Interpersonal Skills at Work*, Prentice Hall

time and with what resources? Group members will equally be checking out what is appropriate behaviour and adjusting accordingly. There is also, at this stage, a strong dependence on any authority in the group as a form of counterbalance to the deeper question which is about 'Why am I here?' or 'Do I really want to be here'? This need to create a sense of self in the group is labelled 'self-lodging' by Denzin (1969): 'If valued portions of self are not lodged, recognised and reciprocated, a dissatisfaction concerning the encounter is likely to be sensed. If self-lodging doesn't take place successfully, the person may fail to take up a rational standpoint.' This supports the paradoxical hypothesis that a group cannot come together until each member has established her or his own separate individuality.

Storming

This stage typically includes conflict and an expression of interpersonal hostility within the group. It is as if any of the uncertainties and deeper emotions from the previous stage have become unfrozen and or projected onto other people of the group. Bennis, Benne and Chin (1985) describe it as a stage of counter-dependence on authority. Differences are asserted and seen as all or nothing, for or against. Issues of personal freedom versus the group authority and leaders of opposing arguments collect followers.

Norming

Emphasis is now placed on the mutual concerns and interrelationships. The freedom/authority conflict of storming has been resolved. Behaviours are now turned to listening, asking opinions, building on others, etc. Personal norms are replaced by group norms, common goals are agreed, ground rules may be established and a sense of open collaboration is created, but not without some compromise on the freedom experienced in Stage 2, and some negotiation.

Performing

Now members settle into, and are reasonably satisfied with, functional roles. Schroder and Harvey (1963) called this positive interdependence with simultaneous autonomy and neutrality. The group acquires a distinct sense of itself as a culture. One role which the group will probably decide is that concerned with its continuity, which naturally leads to the fifth stage.

Informing

In this the final, and sometimes ignored, phase the group starts to give voice to the outside world, communicating, for instance, with other groups, and agreeing how it will further its work.

Lawrence points out that the above stages depend upon certain assumptions which may or may not exist: that the group manages to survive the *storming* stage and does in fact move from stage to stage until they achieve their goal without falling apart; and that problems of outside hierarchy, which might distort the sense of shared purpose, are not imported into the group.

A seven-stage model of group development

Many of the classic studies of group development have involved group leaders who took a passive or non-directive role and did not directly intervene in the group process (Johnson and Johnson 1987), and this contrasts with the typical tutor-led group in higher education. They propose the following seven-stage model for learning groups where there is a leader with clear responsibility for the effective functioning of the group.

1 Defining and structuring procedures

At the first meeting the group will expect the tutor/leader to explain what is expected of them, what the plan and purpose of the meetings is and how the group is going to operate (whether or not this [is] fulfilled is of course a matter of choice). Typically with a learning group, the tutor will clarify the task, explain procedures, and generally set up the group in readiness for its work together.

2 Conforming to procedures and getting acquainted

As the group gets used to the procedures and norms of the group they also become more familiar and relaxed with each other. The group is still dependent on the tutor for direction and they are happy to conform according to the process norms of the group whether explicitly or implicitly expressed. They do not yet feel a personal commitment to the group's goals or to each other.

3 Recognising mutuality and building trust

The group members begin to recognise their interdependence and to build a sense of cooperation and trust. They internalise the sense that group learning is a collaborative venture and participate actively in discussions. There is a feeling of mutual support and trust.

4 Rebelling and differentiating

This stage represents a pulling back from the previous two as members start to resist the responsibilities they had apparently accepted and become counter-dependent, contravening many of the group-learning procedures. Sometimes this may mean returning to a more passive, minimal effort role and forgetting the previously held cooperative ethos. Despite its apparent negativity this stage is important for members in establishing interpersonal boundaries and a sense of autonomy which can lead to a stronger, because self-owned, collaboration. Johnson and Johnson suggest that tutors should regard this rebellion and conflict as a natural and 'deal with both in an open and accepting way'. They recommend:

- Not tightening control and trying to force conformity: reasoning and negotiating.
- Confronting and problem-solving.
- Mediating conflicts while helping to underpin autonomy and individuality.
- Working towards participants taking ownership of procedures and committing themselves to each other's success.

'Coordinating a learning group is like teaching a child to ride a bicycle', they say. You have to run alongside to prevent the child from falling off, giving the child space and freedom to learn how to balance on his or her own.

5   Committing to and taking ownership for the goals, procedures and other members

The group becomes 'our' group, not the tutor's. The group norms of cooperation become internalised and no longer have to be externally imposed: the members are no longer dependent on the tutor as the driving force and find support and help from each other. Friendships develop.

6   Functioning maturely and productively

A sense of collaborative identity develops as the group matures into an effective working unit. Group members learn to operate in different ways in order to achieve group goals and can readily alternate attention between task and maintenance concerns. At this stage they can usually cope with any problems that arise in the group without the help of the tutor who in turn takes on the role of a consultant and resource to the group. Labour is divided according to expertise, members ask for and accept help from each other and leadership is shared among the members.

Johnson and Johnson remark that many discussion groups do not reach this stage either because the tutor does not have the ability to establish cooperative interdependence or group members do not collectively possess the necessary skills to function in this way. Part of the tutor's job is therefore to ensure that group members are acquiring the skills they need to progress to this stage.

7   Terminating

Every group has to come to an end and its members have to move on. The more cohesive and mature a group has become, the more sadness will accompany its ending for both members and tutor. The last meeting must deal with this as a recognisable problem and not avoid it as they leave the group to move on to future experiences.

Most groups, if they are developing effectively, [will] move fairly quickly through the first five stages, devote most time and energy to the mature and productive stage, and then terminate quickly. The skill of the tutor in handing over the 'perceived ownership' of the group goals and procedures as it moves from the first two stages through the rebellion is of course critical.

The five-stage framework for e-groups

Online learning has given specific attention to what the learners should contribute in order to participate effectively. For an online process to be successful, participants need to be supported through a structured developmental process. This involves designing in advance for their participants, and then leading them gently through, during the time the interaction is running. The Salmon five-stage model provides an example of how participants can benefit from increasing skill and comfort from working online and networking with each other, and what the e-moderator needs to do at each stage to help them achieve this success.

Paralleling Johnson and Johnson's seven-stage model, and specific to online computer conferencing, the model (Salmon 2003), is based on and developed from the experience of participants in early computer-mediated conferences (Salmon 2004) (see Figure 2.3). It shows how to motivate online participation, to build learning through appropriate online activities (e-tivities) and to pace e-learners through online courses.

Arranging gradually more demanding participative and interactive tasks provides the action base for the model. We call these 'E-tivities' [...].

Individual access and the induction of participants to online learning are essential prerequisites for online conference participation (stage 1 at the base of the flight of steps). Stage 2 involves individual participants establishing their online identities and then finding others with whom to interact. At stage 3, participants engage in mutual exchange of information. Up to and including stage 3 a form [...] of cooperation occurs whereby each person supports the others participants' goals. At stage 4, course related discussions develop and the interaction becomes more collaborative. At stage 5, participants look for more benefits from the system to help them achieve more personal goals and reflect on the learning processes.

Each stage requires the participants to master certain technical skills (shown in the bottom left of each step). Each stage calls for different e-moderator skills (shown in the right top of each step). The 'interactivity bar' running along the right of the flight of steps suggests the intensity of interactivity that you can expect between the participants at each stage. At first, at stage 1, they interact only with one or two others. After stage 2 the number of others with whom they interact,

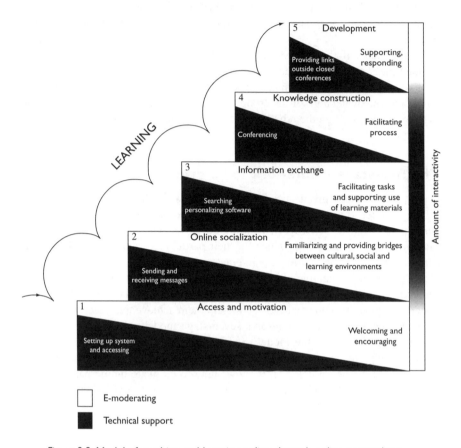

Figure 2.3 Model of teaching and learning online through online networking

and the frequency, gradually increases, although stage 5 often returns to [...] more individual pursuits.

Given appropriate technical support, e-moderation and a purpose for taking part, nearly all participants will progress through these stages of use. There will however be very different responses to how much time they need at each stage before progressing. The model applies to all software. The chief benefit of using the model to design a learning process is that you know how participants are likely to exploit the system at each stage and you can avoid common pitfalls. The results should be higher participation rates and increased participant satisfaction. E-moderators who understand the model and apply it should enjoy their work and find that their work runs smoothly.

Note here that this model is one that is much more accessible to unobtrusive monitoring than might be achieved face-to-face.

[...]

References

Bennis, W., Benne, K. and Chin, R. (1985) *The Planning of Change*, New York: Holt, Rinehart and Winston.

Bligh, D. (1986) *Teach Thinking by Discussion*, Society for Research into Higher Education, London: NFER Nelson.

Bligh, D. (2000) *What's the Point of Discussion?*, Exeter: Intellect Books.

Denzin, W. (1969) Symbolic interaction and ethnomethodology: Proposed synthesis, *American Sociological Review*, 34, December: 922–34.

Galanes, G. (2003) In their own words: An exploratory study of bona fide group leaders, *Small Group Research* 43(6): 741–70.

Guirdham, M. (1990) *Interpersonal Skills at Work*, Englewood Cliffs, NJ: Prentice Hall.

Johnson, D. W. and Johnson, F. P. (1987) *Joining Together: Group theory and group skills*, Englewood Cliffs, NJ: Prentice Hall.

Knowles, H. C. and Knowles, M. (1972) *Introduction to Group Dynamics*, Chicago, IL: Association Press/Folletts.

Salmon, G. K. (2003) E-moderating in higher education, in *Distance Learning and University Effectiveness: Changing educational paradigms for online learning*, ed. C. Howard, K. Schenk and R. Discenza, Idea Group Inc.

Salmon, G. (2004) *E-moderating: The key to teaching and learning online*, 2nd edn, London: Routledge Falmer.

Schellens, T. and Valcke, M. (2004) Fostering knowledge construction in university students through asynchronous discussion groups, *Computers and Education* 46, November: 349–70.

Schroder, H. and Harvey, O. (1963) Conceptual organisation and group structure, in *Motivation and Social Interaction*, ed. O. Harvey, New York: Ronald Press.

Reading 3

Managing computer-supported collaboration

Geoffrey Einon

What is a group?

A group can be defined as two or more people who have:

- a common task or objective;
- an awareness of the group's identity and boundaries;
- a level of interdependence;
- a minimum set of agreed values and norms which regulate their interaction and conduct.

This article focuses on the final criterion in the list above. It considers how an agreed set of values and norms can help a group to achieve its objective. The major issue discussed is the management and co-ordination of group activity when this activity is computer-supported and asynchronous. In this context, 'management and co-ordination' means the set of procedures that a group agrees to follow. Where a group of people has to produce an end product by a particular date, some degree of management and co-ordination is essential. It is unlikely that the task will be completed successfully and on time without some form of management. The question is: How much management, and by whom?

Managing collaborative work

In order to develop a shared product within a specific timeframe, a group needs to:

- agree which individuals will carry out which tasks and responsibilities;
- agree a schedule for when tasks have to be completed;
- agree on what will be acceptable as a final group product.

Carrying out the activities listed above is part of a process which starts with developing a shared understanding of what is needed. The first step is to discuss the requirements and their implications for individual tasks within the group. Group members then need to decide how they are going to collaborate; that is, how to discuss the task and its implications, and then how to carry it out. The list below includes some possible questions to consider.

• What are the components of the task?
• When do the components have to be completed?
• Who will do what?
• How is the progress of the collaboration to be managed?

Individuals tend to have different styles of working and there are likely to be a diversity of approaches within a group. The group therefore needs to find a style of working that suits its members. For example: will the group appoint one chairperson or will it agree that the responsibilities and tasks should be distributed more widely?

Issues in progressing the collaboration

There are a number of issues that have to be faced when collaborating online, particularly when using an asynchronous communication system (such as email or a discussion forum). These issues become apparent when comparing online communication with face-to-face meetings. In a business meeting the chairperson performs the following crucial functions:

1   ensuring that everyone has an opportunity to contribute, and that decisions are made;
2   ensuring that all agenda items are fitted into the meeting's duration.

Although in practice these functions may not be performed as well as they should be, it is worth bearing them in mind when planning online group work. For example, in asynchronous discussions that take place over a period of days or weeks:

1   How do you ensure that group members can contribute, and that group decisions are made?
2   How do you ensure that the project meets its schedule?

These two issues are discussed below ("Encouraging active participation" and "Milestones for monitoring progress").

Encouraging active participation

In a face-to-face meeting, the chairperson can ensure that everyone contributes to the discussion and decisions. When using asynchronous online communication, this can be more difficult. One way of adding a synchronizing structure comes from a version of the 'virtual circle' procedure (Johnson-Lenz and Johnson-Lenz, 1991). In this procedure, the group decides that its deliberations will be broken down into stages. The stages take place over a fixed period: say five days, with each day reserved for a new stage (a 'round' of contributions). The virtual circle sequence is as follows:

1   the chairperson (or facilitator) posts an initial message asking for discussion;
2   all group members post contributions giving their views, responding each day if appropriate;
3   to mark the end of the period, the chairperson (or facilitator) summarizes the discussion and proposes a decision;
4   each group member responds to the summary and proposed decision – by voting if appropriate.

This procedure encourages group members to participate. It also allows the chairperson/facilitator and the group to see who is or isn't contributing to its activities. Two implications of using a virtual circle in this way are that:

•   someone has the responsibility for posting an initial message, and subsequently a summary of the decisions;
•   everyone has a responsibility to contribute usefully to the discussion and decision-making.

Milestones for monitoring progress

A strategy commonly used in project management is to set up 'milestones'. These are dates by which specific tasks, such as decisions or contributions, are scheduled to be completed. The generation of milestones performs two functions. First, it tells team members when contributions are required and when decisions are expected. Second, it helps in monitoring the progress of the collaboration. An implication of the use of milestones is that someone is responsible for monitoring when the individual milestones are achieved. It is also important that decision-making is incorporated as one of the milestones of the collaborative work.

When drawing up timetables with milestones, it is important to include the 'overhead' required to synchronize contributions when groups are using online communication. It is also helpful to take into account that some group members may be less 'available' than others. Holidays and different work or domestic routines may mean that some members cannot contribute as often as others, so some negotiation may be necessary over the nature of individuals' contributions.

Individuals' roles in the collaborative activity

From the preceding discussion, it is clear that a successful collaboration does not just happen; it has to be organized and managed. It is also clear that, over and above the work that each individual has to carry out to meet the requirements of the task, there are administrative and managerial activities.

One of the first jobs for a group is the allocation of tasks to individuals. Once an allocation has been made, individuals can begin their work, and can start dealing with the administrative and managerial tasks. Successful groups often assign roles such as chairperson, secretary, progress-chaser and mediator. The group needs to decide what roles are required, and to allocate them. It is possible to allocate all the roles to one individual, or the roles can be distributed across the group. In either case, the responsibilities could be rotated at each major milestone.

Effective collaboration: overview

This article has indicated some of the issues and procedures that need to be considered when a collaborative activity is conducted using online communication. Agreeing on a set of procedures at the start will help the process of the collaboration. This requires project management decisions to be made, though the type of decision depends on the project. There are no hard-and-fast rules to ensure successful collaboration; learning to work collaboratively is an important part of the challenge. But it should not be a trial – it should be an exciting and enjoyable experience.

Reference

Johnson-Lenz, P. and Johnson-Lenz, T. (1991) 'Post-mechanistic groupware primitives: rhythms, boundaries and containers', *International Journal of Man–Machine Studies*, 34, pp. 395–417.

Collaboration via online discussion forums

Issues and approaches

Karen Kear

The availability of online communication tools means that groups of people can work together even if they are not co-located. In an organisational context, this opens up possibilities for collaborative working where team members may be home-based or may even be in different countries. In an education context, it allows collaborative learning activities to be included in online and distance courses. If asynchronous communication tools such as discussion forums are used, there are further benefits. Group members can communicate when it is convenient (even if they are in different time zones) and there is a permanent record of the communication.

The benefits discussed above are significant, but asynchronous communication tools also have drawbacks. In this article I shall consider some problems that can arise when asynchronous communication tools, and specifically online discussion forums, are used for collaborative work. The issues arose in the context of research on distance learning courses where students used discussion forums for group work, and were then asked to report their experiences and reactions (Kear and Heap, 1999; Kear, 2004). I shall be discussing the specific difficulties that students identified, and also suggesting how these might be avoided or reduced. The issues raised by the students are inter-related, but for convenience I shall discuss them under four headings, as follows:

- time lags;
- information chaos;
- lack of social presence;
- walking out of the virtual room.

Time lags

Communication in an online discussion forum can seem very slow. Users typically wait hours, or days, to get a response to a message they have submitted. One student described this as the 'jet-lag effect'– when reading a message she almost felt that she was in a different time zone from the person who wrote it. These time lags can be frustrating, and can disrupt the flow of the discussion (Wegerif, 1998).

Because of the communication delays, decision making in an asynchronous system such as a discussion forum can be difficult (Sproull and Keisler, 1991 p. 69). Sometimes users feel as if they are going round in circles, trying to discuss all the options and reach a consensus. One remedy is to arrange a face-to-face meeting or telephone conference call, but it can be difficult to find a time when all group members are available. An alternative approach is to agree on timescales for making contributions and coming to decisions via the discussion forum. Using a synchronous communication system such as 'chat' or 'instant messaging', can overcome the problem of time lags. Synchronous systems can speed up communication, and can also make it seem more natural and enjoyable. But all group members need to be online at the same time – which might be inconvenient or impossible.

Information chaos

A specific difficulty that can arise in very active discussion forums is 'information chaos'. There is often too much information to take in, and the information can seem quite disorganised (Hiltz and Turoff, 1985). In a busy discussion forum there will be many messages to keep track of, and if a group member is away for a few days they might have a lot of catching up to do. Because of the asynchronous nature of the communication, there will be parallel conversations going on. When a new topic of discussion arises there is no need to abandon the old one. This can be a benefit compared with face-to-face conversations, but this 'multi-tasking' can be confusing at times.

Forum members need to think carefully about how to manage the discussion, otherwise it can be difficult for participants to work out who is responding to whom. If the parallel conversations are mixed up with each other, the discussion forum can become very muddled. Sensible use of system 'threading' can help to avoid this. Threading means explicitly linking one message to an earlier one using facilities provided by the system (Hiltz and Turoff, 2002). Readers can then 'follow the thread' (Kear, 2001). If a member's input is a reply to an earlier message, or to a particular topic of discussion, the 'reply' option (or equivalent) should be used. If the message starts a new topic of discussion, the group member should start a new discussion thread.

Lack of social presence

A significant difficulty with online communication is that participants don't always get a very good sense of the other people in the group. When you read someone's message, you can't see their expression or gestures, and you can't hear the tone of their voice. This is particularly a problem in the early stages of group work – the 'forming' stage (Tuckman, 1965) – when people are getting to know each other. Many groups find that a face-to-face meeting or some kind of synchronous communication is helpful during this stage.

These issues relate to the concept of 'social presence' – the sense you get of a real person being there (Short, Williams and Christie, 1976). Communication systems can extend the user's presence across space – and, for asynchronous systems, also across time. Different types of communication systems support social presence to different extents. This partly depends on whether the communication medium is a 'rich' one (Daft and Lengel, 1986) such as a video link, or a less rich medium such as text-based online communication. Some communication systems include features which can increase social presence. For example, members may be able to supply a 'user profile' telling other members something about themselves, and perhaps including a photograph. Some systems also have a way of indicating when a group member is currently online.

There are also some simple things that members of a discussion forum can do to enhance their social presence. The tone of a message can be conveyed by careful wording. Messages can include 'smileys' (also called 'emoticons') to represent the tone of what is being said. For example, ;-) could represent a wink, indicating a jokey comment. Paying attention to how other group members might interpret your message will help to avoid the sort of misunderstandings which can result in 'flaming' – sending angry or aggressive messages, which can escalate into a 'flame war'.

Walking out of the virtual room

One further problem which can arise in an online group is that a group member may 'disappear' – or not appear in the first place. This is disruptive to the group's work, and frustrating for the other group members. It is easy for an individual to withdraw from the group, or read messages but not contribute (Haythornthwaite *et al.*, 2000). This creates a difficult situation for the other group members to deal with. In a conventional group working context you could look for the absent person, or stop them when you see them in the corridor, but you can't do that in a discussion forum. If the group finds that a member is absent, the problem needs to be tackled quickly, so the other group members should try to contact them as soon as possible.

To help avoid this situation, there are several things which group members need to consider. The group should try to develop a sense of togetherness – be friendly and welcoming to each other, and try to make the collaboration as enjoyable as possible. Group members will also need to sacrifice some flexibility in what they do and when they do it. The group needs the participation of every member, and it's up to each member to contribute.

Conclusion

Carrying out collaborative work is always a challenge. The nature of online collaboration means that there are additional issues to deal with, beyond those posed in a face-to-face context. However, an awareness of these issues will help group members to address them. By adopting a positive approach, members will gain real benefits from collaborative work – learning from each other, and learning how to work with each other.

References

Daft, R.L. & Lengel, R.H. (1986) 'Organisational information requirements, media richness and structural design', *Management Science* 32, 554–571.

Haythornthwaite, C., Kazmer, M.M., Robins, J., and Shoemaker, S. (2000) 'Community development among distance learners: temporal and technological dimensions', *Journal of Computer Mediated Communication*, 6(1). http://jcmc.indiana.edu/vol6/issue1/haythornthwaite.html [accessed 26th June 2009].

Hilt, S.R. and Turoff, M. (1985) 'Structuring computer-mediated communication systems to avoid information overload', *Communications of the ACM*, 28(7), 680–689.

Hiltz, S.R. and Turoff, M. (2002) 'What makes learning networks effective?', *Communications of the ACM*, 45(4), 56–59.

Kear, K. (2001) 'Following the thread in computer conferences', *Computers & Education*, 37, 81–99.

Kear, K. (2004) 'Peer learning using asynchronous discussion systems in distance education', *Open Learning* 19(2) 151–164.

Kear, K. and Heap, N. (1999) 'Technology-supported groupwork in distance learning', *Active Learning* 10, 21–26.

Short, J., Williams, E. and Christie, B. (1976) *The Social Psychology of Telecommunications*, London: Wiley.

Sproull, L. and Kiesler, S. (1991) *Connections: New Ways of Working in the Networked Organisation*, Cambridge, MA: MIT Press.

Tuckman, B. (1965) 'Developmental sequences in small groups', *Psychological Bulletin*, 62, 384–399.

Wegerif, R. (1998) 'The social dimension of asynchronous learning networks', *Journal of Asynchronous Learning Networks*, 2(1). http://www.sloan-c.org/publications/jaln/v2n1/v2n1_wegerif.asp [accessed 26th June 2009].

Part II

Collaborative technologies

Introduction to Part II

In Part II, consisting of three readings, we look at how collaborative work can be supported through computer and communications technologies. What kind of technologies are best suited to which kind of work? And how does work change through the use of these technologies?

Sometimes collaborative technologies are referred to as *groupware* (since they are forms of software designed to help people work in groups). This part of the Reader draws upon research from the academic discipline of computer-supported cooperative work (CSCW), which is concerned with understanding and developing collaborative technologies. The discipline began in the mid-1980s, when dominant groupware technologies included email, shared editing tools, bulletin boards and video-conferencing.

These technologies were typically developed for personal computers connected by local area networks, well before the wide adoption of the internet. They were generally intended for use within a corporate environment, for a single organisation at a time, but frequently across multiple sites. Nonetheless, the frameworks developed within CSCW still prove highly useful to modern collaborative technologies, often used in quite a different context.

The first reading, by Olson and Olson (2008), gives a very comprehensive overview of the major strands of collaborative technologies. The authors, Gary and Judy Olson, have been at the forefront of the CSCW field for many years, so they are ideally placed to provide that overview. Their article covers a wide range of technologies, including communication tools, coordination support, information repositories, social computing, computer supported cooperative learning, and integrated systems. It is worth observing that the article was originally published in an encyclopaedia of human-computer interaction and as such is extremely comprehensive and readable, with a large number of references.

The second reading (Ackerman 2000, pp. 179–184) takes a less technological stance. It looks at the way collaborative technologies are used in practice, and draws lessons from the many studies of collaboration (using computer technologies as well as more traditional methods) that have been carried out within CSCW. The general argument of the article is that there is a 'socio-technical gap' within collaborative technologies – a gap between the social and technological aspects of the technologies in use. Ackerman claims that the tools are insufficiently well-developed to support the findings from within CSCW about how people best work together. To make this argument, he first of all outlines his understanding of these findings. Because the article is quite long, and only the first part is relevant to this Reader, we have omitted the later parts, in which Ackerman discusses what needs to be done to fill the socio-technical gap. The journal in which the full paper was originally published can be found in many university libraries.

The third reading combines technological issues with issues of technologies in use, looking at evaluation on several different levels. Collaborative technologies (like all information and communication technologies) are not created for their own sake – they are created to be used effectively. But how can we evaluate the effectiveness of a particular collaborative technology? The article by Ramage (2010) was written especially for this Reader although it draws on the author's research going back over a number of years. It presents a method for evaluating a collaborative technology in use, with an example demonstrating a brief evaluation of two contemporary collaborative technologies – blogs and wikis.

Collaborative technologies have had a huge impact upon the way people work together, and continue to develop in interesting ways. Although many tools for collaborative working have only come to prominence in recent years, they have a considerable and very interesting history. We hope that these readings help in focusing understanding of the nature, use, and history of collaborative technologies.

References

Ackerman, M. (2000) 'The intellectual challenge of CSCW: the gap between social requirements and technical feasibility', *Human-Computer Interaction*, 15(2), pp. 179–203.

Olson, G.M. and Olson, J.S. (2008) 'Groupware and computer-supported cooperative work', in Sears, A. and Jacko, J.A. (eds.), *The Human-Computer Interaction Handbook: Fundamentals, Evolving Technologies and Emerging Applications* (2nd edition), New York, Lawrence Erlbaum Associates, pp. 545–558.

Ramage, M. (2010) 'Evaluating collaborative technologies', in Donelan, H., Kear, K. and Ramage, M. (eds.), *Online Communication and Collaboration: A Reader*, London, Routledge, pp. 73–77.

Reading 5

Groupware and computer-supported cooperative work

Gary M. Olson and Judith S. Olson

Introduction

Computing and communication technologies have provided us with useful and powerful information resources, remote instruments, and tools for interacting with each other. These possibilities have also led to numerous social and organizational effects. These tools are of course just the latest in a long line of modern technologies that have changed human experience. Television and radio long ago broadened our awareness of and interest in activities all over the world. The telegraph and telephone enabled new forms of organization to emerge. The new technologies of Computer-Supported Cooperative Work (CSCW)[1] are giving us greater geographical and temporal flexibility in carrying out our activities. They have also given us new modes of socializing.

Groupware is software designed to run over a network in support of the activities of a group or organization. These activities can occupy any of several combinations of same/different places and same/different times. Groupware has been designed for all four of these combinations. Early groupware applications tended to focus on only one of these cells, but more recently groupware that supports several cells and the transitions among them has emerged. We also do not think of groupware as only dealing with groups. Both the individual members of groups and the organizations in which they are embedded affect and are affected by groupware.

CSCW emerged as a formal field of study in the mid-1980s, with conferences, journals, books, and university courses appearing that used this name. There were a number of important antecedents. The earliest efforts to create groupware used timeshared systems but were closely linked to the development of key ideas that propelled the personal computer revolution. Vannever Bush (1945)

From Olson, G. M. and Olson, J. S (2008) 'Group Cooperative Work', in Sears, A. and Jacko, J. A. (eds.), *The Human-Computer Interaction Handbook: Fundamentals, Evolving Technologies and Emerging Applications* (2nd edn). New York: Lawrence Erlbaum Associates, pp. 545–558. Reproduced by permission of Taylor & Francis Books UK.

described a vision of something similar to today's World Wide Web in an influential essay published shortly after the end of World War II. Doug Engelbart's famous demonstration at the 1968 IFIPS meeting in San Francisco included a number of key groupware components (see Engelbart & English, 1968). These components included support for real-time face-to-face meetings, audio and video conferencing, discussion databases, information repositories, and workflow support. Group decision-support systems and computer-supported meeting rooms were explored in a number of business schools (see McLeod, 1992; Kraemer & Pinsonneault, 1990). Work on office automation included many groupware elements, such as group workflow management, calendaring, e-mail, and document sharing (Ellis & Nutt, 1980). A good summary of early historical trends as well as reprints of key early articles appear in Grief's (1988) important anthology of readings.

Today there are a large number of commercial groupware products. In addition, groupware functions are increasingly appearing as options in operating systems or specific applications (e.g., access to meeting-support tools within Microsoft Office products). Groupware functionality has become widespread and familiar. However, there are still many research issues about how to design such systems and what effects they have on the individuals, groups, and organizations that use them.

Adopting groupware in context

Groupware systems are intended to support groups, which are usually embedded in an organization. As a result, there are a number of issues that bear on groupware success. In a justly famous set of papers, Grudin (1988, 1994) pointed out a number of problems that groupware systems have (see also Markus & Connolly, 1990). In brief, he pointed out that developers of groupware systems need to be concerned about the following issues (Grudin, 1994, p. 97):

1   Disparity in work and benefit. Groupware applications often require additional work from individuals who do not perceive a direct benefit from the use of the application.
2   Critical mass and Prisoner's dilemma problems. Groupware may not enlist the "critical mass" of users required to be useful, or can fail because it is never in any one individual's advantage to use it.
3   Disruption of social processes. Groupware can lead to activity that violates social taboos, threatens existing political structures, or otherwise de-motivates users crucial to its success.
4   Exception handling. Groupware may not accommodate the wide range of exception handling and improvisation that characterizes much group activity.
5   Unobtrusive accessibility. Features that support group processes are used relatively infrequently, requiring unobtrusive accessibility and integration with more heavily used features.

6   Difficulty of evaluation. The almost insurmountable obstacles to meaningful, generalizable analysis and evaluation of groupware prevent us from learning from experience.

7   Failure of intuition. Intuitions in product development environments are especially poor for multi-user applications, resulting in bad management decisions and error-prone design processes.

8   The adoption process. Groupware requires more careful implementation (introduction) in the workplace than product developers have confronted.

However, there are reasons for optimism. In a recent survey of the successful adoption of group calendaring in several organizations, Palen and Grudin (2002) observed that organizational conditions in the 1990s were much more favorable for the adoption of group tools than they were in the 1980s. Further, the tools themselves had improved in reliability, functionality, and usability. There is increased "collaboration readiness" and "collaboration technology readiness." But there are still significant challenges in supporting group work at a distance (Olson & Olson, 2000).

Technical infrastructure

Groupware requires networks, and network infrastructure is a key enabler as well as a constraint on groupware. A number of advanced networks are exploring the issues of supporting high-end users (e.g., Abilene, abilene.internet2.edu; National LambdaRail, www.nlr.net; HOPI, networks.internet2.edu/hopi). Wireless networking technology gives users more flexibility. Good access to the Internet is now common in homes, hotels, coffee shops, airports, and many other places. Networking infrastructure is spreading throughout the world. However, heterogeneity in network conditions across both space and time still remains a major technical challenge. For instance, doing web conferencing when some participants are on slow dial-up lines and others are on fast advanced networks requires special coordination. Tanenbaum (2003) is a good resource on the latest developments in networking.

The World Wide Web and its associated tools and standards have had a major impact on the possibilities for groupware (Schatz & Hardin, 1994; Berners-Lee, 1999). Early groupware mostly consisted of stand-alone applications that had to be downloaded and run on each client machine. Increasingly, group tools are written for the web, requiring only a web browser and perhaps some plug-ins. This makes it much easier for the user, and also helps with matters such as version control. It also enables better interoperability across hardware and operating systems.

Security on the Internet is a major challenge for groupware. In some sense the design of Internet protocols are to blame, since the Internet grew up in a culture of openness and sharing (Longstaff et al., 1997; Abbate, 1999; Tanenbaum, 2003). E-commerce and sensitive application domains like medicine have been a driver for advances in security, but there is still much progress to be made (Longstaff et al., 1997; Camp, 2000). Coping with firewalls that block access to certain kinds of organizations can limit the flexibility of web conferencing.

Personal computing was a great enabler of collaborative applications. Today we are liberated from the desktop. Laptops, personal digital assistants, wearables, and cell phones provide access to information and people from almost anywhere. More and more applications are being written to operate across these diverse environments (e.g., Tang et al., 2001; Starner & Rhodes, 2004). These devices vary in computational power, display size and characteristics, network bandwidth, and connection reliability, providing interesting technical challenges to make them all interoperate smoothly. For instance, accessing websites from a cell phone requires special user interface methods to make the tiny displays usable.

Additional flexibility is being provided by the development of infrastructure that lies between the network itself and the applications that run on client workstations, called "middleware." This infrastructure makes it easier to link together diverse resources to accomplish collaborative goals. For instance, the emerging Grid technologies allow the marshalling of powerful, scattered computational resources (Foster & Kesselman, 2004). Middleware provides such services as identification, authentication, authorization, directories, and security in uniform ways that facilitate the interoperability of diverse applications. All of these technical elements are components of cyberinfrastructure (Atkins et al., 2003). There is considerable interest in the development of this infrastructure because of its large impact on research, education, and commerce.

Communication tools

We now turn to a review of specific kinds of groupware, highlighting their various properties and uses. We have grouped this review under several broad headings. We do not aim to be exhaustive, but rather seek to illustrate the variety of kinds of tools that have emerged to support human collaborative activities over networked systems. We also highlight various research issues pertaining to these tools.

E-mail

E-mail has become a ubiquitous communication tool. The early adoption of standards made it possible for messages to be exchanged across networks and different base machines and software applications. E-mail is now also done from cell phones, PDAs, television sets, and kiosks in public sites. Documents of many types can be easily exchanged. Because of its widespread use, it is often called the first successful groupware application (Sproull & Kiesler, 1991; Satzinger & Olfman, 1992; O'Hara-Devereaux & Johnson, 1994; Anderson, Bikson, Law, & Mitchell, 1995). Indeed, it has become so successful that e-mail overload has become a major problem (Whittaker & Sidner, 1996). And of course it has become a vector for viruses, worms, and other invasive software.

Researchers have shown that this widespread use has had a number of effects on how people behave. It has had large effects on communication in organizations: it changes the social network of who talks to whom (Sproull & Kiesler, 1991; DeSanctis, Jackson, Poole, & Dickson, 1996), the power of people who formerly had little voice in decisions (Finholt, Sproull, & Kiesler, 1990), and the tone of what is said and how it is interpreted (Sproull & Kiesler, 1991). For example, with e-mail, people who were shy found a voice; they could overcome their reluctance to speak to other people by composing text, not speech to another face. This invisibility, however, also has a more general effect – without the social cues in the recipient's face being visible to the sender, people will "flame," send harsh or extremely emotive (usually negative) messages (Arrow et al., 1996; Hollingshead, McGrath, & O'Connor, 1993).

As with a number of other "designed" technologies, people use e-mail for things other than the original intent. People use it for managing time, reminding them of things to do, and keeping track of steps in a workflow (Mackay, 1989; Carley & Wendt, 1991; Whittaker & Sidner, 1996). But because e-mail was not designed to support these tasks, it does not do it very well; people struggle with reading signals about whether they have replied or not (and to whom it was cc'd); they manage folders poorly for reminding them to do things, and so forth.

In addition, because e-mail is so widespread, and it is easy and free to distribute a single message to many people, people experience information overload. Many people get hundreds of e-mail messages each day, many of them mere broadcasts of things for sale or events about to happen, much like "classifieds" in the newspaper. Several early efforts to use artificial intelligence techniques to block and/or sort incoming e-mail were tried, and this has continued to be a very active area of work (Malone, Grant, Lai, Rao, & Rosenblitt, 1987; Winograd, 1988). There are two broad classes of uses of e-mail filters. One use is to automatically sort incoming mail into useful categories. This is relatively easy for mail that has simple properties, such as a person's name. It is more difficult for subtle properties. The other major use is to weed out unwanted mail, such as spam. The state-of-the-art in spam filtering is in the range of 80–90% effectiveness in 2005 (e.g., Federal Trade Commission, 2005). Such filters are so good that many institutions automatically filter mail as it comes in to the organization's gateway, sparing users the need to do it in their own clients. Similarly, many clients now come with built-in spam filters that can be tuned by the user (e.g., Google's Gmail).

These problems have led to the "reinvention" of e-mail (Whittaker, Bellotti, & Moody, 2005). For example, given that e-mail is often used in the context of managing projects, systems have been explored that have a more explicit scheme for task management (Whittaker, 2005; Bellotti, Ducheneaut, Howard, Smith, & Grinter, 2005). To deal with problems of e-mail overload, new schemes for filtering e-mail have been explored, such as routing messages differently to different kinds of clients (e.g., cell phone vs. desktop machine; see Schmandt & Marti, 2005). Another approach has been to explore pricing mechanisms for e-mail that are analogous to pricing for regular mail (Kraut, Sunder, Telang, & Morris, 2005).

In such schemes one would pay to send e-mail, with higher prices presumably indicating higher priority, analogous to the difference between first class postage and bulk rates. These schemes are currently exploratory, but are likely to result in new options in future e-mail clients.

Kraut et al. (1998) reported that greater Internet use, which in their sample was mostly e-mail, led to declines in social interactions with family members and an increase in depression and loneliness. Not surprisingly, these results triggered widespread discussion and debate, both over the substance of the results and the methods used to obtain them. Kraut, Gergle, and Fussell (2002) reported new results that suggest these initial negative effects may not persist. Interpersonal communication is one of the principal uses of the Internet, and the possible implications of this kind of communication for social life are important to understand. Indeed, Putnam (2000) has wondered whether the Internet can be a source of social cohesiveness. These kinds of questions need to be addressed by additional large-scale studies of the kind carried out by Kraut and his colleagues (see Resnick, 2002).

Conferencing tools: voice, video, text

There are many options available today for on-line conferencing among geographically dispersed members of a group. So-called computer-mediated communication (CMC) has become widespread. There are three principal modes of interaction, but each has numerous subtypes:

Video + Audio
Full-scale video conferencing room; many options for specific design
Individual desktop video; many options for quality, interface

Audio
Phone conference
Voice over IP (see Federal Communications Commission, 2005)

Text
Instant messaging, chat, SMS on mobile phones

There are many studies that compare face-to-face with various forms of CMC. There are some clear generalizations from such work. The main one is that CMC is more difficult to do than FTF, and requires more preparation and care (Hollingshead et al., 1993; McLeod, 1992; Olson, Olson, & Meader, 1995; Siegel, Dubrovsky, Kiesler, & McGuire, 1986; Straus, 1996, 1997; Straus & McGrath, 1994). A variety of things that come for free in FTF are either difficult to support or outright missing in CMC (Kiesler & Cummings, 2002). Backchannel communication, which is important for modulating conversation, is either weak or nonexistent in CMC. Paralinguistic cues that can soften communication are often missing. Participants in CMC tend to have an informational focus, which means there is usually less socializing, less small talk. Over time this can lead to poorer social integration and organizational effectiveness (Nohria & Eccles, 1992).

CMC often introduces delay. This is well-known to be very disruptive to communication (Egido, 1988; Krauss & Bricker, 1966; O'Conaill, Whittaker, & Wilbur, 1993; Ruhleder & Jordan, 2001; Tang & Isaacs, 1993). Participants will communicate less information, be more frustrated with the communication, and actually terminate communication sessions sooner. Delay can be managed, but it takes special care among the participants and turn-taking widgets in the interface of the tools being used. For instance, if there is delay, then full-duplex open communication will not work, since participants will step all over each other's communication. Either the participants must use a social protocol (e.g., like that used in radio communications with spacecraft), or they must employ a mike-passing procedure with interface indications of who wants to talk next.

While it might seem desirable to always have the maximum communication and tool support possible, it is not always possible or even necessary to do so. Research shows that effective real-time collaboration can take place under a number of different arrangements, depending on the task, the characteristics of the participants, the specific geographical dispersion of the participants, and the processes employed to manage the interactions. There are also organizational effects, especially when the real-time collaborations are embedded in ongoing activities, as they almost always are.

For instance, early work (Williams, 1977) showed that, in referential communication tasks, full-duplex audio is just as effective as FTF. Subsequent research comparing audio and video conferencing (see Finn, Sellen, & Wilbur, 1997; Cadiz et al., 2000 recently found similar results for a tutored video-instruction task) showed that for many tasks audio is sufficient, that video adds nothing to task effectiveness though participants usually report they are more satisfied with video. There are important exceptions, however. Negotiation tasks are more effective with video (Short, Williams, & Christie, 1976). This is probably because the more subtle visual cues to the participants' intentions are important in this kind of task. Further, Veinott, Olson, Olson, and Fu (1999) found that when participants have less common ground video helps. In their case, participants were non-native speakers of English who were doing the task in English. For native speakers, video was no better than audio, but non-native speakers did better when they had video. Again, visual cues to comprehension and meaning likely played an important role. Recently, an experimental study by Daly-Jones, Monk, and Watts (1998) showed that high-quality video resulted in greater conversational fluency over just high-quality audio, especially as group size increased. There was also a higher rated sense of presence in the video conditions.

An important lesson to draw from this literature is that there are two broad classes by which we might assess whether video is important in real-time collaboration. On the one hand, except for tasks like negotiation or achieving common ground, groups are able to get their work done effectively with just high-quality audio. However, for things like satisfaction, conversational fluency, and a sense of presence, video adds value. These kinds of factors might be very important for long-term organizational consequences like employee satisfaction. As of yet, no long-term studies have been done to examine this conjecture.

Audio quality is critical. Ever since early literature review (Egido, 1988), it's been reported over and over again that if the audio is of poor quality participants will develop a workaround. For instance, if the audio in a video conferencing system or in a web conferencing system is poor quality, participants will turn to a phone conference.

The social ergonomics of audio and video are also keys to their success. Many of the failures of audio conferencing, especially over the Internet, result from poor-quality microphones, poor microphone placement, poor speakers, and interfering noises like air conditioning. Getting these details right is essential. Similarly, for video, camera placement can matter a lot. For instance, Huang, Olson, and Olson (2002) found that a camera angle that makes a person seem tall (as opposed to actually being tall) affects how influential a person is in a negotiation task. Apparent height matters a lot. Other aspects of camera placement or arrangement of video displays make a big difference as well, but are not well known.

An exception is eye contact, where studies of FTF communication show that eye contact is a key linguistic and social mediator of communication (Argyle & Cook, 1976; Kendon, 1967). It is very difficult to achieve eye contact in CMC systems. Many attempts have been made (Gale & Monk, 2000; Grayson & Monk, 2003; Monk & Gale, 2002; Okada, Maeda, Ichicawaa, & Matsushita, 1994, Vertegaal, 1999; Vertegaal, Slagter, van der Veer, & Nijholt, 2001), and at least the subjective reports are that these can be effective. But these all require special equipment or setups. And they don't scale very well to multiparty sessions.

While for most situations having at least high-quality audio is essential, there are some special cases where a text-based channel, like chat or instant messaging, can work fine. For instance, in the Upper Atmospheric Research Collaboratory (UARC, later known as the "Space Physics and Aeronomy Research Collaboratory," or SPARC), a chat system worked very well for carrying out geographically distributed observational campaigns, since the flow of events in these campaigns were relatively slow (campaigns went on for several days, key events would take many minutes to unfold). McDaniel, Olson, and Magee (1996) compared chat logs with earlier FTF conversations at a remote site and found many elements of them very similar, including informal socializing. But this kind of ongoing scientific campaign is very unlike the interactions that take place in a typical meeting.

Instant messaging is a new communication modality that is making substantial inroads into organizations. Muller, Raven, Kogan, Millen, and Carey (2003) found in a survey study of three organizations that the introduction of instant messaging led to significantly less use of such communication channels as e-mail, voice-mail, telephone, teleconference, pager, and face-to-face. They also found that instant messaging was used for "substantive business purposes." Furthermore, in one of the organizations where they surveyed users after 24 months of usage they found that the substantive reasons for using IM increased. In a study of IM logs in an organization, Isaacs, Walendowski, Whittaker, Schiano, and Kamm (2002) found that a large proportion of IM conversations involved "complex work discussions." They found that IM users seldom switched to another communication channel once they were engaged in IM. Nardi, Whittaker, and Bradner (2000) observed in a field study that workers used IM for a variety of purposes, not just for information exchange. Such matters as quick questions, scheduling, organizing social interactions, and keeping in touch with others were common uses of IM. Thus, IM has emerged as a significant communication medium in the workplace, and is used even when other, richer communication channels were available.

While IM is a relatively new phenomenon in the workplace, it is clearly established as a useful and widely used tool outside the workplace. This will undoubtedly assist in the development of more sophisticated versions of the tool, as well as its integration into on-line conferencing systems. There is clearly much promise here. We have noticed, for example, that during online conferences IM or chat serves as a backchannel for side conversations or debugging, an extremely useful adjunct to the core audio or video communication taking place in such conferences.

The other key feature of successful remote meetings is the ability to share the objects they are talking about, such as the agenda, the to-do list, the latest draft of a proposal, a view of an object to be repaired, and so on. Many researchers (Fussell, Kraut, & Siegel, 2000; Karsenty, 1999; Kraut, Fussell, & Siegel, 2003; Kraut et al., 2002; Luff, Heath, Kuzuoka, Hindmarsh, & Oyama, 2003; Nardi et al., 1993; Whittaker, 2003; Whittaker, Geelhoed, & Robinson, 1993) have provided experimental evidence of the value of a shared workspace for synchronous audio-supported collaboration. More traditional video conferencing technologies often offer an "object camera," onto which the participants can put a paper agenda, Powerpoint slides, or a manufactured part. More generally, any form of video can also be used to share work objects (Fussell et al., 2000; Nardi et al., 1993). For digital objects, there are now a number of products that will allow meeting participants to share the screen or, in some cases, the remote operation of an application. Some companies are using electronic whiteboards, both in a collocated meeting and in remote meetings to mimic the choreography of people using a physical whiteboard. In some "collaboratories," scientists can even operate remote physical instruments from a distance and jointly discuss the results.

Blogs

Weblogs, more commonly called "blogs," have burst upon the Internet scene in recent years. Blogging software that makes it easy to put up multimedia content has led people to set up sites for all manner of purposes. A site can contain text, pictures, movies, and audio clips. A common social purpose is to keep an on-line diary. Another is to provide commentary on a topic of interest. For instance, blogs played a major role in the 2004 election (Adamic & Glance, 2005). Nardi,

Schiano, Gumbrecht, and Swartz (2004) studied why people blog, as it's sometimes puzzling that people would essentially share personal or private information about themselves through the web.

Coordination support

Meeting support

An early and popular topic in CSCW was the support of face-to-face meetings. A number of systems were developed and tested. While of late the focus has shifted to the support of geographically distributed meetings, the early work on meeting support led to some important and useful conclusions.

Some meeting-support software imposed structure on the process of the meeting, embodying various brainstorming and voting procedures. Group Decision Support Systems (GDSSs) arose from a number of business schools, focusing on large meetings of stakeholders intent on going through a set series of decisions, such as prioritizing projects for future funding (Nunamaker, Dennis, Valacich, Vogel, & George, 1991). With the help of a facilitator and some technical support, the group was led through a series of stages: brainstorming without evaluating, evaluating alternatives from a variety of positions, prioritizing alternatives, and so on. These meetings were held in specialized rooms in which individual computers were embedded in the tables, networked to central services, and summary displays shown "center stage." A typical scenario involved individuals silently entering ideas into a central repository, and after a certain amount of time, they were shown ideas one at a time from others and asked to respond with a new ideas triggered by that one. Later, these same ideas were presented to the individuals who were then asked to rank or rate them according to some fixed criterion, like cost. Aggregates of individuals' opinions were computed, discussed further and presented for vote. The system applied computational power (for voting and rating mechanisms), and networking control (for parallel input) to support typically weak aspects of meetings. These systems were intended to gather more ideas from participants, since one didn't have to wait for another to stop speaking in order to get a turn. And, anonymous voting and rating was intended to insure equal participation, not dominated by those in power.

Evaluations of these GDSSs have been reviewed producing some generalizations about their value (McLeod, 1992; Kraemer & Pinsoneault, 1990; Hollingshead et al., 1993). The systems indeed fulfill their intentions of producing more ideas in brainstorming and having more evaluative comments because of anonymity. Decisions are rated as higher in quality, but the meetings take longer and the participants are less satisfied than those in traditional meetings.

A second class of technologies to support real-time meetings is less structured, more similar to individual workstation support. In these systems, groups are allowed access to a single document or drawing, and can enter and edit into them simultaneously at will. Different systems enforce different "locking" mechanisms (e.g., paragraph or selection locking) so that one person does not enter while another deletes the same thing (Ellis, Gibbs, & Rein, 1991). Some also allow parallel individual work, where participants view and edit different parts of the same document, but can also view and discuss the same part as well. This kind of unstructured shared editor has been shown to be very effective for certain kinds of free-flowing meetings, like design or requirements meetings (Olson, Olson, Storrosten, & Carter, 1993). The rated quality of the meeting products (e.g., a requirements document or plan) was higher when using these technologies than with traditional whiteboard or paper-and-pencil support, but like working in GDSSs, people were slightly less satisfied. The lower satisfaction here and with GDSSs may reflect the newness of the technologies; people may not have yet learned how to persuade, negotiate, or influence each other in comfortable ways, to harness the powers inherent in the new technologies.

These new technologies did indeed change the way in which people worked. They talked less and wrote more, building on each other's ideas instead of generating far-reaching other ideas. The tool seemed to focus the groups on the core ideas, and keep them from going off on tangents. Many participants reported really liking *doing* work *in* the meetings rather than spending time only *talking about* the work.

A third class of meeting room support appears in electronic whiteboards. For example, the LiveBoard (Elrod et al., 1992), SoftBoard and SmartBoard are approximately $4' \times 6'$ rear-projection surfaces that allow pen input, much the way a whiteboard or flipchart does. People at Xerox PARC and Boeing have evaluated the use of these boards in meetings in extended case studies. In both cases, the board was highly valued because of its computational power and the fact that all could see the changes as they were made. At both sites, successful use required a facilitator who was familiar with the applications running to support the meeting. At Xerox, suggestions made in the meeting about additional functionality were built into the system so that it eventually was finely tuned support for their particular needs (Moran et al., 1996). For example, they did a lot of list making of freehand text items. Eventually, the board software recognized the nature of a list and an outline, with simple gestures changing things sensibly. For example, if a freehand text item was moved higher in a list, the other items adjusted their positions to make room for it. The end product was not only a set of useful meeting tools, but also a toolkit to allow people to build new meeting widgets to support their particular tasks.

Meetings are important, though often despised, organizational activities. Laboratory research of the kind just reviewed has shown quite clearly that well-designed tools can improve both work outcomes and participant satisfaction. However, meetings in organizations seldom use such tools. Inexpensive mobile computing and projection equipment combined with many commercial products mean that such tools are within reach of most organizations. But not having these elements readily available in an integrated way probably inhibits their widespread adoption.

While traditional meetings are often viewed as wasteful and frustrating, there can be huge benefits to working together in collocated environments. Kiesler and Cummings (2002) reviewed a number of the characteristics of physical collocation that can benefit performance. In a detailed study of one such situation, Teasley, Covi, Krishnan, and Olson (2002) found that "radical collocation," in which software development teams worked together in a dedicated project room for many weeks, dramatically improved their productivity. Reasons for this included the constant awareness of each other's work status, the associated ability to instantly work on an impasse as a group, and the availability of rich shared artifacts generated by the project.

Workflow

Workflow systems lend technology support to coordinated asynchronous (usually sequential) steps of activities among team members working on a particular task. For example, a workflow system might route a travel reimbursement voucher from the traveler to the approving party to the accounts payable to the bank. The electronic form would be edited and sent to the various parties, their individual to-do-lists updated as they received and/or completed the tasks, and permissions and approval granted automatically as appropriate (e.g., allowing small charges to an account if the charges had been budgeted previously or simply if there was enough money in the account). Not only is the transaction flow supported, but also records are often kept about who did what and when they did it. It is this later feature that has potentially large consequences for the people involved, discussed later.

These workflow systems were often the result of work reengineering efforts, focusing on making the task take less time and to eliminate the work that could be automated. Not only do workflow systems therefore have a bad reputation in that they often are part of workforce reduction plans, but also for those left, their work is able to be monitored much more closely. The systems are often very rigid, requiring, for example, all of a form to be filled in before it can be handed off to the next in the chain. They often require a great deal of rework because of this inflexibility. It is because of the inflexibility and the potential monitoring that the systems fall into disuse (e.g., Abbott & Sarin, 1994).

The fact that workflow can be monitored is a major source of user resistance. In Europe, such monitoring is illegal, and powerful groups of organized workers have made sure that such capabilities are not in workflow systems (Prinz & Kolvenbach, 1996). In the United States, it is not illegal, but many employees complain about its inappropriate use. For example, in one software engineering team where workflow had just been introduced to track bug reports and fixes, people in the chain were sloppy about noting who they had handed a piece of work off to. When it was discovered that the manager had been monitoring the timing of the handoffs to assign praise or blame, the team members were justifiably upset (Olson & Teasley, 1996). In general, managerial monitoring is a feature that is not well received by people being monitored (Markus, 1983). If such monitoring is mandated, workers' behavior will conform to the specifics of what is being monitored (e.g., time to pass an item off to the next in the chain) rather than perhaps to what the real goal is (e.g., quality as well as timely completion of the whole process).

Group calendars

A number of organizations have now adopted online calendars, mainly in order to view people's schedules to arrange meetings. The calendars also allow a form of awareness, allowing people to see if a person who is not present is expected back soon. Individuals benefit only insofar as they offload scheduling meetings to others, like to an administrative assistant, who can write as well as read the calendar. And, in some systems the individual can schedule private time, blocking the time but not revealing to others his or her whereabouts. By this description, on-line calendaring is a classic case of what Grudin (1988) warned against, a misalignment of costs and benefits; the individual puts in the effort to record his/her appointments so that another, in this case a manager or coworker, can benefit from ease of scheduling. However, since the early introduction of electronic calendaring systems, many organizations have found successful adoption (Mosier & Tammaro, 1997; Grudin & Palen, 1995; Palen & Grudin, 2002). Apparently such success requires a culture of sharing and accessibility, something that exists in some organizations and not others (Lange, 1992; Ehrlich, 1987).

Awareness

In normal work, there are numerous occasions in which people find out casually whether others are in and, in some cases, what they are doing. A simple walk down the hall to a printer offers numerous glances into people's offices, noting where their coats are, whether others are talking, whether there is intense work at a computer, and so on. This kind of awareness is unavailable to workers who are remote. Some researchers have offered various technology solutions; some have allowed one to visually walk down the hall at the remote location, taking a five-second glance into each passing office (Bellotti & Dourish, 1997; Fish, Kraut, Root, & Rice, 1993). Another similar system, called "Portholes," provides periodic snapshots instead of full-motion video (Dourish & Bly, 1992). Because of privacy implications, these systems have had mixed success. The places in which this succeeds are those in which the individuals seem to have a reciprocal need to be aware of each other's presence, and a sense of cooperation and coordination. A contrasting case is the instant messaging (IM) system in which the user has control as to what state they wish to advertise to their partners about their availability. The video systems are much more lightweight to the user but more intrusive; the IM ones give the user more control but require intention in action. Another approach investigated by Ackerman, Starr, Hindus, and Mainwaring (1997) looked at shared audio as an awareness tool, though this too has privacy implications.

As mentioned earlier, instant messaging systems provide an awareness capability. Most systems display a list of "buddies" and whether they are currently on-line or not. Nardi et al. (2000) found that people liked this aspect of IM (see also Muller et al., 2003; Isaacs et al., 2002). And, since wireless has allowed constant connectivity of mobile devices like PDAs, this use of tracking others is likely to grow. But again, there are issues of monitoring for useful or insidious purposes, and the issues of trust and privacy loom large (see Godefroid, Herbsleb, Jagadeesan, & Li, 2000).

Another approach to signaling what one is doing occurs at the more micro level. And again, one captures what is easy to capture. When people are closely aligned in their work, there are applications that allow each to see exactly where in the shared document the other is working and what they are doing (Gutwin & Greenberg, 1999). If one is working nearby the other, this signals perhaps a need to converse about the directions each is taking. Empirical evaluations have shown that such workspace awareness can facilitate task performance (Gutwin & Greenberg, 1999).

Studies of attempts to carry out difficult intellectual work within geographically distributed organizations show that one of the larger costs of geographical distribution is the lack of awareness of what others are doing or whether they are even around (Herbsleb, Mockus, Finholt, & Grinter, 2000). Thus, useful and usable awareness tools that mesh well with trust and privacy concerns could be of enormous organizational importance. This is a rich research area for CSCW.

Information repositories

Repositories of shared knowledge

In addition to sharing information generally on the web, in both public and intranet settings, there are applications that are explicitly built for knowledge sharing. The goal in most systems is to capture knowledge that can be reused by others, like instruction manuals, office procedures, training, and "boilerplates," or templates of commonly constructed genres, like proposals or bids. Experience shows, however, that these systems are not easy wins. Again, similar to the case of the on-line calendaring systems described above, the person entering information into the system is not necessarily the one benefiting from it. In a large consulting firm, where consultants were quite competitive in their bid for advancement, there was indeed negative incentive for giving away one's best secrets and insights (Orlikowski & Gash, 1994).

Sometimes subtle design features are at work in the incentive structure. In another adoption of Lotus Notes, in this case to track open issues in software engineering, the engineers slowly lost interest in the system because they assumed that their manager was not paying attention to their contributions and use of the system. The system design, unfortunately, made the manager's actual use invisible to the team. Had they known that he was reading daily what they wrote (though he never wrote anything himself), they would likely have continued to use the system (Olson & Teasley, 1996). A simple design change that would make the manager's reading activity visible to the team would likely have significantly altered their adoption.

The web of course provides marvelous infrastructure for the creation and sharing of information repositories. A variety of tools are appearing to support this. Of particular interest are open source tools that allow for a wider, more flexible infrastructure for supporting information sharing (see www.sakai.org). A major type of collaboratory (see below) are those that provide shared data repositories for a community of scientists. Systematic research on the use of such tools is needed.

Wikis

A wiki is a shared web space that can be edited by anyone who has access to it. They were first introduced by Ward Cunningham in 1995, but have recently become very popular. These can be used in a variety of ways, both for work and for fun. The most famous wiki is Wikipedia (www.wikipedia.org), an online encyclopedia where anyone can generate and edit content. It has grown to have millions of entries, and has versions in at least ten languages. A recent study carried out by *Nature* found that for science articles Wikipedia and the Encyclopedia Britannica were about equally accurate (Giles, 2005). Bryant, Forte, and Bruckman (2005) studied the contributors to Wikipedia, and suggested that a new publishing paradigm was emerging. Viegas, Wattenberg, and Dave (2004) developed imaginative visualizations of Wikipedia authoring and editing behavior over time.

Capture and replay

Tools that support collaborative activity can create traces of that activity that later can be replayed and reflected upon. The Upper Atmospheric Research Collaboratory (UARC) explored the replay of earlier scientific campaign sessions (Olson et al., 2001), so that scientists could reflect upon their reactions to real-time observations of earlier phenomena. Using a VCR metaphor, they could pause where needed, and fast forward past uninteresting parts. This reflective activity could also engage new players who had not been part of the original session. Abowd (1999) has explored such capture phenomena in an educational experiment called Classroom 2000. Initial experiments focused on reusing educational sessions during the term in college courses. We do not yet fully understand the impact of such promising ideas.

Social computing

Social filtering, recommender systems

We often find the information we want by contacting others. Social networks embody rich repositories of useful information on a variety of topics. A number of investigators have looked at whether the process of finding information through others can be automated. The kinds of recommender systems that we find on websites like Amazon.com are examples of the result of such research. The basic principle of such systems is that an individual will tend to like or prefer the kinds of things (e.g., movies, books) that someone who is similar to him/her likes. They find similar people by matching their previous choices. Such systems use a variety of algorithms to match preferences with those of others, and then recommend new items. Resnick and Varian (1997) edited a special issue of the Communication of the ACM on recommender systems that included a representative set of examples. Herlocker, Konstan, and Riedl (2001) used empirical methods to explicate the factors that led users to accept the advice of recommender systems. In short, providing access to explanations for why items were recommended seems to be the key. Cosley, Frankowski, Kiesler, Terveen, and Riedl (2005) studied factors that influence people to contribute data to recommender systems. Recommender systems are emerging as a key element of e-commerce (Schafer, Konstan, & Riedl, 2001). Accepting the output of recommender systems is an example of how people come to trust technical systems. This is a complex topic, and relates to issues like security that we briefly described earlier.

Trust of people via the technology

It has been said that "trust needs touch," and indeed in survey studies, coworkers report that they trust those who are collocated more than those who are remote (Rocco, Finholt, Hofer, & Herbsleb, 2000). Interestingly, those who spend the most time on the phone chatting about non-work related topics with their remote coworkers show higher trust than those they communicate with using only fax and e-mail. But lab studies show that telephone interaction is not as good as face-to-face. People using just the telephone behave in more self-serving, less-trusting ways than they do when they meet face to face (Drolet & Morris, 2000).

What can be done to counteract the mistrust that comes from the impoverished media? Rocco (1998) had people meet and do a team-building exercise the day before they engaged in the social dilemma game with only e-mail to communicate with. These people, happily, showed as much cooperation and trust as those who discussed things face to face during the game. This is important. It suggests that if remote teams can do some face-to-face teambuilding before launching on their project, they will act in a trusting/trustworthy manner.

Since it's not always possible to have everyone on a project meet face to face before they launch into the work, what else will work? Researchers have tried some options, but with mixed success. Zheng, Bos, Olson, Gergle, and Olson

(2001) found that using chat for socializing and sharing pictures of each other also led to trustful relations. Merely sharing a resume did not. When the text is translated into voice, it has no effect on trust, and when it is translated into voice and presented in a moving human-like face, it is even worse than text-chat. (Jensen, Farnham, Drucker, & Kollock, 2000; Kiesler, Sproull, & Waters, 1996). However, Bos, Gergle, Olson, and Olson (2001) found that interactions over video and audio led to trust, albeit of a seemingly more fragile form.

If we can find a way to establish trust without expensive travel, we are likely to see important productivity gains. Clearly the story is not over. However, we must not be too optimistic. In other tasks, video does not produce "being there." There is an overhead to the conversation through video; it requires more effort than working face to face (Olson et al., 1995). And, today's videos over the Internet are both delayed and choppy, producing cues that people often associate with lying. One doesn't trust someone who appears to be lying. Trust is a delicate emotion; today's video might not just do it in a robust enough fashion.

Computer supported cooperative learning

Obviously the range of CSCW systems that we've been describing can be used for a variety of purposes. One special area that has emerged as a subfield with a distinctive identity is education, using the name Computer Supported Cooperative Learning (CSCL). This field first emerged in Europe, but has become quite widespread. This area has its own journals and national meetings (see Koschmann, 1996; Koschmann, Hall, & Miyake, 2002; Koschmann, Suthers, & Chan, 2005).

The emergence of this field has coincided with the emergence of a general trend in education toward collaborative learning, of using working with peers in groups as an effective tool for education (Slavin, 1994). The core idea is that by working together with peers the interactions over problem solving and other learning activities will occur at a level that is most easily understood and engaged by the learners. What CSCL adds to this is a focus on software that can facilitate collaboration, particularly across distance.

Integrated systems

Media spaces

As an extension of video conferencing and awareness systems, some people have experimented with open, continuous audio and video connections between remote locations. In a number of cases, these experiments have been called "Media Spaces." For example, at Xerox, two labs were linked with an open video link between two commons areas (Olson & Bly, 1991), the two locations being Palo Alto, California, and Portland, Oregon. Evaluation of these experiments showed that maintaining organizational cohesiveness at a distance was much more difficult than when members are collocated (Finn et al., 1997). However, some connectedness was maintained. Where many of these early systems were plagued with technical difficulties, human factors limitations, or very large communication costs, in today's situation it might actually be possible to overcome these difficulties, making media a possibility for connecting global organizations. A new round of experimental deployments with new tools is needed.

Collaborative virtual environments

Collaborative virtual environments are 3D embodiments of multi-user domains (MUDs). The space in which people interact is an analog of physical space, with dimensions, directions, rooms, and objects of various kinds. People are represented as avatars – simplified, geometric, digital representations of people, who move about in the 3D space (Singhal & Zyda, 1999). Similar to MUDs, the users in a meeting situation might interact over some object that is digitally represented, like a mock-up of a real thing (e.g., an automobile engine, an airplane hinge, a piece of industrial equipment) or with visualizations of abstract data (e.g., a 3D visualization of atmospheric data). In these spaces, one can have a sense as to where others are and what they are doing, similar to the simplified awareness systems described above. In use, it is difficult to establish mutual awareness or orientation in such spaces (Hindmarsh, Fraser, Heath, Benford, & Greenhalgh, 1998; Park, Kapoor, & Leigh, 2000; Yang & Olson, 2002). There have even been some attempts to merge collaborative virtual environments with real ones, though with limited success so far (Benford, Greenhalgh, Reynard, Brown, & Koleva, 1998).

What people seem to want is more like the Holodek in "Star Trek." These environments are complicated technically, and perhaps even more complicated socially. In real life, we have developed interesting schemes that trigger behavior and interpretation of others' behavior as a function of real distance, a field called "Proxemics" (Hall, 1982). Only when these subtle behaviors are incorporated into the virtual environment will we have a chance of simulating appropriate interhuman behavior in the virtual 3D world.

Collaboratories

A collaboratory is a laboratory without walls (Finholt & Olson, 1997). From a National Research Council report, a collaboratory is supposed to allow "the nation's researchers [to] perform their research without regard to geographical location – interacting with colleagues, accessing instrumentation, sharing data and computational resources [and] accessing information in digital libraries" (National Research Council 1993, p. 7). Starting in the early 1990s, these capabilities have been configured into support packages for a number of specific sciences (see Finholt, 2002). The Science of Collaboratories project (www.scienceofcollaboratories.org) has identified more than 200 existing collaboratories and is drawing lessons about why some succeed and others don't (Olson et al., 2004).

A number of companies have also experimented with similar concepts, calling them "virtual collocation." The goal there is to support geographically dispersed teams as they carry out product design, software engineering, financial reporting, and almost any business function. In these cases, suites of off-the-shelf groupware tools have been particularly important and have been used to support round-the-clock software development among overlapping teams of engineers in time zones around the world (Carmel, 1999). There have been a number of such efforts, and it is still unclear as to their success or what features make their success more likely (Olson & Olson, 2000).

Conclusions

Groupware functionality is steadily becoming more routine in commercial applications. Similarly, suites of groupware functions are being written into operating systems. Many of the functions we have described in this article are becoming ordinary elements of infrastructure in networked computing systems.

Prognosticators looking at the emergence of groupware and the convergence of computing and communication media have forecast that distance will diminish as a factor in human interactions (e.g., Cairncross, 1997). However, to paraphrase Mark Twain, the reports of distance's death are greatly exaggerated. Even with all our emerging information and communications technologies, distance and its associated attributes of culture, time zones, geography, and language will continue to affect how humans interact with each other. Emerging distance technologies will allow greater flexibility for those whose work must be done at a distance, but we believe (see Olson & Olson, 2000) that distance will continue to be a factor in understanding these work relationships.

Acknowledgments

Preparation of this chapter was facilitated by several grants from the National Science Foundation (research grants IIS-9320543, IIS-9977923, ATM-9873025, IIS-0085951 and cooperative agreement IRI-9216848). We are also grateful to several anonymous reviewers for helpful comments on an earlier draft.

Note

1 This name contains several anachronisms. "Computer" is no longer confined to the familiar desktop device. "Cooperative" does not mean we ignore competitive uses of technology. "Work" is only one of a number of venues that CSCW researchers study.

References

Abbate, J. (1999). *Inventing the Internet.* Cambridge, MA: MIT Press.

Abbott, K. R., & Sarin, S. K. (1994). Experiences with workflow management: Issues for the next generation. *Proceedings of the Conference on Computer Supported Cooperative Work* (pp. 113–120). Chapel Hill, NC: ACM Press.

Abowd, G. D. (1999). Classroom 2000: An experiment with the instrumentation of a living educational environment. *IBM Systems Journal, 38,* 508–530.

Ackerman, M. S., Starr, B., Hindus, D., & Mainwaring, S. D. (1997). Hanging on the 'wire': A field study of an audio-only media space. *ACM Transactions on Computer-Human Interaction, 4*(1), 39–66.

Adamic, L. A., & Glance, N. (2005). The political blogosphere and the 2004 U.S. election: Divided they blog. Presented at LinkKDD-2005, Chicago, IL. Retrieved March 13, 2007, from www.blogpulse.com/papers/2005/.

Anderson, R. H., Bikson, T. K., Law, S. A., & Mitchell, B. M. (1995). *Universal access to e-mail: Feasibility and societal implications.* Santa Monica, CA: Rand.

Argyle, M., & Cook, M. (1976). *Gaze and mutual gaze.* New York: Cambridge University Press.

Arrow, H., Berdahl, J. L., Bouas, K. S., Craig, K. M., Cummings, A., Lebei, L., McGrath, J. E., O'Connor, K. M., Rhoades, J. A., & Schlosser, A. (1996). Time, technology, and groups: An integration. *Computer Supported Cooperative Work, 4,* 253–261.

Atkins, D. E., Droegemeier, K. K., Feldman, S. I., Garcia-Molina, H., Klein, M. L., Messerschmitt, D. G., Messina, P., Ostriker, J. P., & Wright, M. H. (2003). *Revolutionizing science and engineering through cyberinfrastructure.* Report of the National Science Foundation Blue-Ribbon Advisory Panel on Cyberinfrastructure. National Science Foundation. Arlington, VA.

Bellotti, V., & Dourish, P. (1997). Rant and RAVE: Experimental and experiential accounts of a media space. In K. E. Finn, A. J. Sellen, & S. B. Wilbur (Eds.), *Video-mediated communication* (pp. 245–272). Mahwah, NJ: Lawrence Erlbaum Associates.

Bellotti, V., Ducheneaut, N., Howard, M., Smith, I., & Grinter, R. E. (2005). Quality versus quantity: E-mail centric task management and its relation with overload. *Human-Computer Interaction, 20,* 89–138.

Benford, S., Greenhalgh, C., Reynard, G., Brown, C., & Koleva, B. (1998). Understanding and constructing shared spaces with mixed-reality boundaries. *ACM Transactions on Computer-Human Interaction, 5,* 185–223.

Berners-Lee, T. (1999). *Weaving the web.* New York: Harper Collins.

Bos, N., Gergle, D., Olson, J. S., & Olson, G. M. (2001). *Being there vs. seeing there: Trust via video.* Short Paper presented at the Conference on Human Factors in Computing Systems: CHI-2001. Seatle, WA.

Bryant, S. L., Forte, A., & Bruckman, A. (2005). Becoming Wikipedian: Transformation of participation in a collaborative online encyclopedia *Proceedings of GROUP 2005* (pp. 1–10). New York: ACM.

Bush, V. (1945). As we may think. *Atlantic Monthly, 176*(1), 101–108.

Cadiz, J., Balachandran, A., Sanocki, E., Gupta, A., Grudin, J., & Jancke, G. (2000). *Distance learning through distributed collaborative video viewing.* Paper presented at the CSCW 2000, New York.

Cairncross, F. (1997). *The death of distance: How the communications revolution will change our lives.* Boston: Harvard Business School Press.

Camp, L. J. (2000). *Trust and risk in Internet commerce*. Cambridge, MA: MIT Press.

Carley, K., & Wendt, K. (1991). Electronic mail and scientific communication: A study of the Soar extended research group. *Knowledge: Creation, Diffusion, Utilization, 12*, 406–440.

Carmel, E. (1999). *Global software teams*. Upper Saddle River, NJ: Prentice-Hall.

Cosley, D., Frankowski, D., Kiesler, S., Terveen, L., & Riedl, J. (2005). How oversight improves member-maintained communities. *Proceedings of CHI 2005* (pp. 11–20). New York: ACM.

Daly-Jones, O., Monk, A., & Watts, L. (1998). Some advantages of video conferencing over high-quality audio conferencing: fluency and awareness of attentional focus. *International Journal of Human-Computer Studies, 49*(1), 21–58.

DeSanctis, G., Jackson, B. M., Poole, M. S., & Dickson, G. W. (1996). Infrastructure for telework: Electronic communication at Texaco. *Proceedings of SIGCPR/SIGMIS '96* (pp. 94–102). New York: ACM.

Dourish, P., & Bly, S. (1992). Portholes: Supporting awareness in a distributed work group. *Proceedings of CHI 92* (pp. 541–547). Monterey, CA: ACM Press.

Drolet, A. L. & Morris, M. W. (2000). Rapport in conflict resolution: Accounting for how nonverbal exchange fosters coordination on mutually beneficial settlements to mixed motive conflicts. *Journal of Experimental Social Psychology, 36*(1), 26–50.

Egido, C. (1988). *Video conferencing as a technology to support group work: A review of its failure*. Paper presented at the CSCW '88, New York.

Ehrlich, S. F. (1987). Strategies for encouraging successful adoption of office communication systems. *ACM Transactions on Office Information Systems, 5*, 340–357.

Ellis, C. A., Gibbs, S. J., & Rein, G. L. (1991). Groupware: Some issues and experiences, *CACM, 34*(1), 38–58.

Ellis, C., & Nutt, G. (1980). Office information systems and computer science. *Computing Surveys, 12*(1), 27–60.

Elrod, S., Bruce, R., Gold, R., Goldberg, D., Halasz, F., Janssen, W., Lee, D., McCall, K., Pedersen, E., Pier, K., Tang, J., & Welch, B. (1992). LiveBoard: A large interactive display supporting group meetings, presentations, and remote collaboration. *Proceedings of CHI'92* (pp. 599–607). Monterey, CA: ACM Press.

Engelbart, D., & English, W. (1968). A research center for augmenting human intellect. *Proceedings of FJCC, 33*, 395–410.

Federal Communications Commission (2005). *Voice over internet protocol*. Retrieved January 28, 2006, from http://www.fcc.gov/voip/

Federal Trade Commission (2005, November). *Email address harvesting and the effectiveness of anti-spam filters*. Report by Federal Trade Commission, Division of Marketing Practices. Washington, DC.

Finholt, T. A. (2002). Collaboratories. In B. Cronin (Ed.), *Annual Review of Information Science and Technology*.

Finholt, T. A., & Olson, G. M. (1997). From laboratories to collaboratories: A new organizational form for scientific collaboration. *Psychological Science, 8*, 28–36.

Finholt, T., Sproull, L., & Kiesler, S. (1990). Communication and performance in ad hoc task groups. In J. Galegher, R. Kraut, & C. Egido (Eds.), *Intellectual teamwork: Social and technological foundations of cooperative work* (pp. 291–325). Hillsdale, NJ: Lawrence Erlbaum Associates.

Finn, K., Sellen, A., & Wilbur, S. (Eds.) (1997). *Video-mediated communication*. Hillsdale, NJ: Lawrence Erlbaum Associates.

Fish, R. S., Kraut, R. E., Root, R. W., & Rice, R. E. (1993). Video as a technology for informal communication. *Communications of the ACM, 36*(1), 48–61.

Foster, I., & Kesselman, C. (2004). *The Grid: Blueprint for a new computing infrastructure* (2nd ed.). San Francisco: Morgan Kaufmann.

Fussell, S. R., Kraut, R. E., & Siegel, J. (2000). *Coordination of communication: Effects of shared visual context on collaborative work.* Paper presented at the CSCW 2000, New York.

Gale, C., & Monk, A. (2000). Where am I looking? The accuracy of video-mediated gaze awareness. *Perception & Psychophysics, 62*, 586–595.

Giles, J. (2005). Internet encyclopaedias go head to head. *Nature, 438*, 900–901.

Godefroid, P., Herbsleb, J. D., Jagadeesan, L. J., & Li, D. (2000). Ensuring privacy in presence awareness systems: An automated verification approach. *Proceedings of CSCW 2000* (pp. 59–68). New York: ACM.

Grayson, D. M., & Monk, A. (2003). Are you looking at me? Eye contact and desktop video conferencing. *ACM Transactions on Computer-Human Interaction, 10*(3), 221–243.

Greif, I. (Ed.) (1988). *Computer-supported cooperative work: A book of readings.* San Mateo, CA: Morgan Kaufmann.

Grudin, J. (1988). Why CSCW applications fail: Problems in the design and evaluation of organizational interfaces. *Proceedings of the Conference on Computer Supported Cooperative Work* (pp. 85–93). Portland, OR: ACM Press.

Grudin, J. (1994). Groupware and social dynamics: Eight challenges for developers. *Communications of the ACM, 37*(1), 92–105.

Grudin, J., & Palen, L. (1995). Why groupware succeeds: Discretion or mandate? *Proceedings of the European Computer Supported Cooperative Work* (pp. 263–278). Stockholm, Sweden: Springer.

Gutwin, C., & Greenberg, S. (1999). The effects of workspace awareness support on the usability of real-time distributed groupware. *ACM Transactions on Computer-Human Interaction, 6*, 243–281.

Hall, E. T. (1982). *The Hidden Dimension.* New York: Anchor Doubleday Books.

Herbsleb, J. D., Mockus, A., Finholt, T. A., & Grinter, R. E. (2000). Distance, dependencies, and delay in a global collaboration. *Proceedings of CSCW 2000* (pp. 319–328). New York: ACM.

Herlocker, J. L., Konstan, J. A., & Riedl, J. (2000). Explaining collaborative filtering recommendations. *Proceedings of CSCW 2000* (pp. 241–250). New York: ACM.

Hindmarsh, J., Fraser, M., Heath, C., Benford, S., & Greenhalgh, C. (1998). Fragmented Interaction: Establishing Mutual Orientation in Virtual Environments, *Proceedings of Conference on Computer-Supported Cooperative Work* (pp. 217–226). Portland, OR: ACM Press.

Hollingshead, A. B., McGrath, J. E., & O'Connor, K. M. (1993). Group performance and communication technology: A longitudinal study of computer-mediated versus face-to-face work. *Small Group Research, 24*, 307–333.

Huang, W., Olson, J. S., & Olson, G. M. (2002). *Camera angle affects dominance in video-mediated communication.* Paper presented at the CHI 2002, New York.

Isaacs, E., Walendowski, A., Whittaker, S., Schiano, D. J., & Kamm, C. (2002). *The character, functions, and styles of instant messaging in the workplace.* Paper presented at the CSCW 2002, New York.

Jensen, C., Farnham, S. D., Drucker, S. M., & Kollock, P. (2000). The effect of communication modality on cooperation in on-line environments. *Proceedings of CHI '2000.* (pp. 470–477). New York: ACM Press.

Karsenty, L. (1999). Cooperative work and shared visual context: An empirical study of comprehension problems in side-by-side and remote help dialogues. *Human-Computer Interaction, 14,* 283–315.

Kendon, A. (1967). Some functions of gaze direction in social interaction. *Acta Psychologia, 26,* 22–63.

Kiesler, S., & Cummings, J. N. (2002). What do we know about proximity and distance in work groups? A legacy of research. In P. J. Hinds & S. Kiesler (Eds.), *Distributed work* (pp. 57–80). Cambridge, MA: MIT Press.

Kiesler, S., Sproull, L., & Waters, K. (1996). Prisoner's dilemma experiment on cooperation with people and human-like computers. *Journal of Personality and Social Psychology, 70*(1), 47–65.

Koschmann, T. (1996). *CSCL: Theory and practice of an emerging paradigm.* Lawrence Erlbaum Associates. Hillsdale, NJ.

Koschmann, T., Hall, R., & Miyake, N. (2002). *CSCW 2: Carrying forward the conversation.* Lawrence Erlbaum Associates. Hillsdale, NJ.

Koschmann, T., Suthers, D. D., & Chan, T. (2005). *Computer supported collaborative learning 2005: The next 10 years!* Lawrence Erlbaum Associates. Hillsdale, NJ.

Kraemer, K. L., & Pinsonneault, A. (1990). Technology and groups: Assessments of empirical research. In J. Galegher, R. Kraut, & C. Egido (Eds.), *Intellectual teamwork: Social and technological foundations of cooperative work* (pp. 373–405). Hillsdale, NJ: Lawrence Erlbaum Associates.

Krauss, R. M., & Bricker, P. D. (1966). Effects of transmission delay and access delay on the efficiency of verbal communication. *Journal of the Acoustical Society, 41,* 286–292.

Kraut, R. E., Fussell, S. R., & Siegel, J. (2003). Visual information as a conversational resource in collaborative physical tasks. *Human-Computer Interaction, 18*(1–2), 13–39.

Kraut, R. E., Gergle, D., & Fussell, S. R. (2002). *The use of visual information in shared visual spaces: Informing the development of virtual co-presence.* Paper presented at the CSCW 2002, New York.

Kraut, R., Kiesler, S., Boneva, B., Cummings, J., Helgeson, V. & Crawford, A. (2002). Internet paradox revisited. *Journal of Social Issues, 58*(1), 49–74.

Kraut, R., Patterson, M., Lundmark, V., Kiesler, S., Mukopadhyay, T., & Scherlis, W. (1998). Internet paradox: A social technology that reduces social involvement and psychological well-being. *American Psychologist, 53,* 1071–1031.

Kraut, R. E., Sunder, S., Telang, R., & Morris, J. (2005). Pricing electronic mail to solve the problem of spam. *Human-Computer Interaction, 20,* 195–223.

Lange, B. M. (1992). Electronic group calendaring: Experiences and expectations. In D. Coleman (Ed.) *Groupware* (pp. 428–432). San Mateo, CA: Morgan Kaufmann.

Longstaff, T. A., Ellis, J. T., Hernan, S. V., Lipson, H. F., McMillan, R. D., Pesanti, L. H., & Simmel, D. (1997). Security on the Internet. In *The Froehlich/Kent Encyclopedia of Telecommunications* (Vol. 15, pp. 231–255). New York: Marcel Dekker.

Luff, P., Heath, C., Kuzuoka, H., Hindmarsh, J., & Oyama, S. (2003). Fractured ecologies: Creating environments for collaboration. *Human-Computer Interaction, 18*(1–2), 51–84.

Mackay, W. E. (1989). Diversity in the use of electronic mail: A preliminary inquiry. *ACM Transactions on Office Information Systems, 6,* 380–397.

Malone, T. W., Grant, K. R., Lai, K. Y., Rao, R., & Rosenblitt, D. A. (1989). The information lens: An intelligent system for information sharing and coordination. In M. H. Olson (Ed.). *Technological support for work group collaboration* (pp. 65–88). Hillsdale, NJ: Lawrence Erlbaum Associates.

Markus, M. L. (1983). *Systems in Organization: Bugs and Features.* San Jose, CA: Pitman.

Markus, M. L., & Connolly, T. (1990). Why CSCW applications fail: Problems in the adoption of interdependent work tools. *Proceedings of the Conference on Computer Supported Cooperative Work* (pp. 371–380). Los Angeles, CA: ACM Press.

McDaniel, S. E., Olson, G. M., & Magee, J. S. (1996). Identifying and analyzing multiple threads in computer-mediated and face-to-face conversations. *Proceeding of the ACM Conference on Computer Supported Cooperative Work* (pp. 39–47). Cambridge, MA: ACM Press.

McLeod, P. L. (1992). An assessment of the experimental literature on electronic support of group work: Results of a meta-analysis. *Human-Computer Interaction, 7,* 257–280.

Monk, A., & Gale, C. (2002). A look is worth a thousand words: Full gaze awareness in video-mediated communication. *Discourse Processes, 33*(3), 257–278.

Moran, T. P., Chiu, P., Harrison, S., Kurtenbach, G., Minneman, S., & van Melle, W. (1996). Evolutionary engagement in an ongoing collaborative work process: A case study. *Proceeding of the ACM Conference on Computer Supported Cooperative Work* (pp. 150–159). Cambridge, MA: ACM Press.

Mosier, J. N., & Tammaro, S. G. (1997). When are group scheduling tools useful? *Computer Supported Cooperative Work, 6,* 53–70.

Muller, M. J., Raven, M. E., Kogan, S., Millen, D. R., & Carey, K. (2003). *Introducing chat into business organizations: Toward an instant messaging maturity model.* Paper presented at the GROUP '03, New York.

Nardi, B. A., Schwarz, H., Kuchinsky, A., Leichner, R., Whittaker, S., & Sclabassi, R. (1993). *Turning away from talking heads: The use of video-as-data in neurosurgery.* Paper presented at the CHI 93, New York.

Nardi, B. A., Whittaker, S., & Bradner, E. (2000). Interaction and outeraction: Instant messaging in action. *Proceedings of the ACM Conference on Computer Supported Cooperative Work* (pp. 79–88). Philadelphia, PA: ACM Press.

Nardi, B. A., Schiano, D. J., Gumbrecht, M., & Swartz, L. (2004). Why we blog? *Communications of the ACM, 47*(12), 41–46.

National Research Council. (1993). *National collaboratories: Applying information technology for scientific research.* Washington, D.C.: National Academy Press.

Nohria, N., & Eccles, R. G. (Eds.). (1992). *Networks and organizations: Structure, form, and action.* Boston: Harvard Business School Press.

Nunamaker, J. F., Dennis, A. R., Valacich, J. S., Vogel, D. R., & George, J. F. (1991). Electronic meeting systems to support group work. *Communications of the ACM, 34*(7), 40–61.

O'Conaill, B., Whittaker, S., & Wilbur. S. (1993). Conversations over videoconferences: An evaluation of the spoken aspects of video mediated communication. *Human-Computer Interaction, 8,* 389–428.

O'Hara-Devereaux, M., & Johansen, R. (1994). *Global work: Bridging distance, culture & time.* San Francisco: Jossey-Bass.

Okada, K., Maeda, F., Ichicawaa, Y., & Matsushita, Y. (1994). *Multiparty videoconferencing at virtual social distance: MAJIC design.* Paper presented at the CSCW 94, New York.

Olson, G. M., & Olson, J. S. (2000). Distance matters. *Human-Computer Interaction, 15*, 139–179.

Olson, G. M., Atkins, D., Clauer, R., Weymouth, T., Prakash, A., Finholt, T., Jahanian, F., & Rasmussen, C. (2001). Technology to support distributed team science: The first phase of the Upper Atmospheric Research Collaboratory (UARC) In G. M. Olson, T. Malone, & J. Smith (Eds.), *Coordination theory and collaboration technology* (pp. 761–783). Hillsdale, NJ: Lawrence Erlbaum Associates.

Olson, G. M., Olson, J. S., Bos, N., & the SOC Data Team (2004). International collaborative science on the net. In W. Blanpied (Ed.), *Proceedings of the Trilateral Seminar on Science, Society and the Internet* (pp. 65–77). Arlington, VA: George Mason University.

Olson, J. S., Olson, G. M., & Meader, D.K. (1995). What mix of video and audio is useful for remote real-time work? *Proceedings of CHI '95* (pp. 362–368). Denver, CO: ACM Press.

Olson, J. S., Olson, G. M., Storrøsten, M., & Carter, M. (1993). Group work close up: A comparison of the group design process with and without a simple group editor. *ACM Transactions on Information Systems, 11*, 321–348.

Olson, J. S., & Teasley, S. (1996). Groupware in the wild: Lessons learned from a year of virtual collocation. *Proceeding of the ACM Conference on Computer Supported Cooperative Work* (pp. 419–427). Cambridge, MA: ACM Press.

Olson, M. H., & Bly, S. A. (1991). The Portland experience: A report on a distributed research group. *International Journal of Man-Machine Studies, 34*, 211–228.

Orlikowski, W. J., & Gash, D. C. (1994). Technological frames: Making sense of information technology in organizations. *ACM Transactions on Information Systems, 12*, 174–207.

Palen, L., & Grudin, J. (2002). Discretionary adoption of group support software: lessons from calendar applications. In B. E. Munkvold (Ed.), *Implementing collaboration technologies in industry* (pp. 159–180). Springer-Verlag. London.

Park, K. S., Kapoor, A., & Leigh, J. (2000). Lessons learned from employing multiple perspective in a collaborative virtual environment for visualizing scientific data. *Proceedings of ACM CVE'2000 Conference on Collaborative Virtual Environments* (pp. 73–82). San Francisco, CA: ACM Press.

Prinz, W., & Kolvenbach, S. (1996). Support for workflows in a ministerial environment. *Proceedings of the Conference on Computer Supported Cooperative Work* (pp. 199–208). Cambridge, MA: ACM Press.

Putnam, R. D. (2000). *Bowling alone: The collapse and revival of American community*. New York: Simon & Schuster.

Resnick, P. (2002). Beyond bowling together: SocioTechnical capital. In J. M. Carroll (Ed.), *Human-computer interaction in the new millennium* (pp. 647–672). New York: ACM Press.

Resnick, P., & Varian, H. R. (Eds.) (1997). Special section: Recommender systems. *Communications of the ACM, 40*(3), 56–89.

Rocco, E. (1998) Trust breaks down in electronic contexts but can be repaired by some initial face-to-face contact. *Proceedings of CHI'98* (pp. 496–502). Los Angeles, CA: ACM Press.

Rocco, E., Finholt, T., Hofer, E. C., & Herbsleb (2000). *Designing as if trust mattered*. (CREW Technical Report). University of Michigan, Ann Arbor.

Ruhleder, K., & Jordan, B. (2001). Co-constructing non-mutual realities: Delay-generated trouble in distributed interaction. *Computer Supported Cooperative Work, 10*(1), 113–138.

Satzinger, J., & Olfman, L. (1992). A research program to assess user perceptions of group work support. *Proceeding of CHI'92* (pp. 99–106). Monterey, CA: ACM Press.

Schafer, J. B., Konstan, J., & Riedl, J., (2001). Electronic commerce recommender applications. *Journal of Data Mining and Knowledge Discovery, 5*(1/2), 115–152.

Schatz, B. R., & Hardin, J. B. (1994). NCSA Mosaic and the World Wide Web: Global hypermedia protocols for the internet. *Science, 265*, 895–901.

Schmandt, C., & Marti, S. (2005). Active Messenger: E-mail filtering and delivery in a heterogeneous network. *Human-Computer Interaction, 20*, 163–194.

Short, J., Williams, E., & Christie, B. (1976). *The social psychology of telecommunications.* New York: Wiley.

Siegel, J., Dubrovsky, V., Kiesler, S., & McGuire, T. W. (1986). Group processes in computer-mediated communication. *Organizational Behavior and Human Decision Processes, 37*(2), 157–187.

Singhal, S., & Zyda, M. (1999). *Networked virtual environments: Design and implementation.* New York: Addison-Wesley.

Slavin, R. E. (1994). *Cooperative learning: Theory, research, and practice* (2nd ed.). Boston: Allyn & Bacon.

Sproull, L., & Kiesler, S. (1991). *Connections: New ways of working in the networked organization.* Cambridge, MA: MIT Press.

Starner, T., & Rhodes, B. (2004). Wearable computer. In W. S. Bainbridge (Ed.), *Berkshire encyclopedia of human-computer interaction* (Vol. 2, pp. 797–802). Great Barrington, MA.: Berkshire Publishing Group.

Straus, S. G. (1996). Getting a clue: The effects of communication media and information distribution on participation and performance in computer-mediated and face-to-face groups. *Small Group Research, 1*, 115–142.

Straus, S. G. (1997). Technology, group process, and group outcomes: Testing the connections in computer-mediated and face-to-face groups. *Human-Computer Interaction, 12*(3), 227–266.

Straus, S. G., & McGrath, J. E. (1994). Does the medium matter: The interaction of task and technology on group performance and member reactions. *Journal of Applied Psychology, 79*, 87–97.

Tanenbaum, A. S. (2003). *Computer networks* (4th ed.). Upper Saddle River, NJ: Prentice Hall PTR.

Tang, J. C., & Isaacs, E. (1993). Why do users like video? *Computer Supported Cooperative Work, 1*(3), 163–196.

Tang, J. C., Yankelovich, N., Begole, J., van Kleek, M., Li, F., & Bhalodia, J. (2001). ConNexus to Awarenex: Extending awareness to mobile users. *Proceedings of CHI 2001* (pp. 221–228). New York: ACM.

Teasley, S. D., Covi, L. A., Krishnan, M. S., & Olson, J. S. (2002). Rapid software development through team collocation. *IEEE Transactions on Software Engineering, 28*, 671–683.

Veinott, E., Olson, J. S., Olson, G. M., & Fu, X. (1999). Video helps remote work: Speakers who need to negotiate common ground benefit from seeing each other. *Proceedings of the Conference on Computer-Human Interaction, CHI'99* (pp. 302–309). Pittsburgh, PA: ACM Press.

Vertegaal, R. (1999). *The GAZE groupware system: Mediating joint attention in multiparty communication and collaboration.* Paper presented at the CHI 99, New York.

Vertegaal, R., Slagter, R., van der Veer, G., & Nijholt, A. (2001). *Eye gaze patterns in conversations: There is more to conversational agents than meets the eye.* Paper presented at the CHI 2001, New York.

Viegas, F. B., Wattenberg, M., & Dave, K. (2004). Studying cooperation and conflict between authors with history flow visualizations. *Proceedings of CHI 2004* (pp. 575–582). New York: ACM.

Wellman, B. (2001). *Design considerations for social networkware: Little boxes, glocalization, and networked individualism.* Draft ms.

Whittaker, S. (2005). Supporting collaborative task management in e-mail. *Human-Computer Interaction, 20,* 49–88.

Whittaker, S., Bellotti, V., & Moody, P. (2005). Introduction to this special issue on revisiting and reinventing e-mail. *Human-Computer Interaction, 10,* 1–9.

Whittaker, S., Geelhoed, E., & Robinson, E. (1993). Shared workspaces: How do they work and when are they useful? *International Journal of Man-Machine Studies, 39*(5), 813–842.

Whittaker, S., & Sidner, C. (1996). Email overload: Exploring personal information management of email. *Proceeding of CHI'96* (pp. 276–283). Vancouver, BC: ACM Press.

Williams, E. (1977). Experimental comparisons of face-to-face and mediated communication: A review. *Psychological Bulletin, 84,* 963–976.

Winograd, T. (1988). A language/action perspective on the design of cooperative work. *Human Computer Interaction, 3,* 3–30.

Yang, H., & Olson, G. M. (2002). Exploring collaborative navigation: The effect of perspectives on group performance. *Proceedings of CVE'02* (pp. 135–142). New York: ACM Press.

Zheng, J., Bos, N., Olson, J. S., Gergle, D. & Olson, G. M. (2001). Trust without touch: Jump-start trust with social chat. *Paper presented at the Conference on Human Factors in Computing Systems CHI-01.* Seattle, WA: ACM Press.

The intellectual challenge of CSCW

The gap between social requirements and technical feasibility

Mark S. Ackerman

Abstract   Over the last 10 years, Computer-Supported Cooperative Work (CSCW) has identified a base set of findings. These findings are taken almost as assumptions within the field. In summary, they argue that human activity is highly flexible, nuanced, and contextualized and that computational entities such as information sharing, roles, and social norms need to be similarly flexible, nuanced, and contextualized. However, current systems cannot fully support the social world uncovered by these findings. In this article I argue that there is an inherent gap between the social requirements of CSCW and its technical mechanisms. The *social–technical gap* is the divide between what we know we must support socially and what we can support technically. Exploring, understanding, and hopefully ameliorating this social–technical gap is the central challenge for CSCW as a field and one of the central problems for human–computer interaction. Indeed, merely attesting the continued centrality of this gap could be one of the important intellectual contributions of CSCW. I also argue that the challenge of the social–technical gap creates an opportunity to refocus CSCW.

Introduction

Over the last 10 years, Computer-Supported Cooperative Work (CSCW) has identified a base set of findings. These findings are taken almost as assumptions within the field. Indeed, many of these findings have been known and have been debated within computer science, information science, and information technology for over 20 years. I discuss the findings at length later, but in summary, they argue that human activity is highly flexible, nuanced, and contextualized and that computational entities such as information transfer, roles, and policies need to be similarly flexible, nuanced, and contextualized.

Simply put, we do not know how to build systems that fully support the social world uncovered by these findings. I argue here that it is neither from lack of

Ackerman, M. S. (2000) 'The intellectual challenge of CSCW: the gap between social requirements and technical feasibility', *Human-Computer Interaction*, 15(2), pp. 179–203. Lawrence Erlbaum Associates Inc.

trying nor from lack of understanding by technical people. Numerous attempts have been made, not only within CSCW, but within many other subfields of computer science to bridge what I call here the *social–technical gap*, the great divide between what we know we must support socially and what we can support technically. Technical systems are rigid and brittle – not only in any intelligent understanding, but also in their support of the social world.

Researchers and computer professionals have edged toward a better understanding of this social–technical gap in the last 10 years, and CSCW systems have certainly become more sophisticated. We have learned to construct systems with computer-mediated communication (CMC) elements to allow people enough communicative suppleness; yet, these systems still lack much computational support for sharing information, roles, and other social policies. Important CSCW technical mechanisms (e.g., floor or session control) lack the flexibility required by social life. The social–technical gap still exists and is wide. Exploring, understanding, and hopefully ameliorating this social–technical gap is the central challenge for CSCW as a field and one of the central problems for human–computer interaction (HCI). Other areas of computer science dealing with users also face the social–technical gap, but CSCW, with its emphasis on augmenting social activity, cannot avoid it. I also argue later that the challenge of the social–technical gap creates an opportunity to refocus CSCW as a Simonian science of the artificial (where a science of the artificial is suitably revised from Simon's strictly empiricist grounds).

This article proceeds in three parts. First, I provide an overview of CSCW, briefly reviewing the major social and technical findings of the field, particularly with regard to the construction of computational systems. Next, I argue that there is an inherent gap between the social requirements of CSCW and its technical mechanisms; I demonstrate this through a discussion of a particular CSCW research problem, privacy in information systems. Finally, I discuss potential resolutions for the social–technical gap. In the section, the requirements for a science of the artificial are evaluated, along with the need for such a viewpoint for CSCW.

A biased summary of CSCW findings

Most of this section will be obvious to CSCW researchers but might be a useful overview for non-CSCW researchers. This section does not attempt to be a complete summary of CSCW assumptions and findings; rather, the emphasis is on those social aspects most germane to the social–technical gap.

Although March and Simon's (1958; Simon, 1957) limited rational actor model underlies CSCW, as it does for most of computer science, CSCW researchers also tend to assume the following:

• Social activity is fluid and nuanced, and this makes systems technically difficult to construct properly and often awkward to use. A considerable range of social inquiry has established that the details of interaction matter (Garfinkel, 1967; Strauss, 1993) and that people handle this detail with considerable agility (Garfinkel, 1967; Heritage, 1984; Suchman, 1987). (In this article, following Strauss, 1991, and others, I use *nuanced* narrowly to denote the depth of detail as well as its fine-grained quality. Connotations to the term include agility and smoothness in the use of the detail.) People's emphases on which details to consider or to act on differ according to the situation (Suchman, 1987). Yet, systems often have considerable difficulty handling this detail and flexibility.

For example, Goffman (1961, 1971) noted that people have very nuanced behavior concerning how and with whom they wish to share information. People are concerned about whether to release this piece of information to that person at this time, and they have very complex understandings of people's views of themselves, the current situation, and the effects of disclosure. Yet, access control systems often have very simple models. As another example, because people often lack shared histories and meanings (especially when they are in differing groups or organizations), information must be recontextualized to reuse experience or knowledge. Systems often assume a shared understanding of information.

One finding of CSCW is that it is sometimes easier and better to augment technical mechanisms with social mechanisms to control, regulate, or encourage behavior (Sproull & Kiesler, 1991). An example is the use of chat facilities to allow norm creation and negotiation in commercial CSCW systems.

- Members of organizations sometimes have differing (and multiple) goals, and conflict may be as important as cooperation in obtaining issue resolutions (Kling, 1991). Groups and organizations may not have shared goals, knowledge, meanings, and histories (Heath & Luff, 1996; Star & Ruhleder, 1994).

If there are hidden or conflicting goals, people will resist concretely articulating their goals. On the other hand, people are good at resolving communicative and activity breakdowns (Suchman, 1987).

Without shared meanings or histories, meanings will have to be negotiated (Boland, Tenkasi, & Te'eni, 1994). As well, information will lose context as it crosses boundaries (Ackerman & Halverson, 2000). Sometimes this loss is beneficial in that it hides the unnecessary details of others' work. Boundary objects (Star, 1989) are information artifacts that span two or more groups; each group will attach different understandings and meanings to the information. Boundary objects let groups coordinate because the details of the information used in one group need not be understood completely by any other group.

An active area of CSCW research is in finding ways to manage the problems and trade-offs resulting from conflict and coordination (Malone & Crowston, 1994; Schmidt & Simone, 1996).

- Exceptions are normal in work processes. It has been found that much of office work is handling exceptional situations (Suchman & Wynn, 1984). In addition, roles are often informal and fluid (Strauss, 1993). CSCW approaches to workflow and process engineering primarily try to deal with exceptions and fluidity (e.g., Katzenberg, Pickard, & McDermott, 1996).
- People prefer to know who else is present in a shared space, and they use this awareness to guide their work (Erickson et al., 1999). For example, air traffic controllers monitor others in their workspace to anticipate their future workflow (Bentley et al., 1992; Hughes, King, Rodden, & Andersen, 1994). This effect has also been found in other control room settings and trading floors (Heath, Jirotka, Luff, & Hindmarsh, 1994). An active area of research is adding awareness (i.e., knowing who is present) and peripheral awareness (i.e., low-level monitoring of others' activity) to shared communication systems. Recent research is addressing the trade-offs inherent in awareness versus privacy, and in awareness versus disturbing others (Hudson & Smith, 1996).
- Visibility of communication exchanges and of information enables learning and greater efficiencies (Hutchins, 1995). For example, copilots learn from observing pilots work (i.e., situated learning, learning in a community of practice). However, it has been found that people are aware that making their work visible may also open them to criticism or management; thus, visibility may also make work more formal and reduce sharing. A very active area of CSCW is trying to determine ways to manage the trade-offs in sharing. This is tied to the issue of incentives, discussed later.
- The norms for using a CSCW system are often actively negotiated among users. These norms of use are also subject to renegotiation (Strauss, 1991). CSCW systems should have some secondary mechanism or communication back channel to allow users to negotiate the norms of use, exceptions, and breakdowns among themselves, making the system more flexible.
- There appears to be a critical mass problem for CSCW systems (Markus, 1990). With an insufficient number of users, people will not use a CSCW system. This has been found in e-mail, synchronous communication, and calendar systems. There also appears to be a similar problem with communication systems if the number of active users falls beneath a threshold (called the "melt-down" problem in Ackerman & Palen, 1996). Adoption of CSCW systems is often more difficult than for single-user systems because CSCW systems often require initial buy-in from groups of people, rather than individuals, as well as continued buy-in.
- People not only adapt to their systems, they adapt their systems to their needs (coevolution; Orlikowski, 1992a; O'Day, 1996). These adaptations can be quite sophisticated. People may use systems in ways completely unanticipated by the designers. One CSCW finding is that people will need to change their categories over time (Suchman, 1994). System designers should assume that people will try to tailor their use of a system.

- Incentives are critical. A classic finding in CSCW, for example, is that managers and workers may not share incentive or reward structures; systems will be less used than desired if this is true (Grudin, 1989). Another classic finding is that people will not share information in the absence of a suitable organizational reward structure (Orlikowski, 1992b). Even small incremental costs in collaborating must be compensated (either by reducing the cost of collaboration or offering derived benefits). Thus, many CSCW researchers try to use available data to reduce the cost of sharing and collaborative work.

Not every CSCW researcher would agree with all of the aforementioned assumptions and findings, and commercial systems (e.g., workflow systems) sacrifice one or more of them. The previous list provides an ideal type of what needs to be provided. Because some of the idealization must be ignored to provide a working solution, this trade-off provides much of the tension in any given implementation between "technically working" and "organizationally workable" systems. CSCW as a field is notable for its attention and concern to managing this tension.

[...]

References

Ackerman, M. S., & Halverson, C. (2000). Re-examining organizational memory. *Communications of the ACM, 43*(1), 58–63.

Ackerman, M. S., & Palen, L. (1996). The zephyr help instance: Promoting ongoing activity in a CSCW system. *Proceedings of the CHI'96 Conference on Human Factors in Computing Systems*, 268–275. New York: ACM.

Bentley, R., Rodden, T., Sawyer, P., Sommerville, I., Hughes, J., Randall, D., & Shapiro, D. (1992). Ethnographically-informed systems design for air traffic control. *Proceedings of the CSCW'92 Conference on Computer Supported Cooperative Work*, 123–129. New York: ACM.

Boland, R. J., Jr., Tenkasi, R. V., & Te'eni, D. (1994). Designing information technology to support distributed cognition. *Organization Science, 5*, 456–475.

Erickson, T., Smith, D. N., Kellogg, W. A., Laff, M., Richards, J. T., & Bradner, E. (1999). Socially translucent systems: Social proxies, persistent conversation, and the design of "babble." *Proceedings of the CHI'99 Conference on Human Factors in Computing Systems*, 72–79. New York: ACM.

Garfinkel, H. (1967). *Studies in ethnomethodology*. Englewood Cliffs, NJ: Prentice Hall.

Goffman, E. (1961). *The presentation of self in everyday life*. New York: Anchor-Doubleday.

Goffman, E. (1971). *Relations in public*. New York: Basic Books.

Grudin, J. (1989). Why groupware applications fail: Problems in design and evaluation. *Office: Technology and People, 4*, 245–264.

Heath, C., Jirotka, M., Luff, P., & Hindmarsh, J. (1994). Unpacking collaboration: The interactional organisation of trading in a city dealing room. *Computer Supported Cooperative Work Journal, 3*(2), 147–165.

Heath, C., & Luff, P. (1992). Collaboration and control: Crisis management and multimedia technology in London underground line control rooms. *Computer Supported Cooperative Work Journal, 1*(1), 69–94.

Heath, C., & Luff, P. (1996). Documents and professional practice: "Bad" organizational reasons for "good" clinical records. *Proceedings of the CSCW'96 Conference on Computer Supported Cooperative Work*, 354–363. New York: ACM.

Heritage, J. (1984). *Garfinkel and ethnomethodology*. Cambridge, England: Polity.

Hudson, S. E., & Smith, I. (1996). Techniques for addressing fundamental privacy and disruption tradeoffs in awareness support systems. *Proceedings of the CSCW'96 Conference on Computer Supported Cooperative Work*, 248–257. New York: ACM.

Hughes, J., King, V., Rodden, T., & Andersen, H. (1994). Moving out from the control room: Ethnography in system design. *Proceedings of the CSCW'94 Conference on Computer Supported Cooperative Work*, 429–439. New York: ACM.

Hutchins, E. (1995). How a cockpit remembers its speeds. *Cognitive Science, 19*, 265–288.

Katzenberg, B., Pickard, F., & McDermott, J. (1996). Computer support for clinical practice: Embedding and evolving protocols of care. *Proceedings of the CSCW'96 Conference on Computer Supported Cooperative Work*, 364–369. New York: ACM.

Kling, R. (1991). Cooperation, coordination and control in computer-supported work. *Communications of the ACM, 34*(12), 83–88.

Malone, T. W., & Crowston, K. (1994). The interdisciplinary study of coordination. *ACM Computing Surveys, 26*(1), 87–119.

March, J. G., & Simon, H. A. (1958). *Organizations*. New York: Wiley.

Markus, M. L. (1990). Toward a "critical mass" theory of interactive media. In J. Fulk & C. Steinfield (Eds.), *Organizations and communication technology* (pp. 194–218). Newbury Park, CA: Sage.

O'Day, V. L., Bobrow, D. G., & Shirley, M. (1996). The socio-technical design circle. *Proceedings of the CSCW'96 Conference on Computer-Supported Cooperative Work*, 160–169. New York: ACM.

Orlikowski, W. J. (1992a). The duality of technology: Rethinking the concept of technology in organizations. *Organization Science, 3*, 398–427.

Orlikowski, W. J. (1992b). Learning from notes: Organizational issues in groupware implementation. *Proceedings of the CSCW'92 Computer Supported Cooperative Work*, 362–369. New York: ACM.

Schmidt, K., & Simone, C. (1996). Coordination mechanisms: Towards a conceptual foundation of CSCW systems design. *Computer Supported Cooperative Work Journal, 5*(2/3), 155–200.

Simon, H. A. (1957). *Administrative behavior*. New York: Macmillan.

Sproull, L., & Kiesler, S. (1991). *Connections: New ways of working in the networked organization*. Cambridge, MA: MIT Press.

Star, S. L. (1989). The structure of ill-structured solutions: Boundary objects and heterogeneous distributed problem solving. In L. Gasser & M. Huhns (Eds.), *Distributed artificial intelligence* (pp. 37–54). San Mateo, CA: Kaufmann.

Star, S. L., & Ruhleder, K. (1994). Steps toward an ecology of infrastructure: Complex problems in design and access for large-scale collaborative systems. *Proceedings of the CSCW'94 Conference on Computer Supported Cooperative Work*, 253–264. New York: ACM.

Strauss, A. (1991). *Creating sociological awareness: Collective images and symbolic representations*. New Brunswick, NJ: Transaction.

Strauss, A. L. (1993). *Continual permutations of action*. New York: Aldine de Gruyter.

Suchman, L. A. (1987). *Plans and situated actions: The problem of human–computer communication*. New York: Cambridge University Press.

Suchman, L. (1994). Do categories have politics? *Computer Supported Cooperative Work Journal, 2*, 177–190.

Suchman, L., & Wynn, E. (1984). Procedures and problems in the office. *Office: Technology and People, 2*, 133–154.

Evaluating collaborative technologies – a simple method

Magnus Ramage

Collaborative technologies are complex and multi-faceted, and evaluating them (understanding how effective they are in use) is difficult. This is partly because they are complicated technical systems, comprising software, hardware and communications components; but also because they have effects upon individuals, groups and organisations. Thus to evaluate collaborative technologies in use requires us to take into account all of these different aspects.

In research I carried out on evaluation (Ramage 1999), I presented a simple method for doing this. The method starts by observing that the main issues to be considered in evaluation are not just interconnected but also occur as a series of layers. It doesn't make sense to ask about the usability of a piece of software if it perpetually crashes, and it doesn't make sense to ask about the effects on an organisation if the technology is unusable.

The kind of evaluation I am considering here is not solely technical, but crosses a range of different issues, and draws on a number of different academic disciplines (including computer science, psychology, management and sociology). This approach is applicable both to technologies in a particular context of use (e.g. implemented in a given organisation) and to a technology considered for any context.

It is worth observing that before any evaluation can be carried out, those performing it need to be clear as to what its *purpose* is. Each of the following activities can legitimately be called evaluation (as can others): studying the impact of an existing collaborative system in use in an organisation; developing a new piece of software and trying it out with potential users as part of the development process; examining a potential purchase of a piece of off-the-shelf software to be used in an organisation; a comparison of a series of different tools to look at their strengths and weaknesses. Which of these types of evaluation is being followed will make a big difference as to the way in which the evaluation is carried out, and how its results are used. However this method will help in a range of different types of evaluation.

The layers that I use are illustrated in Figure 7.1 below (updated slightly from my original work). These layers are very blurred, and various issues could appear

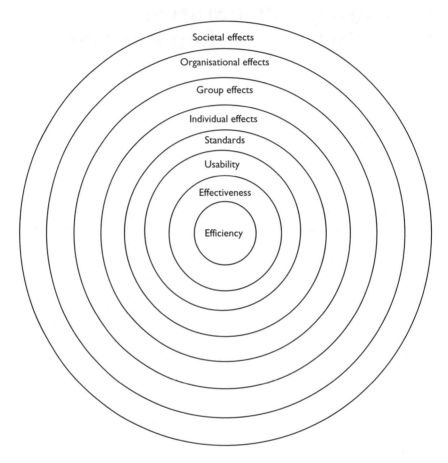

Figure 7.1 Layers of evaluation

in more than one layer, but they serve as a way to make sense of the wide range of issues involved. The layers can be described as follows:

- *Efficiency*: this layer is concerned with technical issues – whether the technology works as planned without crashing, whether the software is fast enough on the hardware used, etc.
- *Effectiveness*: even if the technology works well technically, it may not be doing what users and other key stakeholders actually need. This is the distinction sometimes drawn, originally by Peter Drucker (1974, p.45), between 'doing things right' (efficiency) and 'doing the right things' (effectiveness).
- *Usability*: issues here are concerned with how easy the technology is to use. In the first place this is to do with the user interface design, but it also relates to accessibility issues for people with disabilities, and its use across a range of devices (such as mobile phones).

- *Standards*: in many situations, technology has to comply with standards set by government agencies (for example on accessibility issues or on interference by wireless devices). These will differ from one country to another, and their nature will depend on the application domain.
- *Individual effects*: what impact does the technology have on the individuals using it? What does it do to their work?
- *Group effects*: what effect does the technology have on the group in which its users work (e.g. the cohesion of the group)? Does it make the group more or less effective?
- *Organisational effects*: if the group using the technology is based in a particular organisation (whether private or public sector), what effect does the technology have on the organisation? Is it positive or negative?
- *Societal effects*: does the technology have an impact on the wider society? If so, what kind of impact, and is it positive or negative?

The issues can be represented as a set of concentric circles or layers, rather like an onion (hence I have often referred to this as the onion model of evaluation).

It's worth noting that although this implies an order in which we might consider the issues, it doesn't mean that the inner layers are more important than the outer ones. However, we can also say that in moving out through the layers, we are looking at wider (and progressively less technical) issues.

The method in practice

As an example of this method in practice, consider the comparison between two currently popular collaborative technologies – blogs and wikis. They are designed for slightly different situations – blogs tend to be more individually focused, and wikis more collectively focused. However, both enable collaborative working in their different ways. The results of my example are shown in Table 7.1.

Table 7.1 Example of the evaluation method in use

Criterion	Blogs	Wikis
Efficiency	Low resource; can be hosted on own server or via third-party websites. Need to have moderately good internet connection.	Low resource; can be hosted on own server or via third-party websites. Need access to a PC with a moderately good internet connection.
Effectiveness	Editing sometimes possible with mobile devices, though commenting sometimes not. It is often better for one person to start a blog and others to comment, though some collective blogs exist and these blend into discussion forums.	An easy way for a group to create a collective website and share their ideas. Wiki tools typically store the revision history well and allow for discussion of pages as well as their creation.

Table 7.1 Continued

Criterion	Blogs	Wikis
Usability	Generally easy to use, well-designed interfaces. Can sometimes be difficult to find particular messages or threads.	Requires a higher level of technical ability than blogs, with use of formatting codes. Sites are usually well laid-out with plenty of documentation available.
Standards	Few relevant standards exist, though some countries have accessibility standards. Generally blogs, being text-based, work well with screen readers.	Accessibility standards will be the main relevant ones. Editing may not always be entirely accessible, although finished sites are often simple and consistent in appearance.
Individual effects	Individuals who have their own blog and post messages regularly often have a good outlet for their ideas and opinions, though need to take care about expectations (will anyone read them?) and how widely they tell people about their personal ideas.	Contributing to a large wiki can be satisfying for an individual, who is able to have an effect upon a larger project. The fact that anyone can edit entries means that individuals' work can be lost (regularly an issue on public wikis such as Wikipedia).
Group effects	Can be an excellent way for individuals in a group to share their ideas with others and to get comments. If just a few people in a group are blogging, it could make them out as unusual in a way that may or not be good for them.	Wikis are an easy way for a group to work together, but they need to agree a way of working to reduce the potential for conflicts.
Organisational effects	Similar to group effects on a larger scale. Some organisations have been quite hostile to their staff revealing things about them in their blogs; others find them an extremely useful piece of public relations.	Wikis can be a useful organisational tool, especially in small organisations, for easy creation of websites. The results are less flexible than some organisations may wish, and the finished websites may seem too alike.
Societal effects	Blogs are often said to have widened the range of people able to publish ideas, especially on political matters, and to have narrowed the gap between politicians and the public. However, they can lead to self-reinforcing debates (the so-called 'echo chamber').	Wikis as a general technology have had little societal effect, but Wikipedia in particular has had considerable effect. It is the subject of some debate as to whether it democratises knowledge or trivialises it, and the quality of the entries is likewise widely debated.

Conclusion

Evaluating collaborative technologies is not easy. There are many different kinds of issues to be taken into account. Ultimately this kind of evaluation is not so much about establishing that a particular technology is right or wrong, but how useful it is in a particular situation. I have found that the evaluation *process* is as important as the outcome of the evaluation, and that the different stakeholders involved learn many different things from that process. The method given here is a simple way of beginning that evaluation process.

References

Drucker, P. (1974) *Management: tasks, responsibilities, practices*, New York: Harper & Row.

Ramage, M. (1999) The learning way: evaluating co-operative systems, unpublished PhD thesis, University of Lancaster, UK.

Part III

Wikis and instant messaging

Introduction to Part III

Part III builds on concepts and technologies presented in Part II, through the use of three readings. We start by considering the differences between asynchronous and synchronous communication technologies. We then go on to explore two particular technologies, one asynchronous and one synchronous, in greater depth. These two technologies are wikis and instant messaging.

The first reading has been written for this reader by Helen Donelan and introduces the main communication technologies, including those that have gained popularity over the past few years (Donelan, 2010). The reading classifies technologies as either asynchronous (different time) or synchronous (same time) and compares the communication and collaboration supported. Comparisons are also made with other types of interaction such as face-to-face conversation. The concept of 'media richness'– a term that is explored in more detail in Part V – is used to compare interactions.

The second and third readings each explore a different technology in more depth. The use of wikis and instant messaging has become widespread over the past decade, both for personal and professional purposes. They have very different features, usage patterns, benefits and drawbacks. The two readings enable these differences to be explored.

The second reading by O'Leary (2008), originally published in the IEEE magazine, *Computer*, describes how wikis are used and implemented, their advantages and their limitations. Wikis are web pages where many people can contribute new content or modify existing content. They therefore enable asynchronous online collaboration and content generation. Editing permission can be granted to anyone with access to the web, or alternatively, restricted to a closed group. Either way, they are designed to allow content to be generated and shared quickly and easily through online collaboration. Although the first wiki was implemented in 1994, it was only really after Wikipedia, now the most well known wiki application, was launched in 2001 that wikis really started to gain prominence.

The third and final reading by Nardi *et al.* (2000) is about instant messaging (IM). IM allows text-based, synchronous communication between two or more people. Users of IM systems can create their own list of contacts and be notified when contacts are online. Messages usually appear in pop-up windows and tend to have a conversational feel. The use of shorthand and emoticons (images or combinations of symbols representing the current emotions of the writer ☺) help to speed up the typing of messages and convey the intended mood. Instant messaging has been around in some form for decades, but gained popularity as a social communication tool in the mid-to-late 1990s through products such as ICQ, AOL Instant Messenger (AIM), Windows Live Messenger (originally MSN Messenger), Yahoo! Messenger and (from 2005), Google Talk. IM also tends to appear as an additional feature within other types of communication and collaboration software packages. For example, Skype, an application that enables voice calls to be made over the Internet, includes an IM feature. IBM's Lotus Notes incorporates a business application of IM. Lotus Notes is a collaborative software application encompassing email, databases, shared documents, and its own enterprise grade IM, Lotus Sametime.

Nardi *et al.*'s article on IM is from a CSCW (computer-supported cooperative work) conference, and presents results from a research study into the use of instant messaging in the workplace. The reading illustrates some positive examples of informal communication and information exchange. However, in some situations IM can have negative impacts. Intrusion and distraction are well-known problems associated with the use of IM as frequent message alerts can distract from thought processes.

Part III focuses on two technologies: wikis and instant messaging. Both of these are now commonly used in workplace and learning settings as well as for personal purposes, but support very different online activities. The readings in this part highlight the different online communication and collaboration that is supported by these different technologies.

References

Donelan, H. (2010) 'Asynchronous and synchronous communication technologies', in Donelan, H., Kear, K. and Ramage, M. (eds.), (2010) *Online Communication and Collaboration*, London: Routledge, pp. 83–88.

Nardi, B. A., Whittaker, S. and Bradner, E. (2000) 'Interaction and outeraction: instant messaging in action', *Proceedings of the 2000 ACM conference on computer supported cooperative work*, Philadelphia, Pennsylvania, pp. 79–88.

O'Leary, D. E. (2007) 'Wikis: "from each according to his knowledge" ', *IEEE Computer*, 41(2), pp. 34–41.

Asynchronous and synchronous communication technologies

Helen Donelan

Introduction

There are many different technologies that enable us to communicate online. These have widely different properties and support different types of interaction, from basic text-based communication to advanced collaboration and information exchange activities. There are several different dimensions that can be used to classify or compare these technologies. For example:

- whether communication occurs synchronously (same time) or asynchronously (different time);
- the geographical distribution of participants (same place or different place);
- the number of participants and pattern of communication (one-to-one, one-to-many or group discussion);
- whether conversations and content are displayed publicly or kept private to those communicating.

This article introduces the major communication and collaboration technologies and focuses on the first dimension above to provide a comparison of their key benefits and drawbacks. Whilst comparisons are made primarily between synchronous and asynchronous technologies, the number of participants is also considered. Comparisons are also made with other types of interaction such as face-to-face and paper-based communication.

The term 'asynchronous' means that discussions do not occur in real-time. Participants can catch up with discussions by reading the trail of past messages and can make contributions at any time (Wallace, 1999, p. 5). This category includes email, discussion forums (sometimes called electronic bulletin boards or computer conferences), blogs and wikis. 'Synchronous' communication technologies require people to be online at the same time, and enable immediate response to messages as discussions occur in real-time. This category includes chat rooms, instant messaging and shared whiteboards. It also includes IP telephony and video conferencing where the communication, instead of being text based, is in audio and video format. This article focuses on text based technologies, although some mention is made of tools providing audio and video based communication.

Asynchronous technologies

The most well-known asynchronous communication technology is currently email. The use of email has grown enormously over the past two decades and it has become indispensable to many for both social and work-based communications. Email was originally seen as a method for bypassing the normal, more formal channels of letters and meetings, but has gained widespread acceptance as a method for undertaking business communications (Wallace, 2004, p. 90). Email messages tend to be more informal, both in content and structure, than paper based messages, although different styles are easily adopted (Wallace, 2004, p. 91). As with spoken communications, email can be used to convey a message to a single recipient (one-to-one) or multiple recipients (one-to-many). Electronic mailing lists or listservs (a software program for setting up and maintaining mailing lists) are a common method for distributing messages to many recipients. As with spoken communications, the size of the audience will influence the style adopted. People act differently in a one-to-one discussion (and equally a one-to-one email) than when addressing a larger audience (or sending an email to many recipients).

Email was originally seen as an efficient method for facilitating workplace communications. This was first due to the reduction in time needed to send and receive messages compared with paper based methods. Another reason email was seen as efficient was because it avoided the need for two (or more) people to be available at the same time for face-to-face or phone conversation to take place. However, many people now see email as having grown inefficient due to the volume of messages received – much of it often being spam (unwanted junk email), and the overload of information. In addition, younger people are beginning to express preferences for other online tools such as instant messaging (Lenhart, Madden and Hitlin, 2005, pp. 15–17) and social network sites (Lenhart & Madden, 2007). The role of email in the work place, therefore, is changing as other technologies start to play a larger role.

Another example of an asynchronous environment is a discussion forum. Here, group discussions are supported and ongoing conversations are organised into parallel discussion topics known as threads. These threads may comprise questions, responses, challenges or simply comments that are posted by participants. Individual messages need not be long to demonstrate a high level of activity in these forums. It is more important that each message should address issues raised by earlier messages and the conversation should progress. The asynchronicity of these environments enables a level of flexibility as to when participants contribute to discussions. However, this can also result in erratic activity. Discussions may be long and drawn out, depending on how often and when people visit the forum and respond. Some messages may receive many replies and others may be ignored (Wallace, 1999, p. 5).

Asynchronous discussion forums are discussed by Swan (2002) in the context of online learning communities. She reports that students can perceive online discussion to be more impartial and democratic than face-to-face classroom discussions. The asynchronous environment enables participants to consider others' comments before replying and therefore creates a culture that promotes reflection and learning. More generally, an advantage of asynchronous tools such as discussion forums is that they encourage and enable participation from all, not just the most confident. Postings are often well thought out and explained, as the contributor has time to collect their thoughts and reflect on past comments. In terms of drawbacks, users can have difficulty catching up with discussions when many messages have been posted since the user last logged on. Additionally, participants may wait long periods of time before receiving a response. Wegerif (1998) reported that a student on a distance learning course described using the course's discussion forum as 'isolating and unnerving' as they felt that they were sending messages 'out into silence'.

A more recent asynchronous communication technology is the weblog or blog. Blogs are journals published on the web for general consumption. They can be used to record the author's thoughts, experiences and philosophies and are usually text-based, although audio and video blogs are now beginning to emerge. Personal blogs, acting as online personal journals, tend to be focused more on one-to-many communication, rather than explicitly encouraging collaboration or discussion. However, feedback on blog posts can be facilitated through a number of options. Blogs written by authors wishing to disseminate and bring attention to more public issues, and to encourage debate, are also now commonplace. Some well recognised public blogs are very active and can attract a great deal of feedback from many contributors. Blogs can also be used to document the progress of a particular project or activity.

The wiki is another asynchronous technology. Wikis are collaborative websites now commonly used as a way for multiple users to create content or share knowledge online. Wikis can be publicly available websites that allow anyone to edit their content, such as Wikipedia, the web-based encyclopedia. Alternatively, they can be set up within smaller learning and workplace environments, to allow a specific set of contributors to pool their knowledge. Benefits of wikis include: they can be an efficient means to draw on knowledge from a network of people; they can be accurate as they draw on many sources of expertise; and they can encourage communities to develop (O'Leary, 2008). Drawbacks tend to be associated with the lack of authority or control. This can make it difficult to prevent people making contributions that may be inaccurate, biased, unreasonable or even commercially damaging. The lack of control can also mean that one person's contribution is overwritten almost immediately by another person, although the use of revision histories tends to make it straightforward to revert back to earlier versions.

Synchronous technologies

'Synchronous' technologies enable discussions to occur in real-time. Chat facilities, such as instant messaging (IM) and chat rooms, are examples of synchronous communication technologies. These are used for a wide range of purposes including learning, socialising, networking and gaming. As with asynchronous technologies some of these primarily support one-to-one exchanges whilst others facilitate group discussion. Instant messaging products tend to focus on one-to-one exchanges, although some do enable communication among groups. Users of chat rooms visit a virtual "room" to converse with others, although features may also enable one-to-one exchanges. Online chat is typically similar in style to face-to-face chat. There are multiple short, informal messages, typed quickly in response to previous messages.

Shared whiteboards are another example of a synchronous technology. These enable those logged in to view text and images posted by others as they are created. They enable concepts to be explained in the same way a classroom based whiteboard might be used. Many educational tools now encompass several technologies, such as an interactive whiteboard, instant messaging, and audio and/or video, to provide a real-time virtual classroom. Some tools also have features that allow sessions to be recorded. Whilst all the original technologies were synchronous in nature, these recording facilities introduce an asynchronous element in that sessions may be revisited later.

Synchronous technologies have the benefit of enabling users to give or receive an immediate response. They create an awareness of presence, knowing that recipients are actually around and able to respond immediately to questions. This contrasts with asynchronous communication, where users are uncertain as to whether a message will be received, read or replied to. Synchronous technologies are more spontaneous and can create opportunities for developing personal relationships with fellow participants more quickly than in asynchronous environments. They are particularly useful for discussing specific issues that need to be addressed within a given time frame.

However, synchronous communication also has drawbacks. There are practical issues, in that everyone wanting to participate must be online at the same time. Messages, although spontaneous and instantaneous, may not always be well thought out. For people who are not typing in their first language or people unfamiliar with the user interfaces involved, it may be difficult to keep up with the flow of a conversation. This can incite feelings of frustration both from the individual concerned and fellow participants. In addition, discussions may be dominated by a small number of assertive contributors, with less confident members feeling unable to participate. With less time to contemplate and compose responses than in asynchronous environments, responses can unintentionally appear hostile, and misunderstandings may easily alienate people. A common phenomenon in chat rooms is the presence of so called "lurkers", people who follow the interactions but never contribute anything. Although this is also applicable to asynchronous technologies, it may be more obvious and disconcerting to participants in a real-time environment.

Media richness

Communication technologies can be compared in terms of their media richness (Wallace, 2004, p. 83) – that is, their ability to transmit communication cues. Cues include things like facial expression, body language, gestures and tone of voice – aspects that can add a lot of meaning on top of the actual content of a message. At the bottom end of the media richness scale are text-based technologies, such as email and instant messaging, where most communication cues are missing. At the other end of the scale are face-to-face interactions. The ultimate richness of face-to-face is due to the ability to communicate in a real-time environment using not only words but also gestures, tone of voice and body language (Wallace, 2004, p. 83). In between are communication technologies such as audio and video conferencing. These provide richer channels than the text-based technologies because of their ability to transmit cues such as tone of voice, and in the case of video, gestures and body language.

There are, however, ways of adding meaning or emotion to the content of text-based communications. The use of emoticons (or smiley faces) to portray the feelings of the sender at the time of writing, or how a comment is meant to be taken, are now commonplace. Internet slang or abbreviations have evolved and are used across a range of technologies such as email, discussion forums and IM. For example, some commonly used abbreviations include: LOL – laugh out loud; and IMHO – in my honest/humble opinion. Capital letters have come to represent shouting and multiple exclamation or question marks can be used to stress a point. These techniques help to compensate for a technology's intrinsic lack of richness.

Summary

There are many different technologies that are used to support a diverse range of online communication and collaboration activities. These activities range from one-to-one, asynchronous, text-based interactions to those that involve many users collaborating and generating multimedia content. Some communication technologies are "richer" than others in terms of their ability to convey meaning or feeling, and this can be a key factor used to select a technology appropriate for its intended use. Other factors such as availability, practicality and cost also play an important part in the decision.

There are an increasing number of products offering a combination of technologies within one user interface and these are getting closer to reproducing the richness of face-to-face interaction. These products blur the distinction between asynchronous and synchronous communication as some enable both. In addition, users are adapting technologies to suit their immediate needs – for example using synchronous technologies asynchronously and vice versa.

References

Lenhart, A. and Madden, M. (2007) 'Social networking websites and teens' *Pew Internet and American Life Project*, January 7. Available from: http://www.pewinternet.org/Reports/2007/Social-Networking-Websites-and-Teens.aspx retrieved 7 May 2009.

Lenhart, A., Madden, M. and Hitlin, P. (2005) 'Youth are leading the transition to a fully wired and mobile nation' *Pew Internet and American Life Project*, July 27. Available from: http://www.pewinternet.org/Reports/2005/Teens-and-Technology.aspx retrieved 7 May 2009.

O'Leary, D. E. (2008) 'Wikis: "from each according to his knowledge"' *IEEE Computer*, 41(2), February, pp. 34–41.

Swan, K. (2002) 'Building learning communities in online courses: the importance of interaction', *Education, Communication and Information*, 2(1), pp. 23–49.

Wallace, P. (1999) *The Psychology of the Internet*, Cambridge: Cambridge University Press.

Wallace, P (2004) *The Internet in the Workplace: How New Technology is Transforming Work*, Cambridge: Cambridge University Press.

Wegerif, R. (1998) 'The social dimension of asynchronous learning networks', *Journal of Asynchronous Learning*, 2(1), pp. 34–49.

Reading 9

Wikis: 'from each according to his knowledge'

Daniel E. O'Leary

Abstract Wikis offer tremendous potential to capture knowledge from large groups of people, making tacit, hidden content explicit and widely available. They also efficiently connect those with information to those seeking it.

Much has been written about wikis in recent years by researchers, journalists, bloggers, and wiki software vendors. Not surprisingly, most of this information appears in wikis themselves. Given the explosive growth in wiki applications and the controversies surrounding the technology, it is useful to sort through the claims and criticisms to better understand what wikis are, how they are used, their advantages and limitations, and various issues surrounding their implementation.

What is a wiki?

In 1994, Ward Cunningham implemented the first wiki, the WikiWikiWeb, to promote the exchange of ideas among fellow programmers on his consultancy's website (http://en.wikipedia.org/wiki/Ward_Cunningham). [...] the WikiWikiWeb was written in Perl and based on a HyperCard stack Cunningham wrote in the late 1980s. Today, wiki software applications are based on numerous languages, including Java, Lisp, PHP, Smalltalk, Python, and Ruby (http://en.wikipedia. org/wiki/List_of_wiki_software).

"Wiki" is Hawaiian for quick, and, as the term suggests, the technology's initial goal was to give users the ability to quickly put content on the Web. Today, however, a wiki's purpose depends on who you ask and what kind of application is being developed. In general, wikis are designed to facilitate quick and easy content

* generation,
* collaboration, and
* distribution.

From O'Leary, D.E. (2008). 'Wikis: "From Each According to His Knowledge"', *IEEE Computer*, 41(2), Feb, pp. 34–41. IEEE Computer Society Publications.

With wikis, multiple users can connect virtually in time or space – from private communities within enterprises to the general public – to create, update, and share knowledge with others.

Wikis typically allow users to

- add new content,
- link to other related content,
- edit existing content,
- organize and structure content,
- view content, and
- access a history of contributed content.

Most wiki contributions are written, but they can include media such as images, videos, and sound files. Web-based documents are created collaboratively in a simplified markup language, or "wikitext," using a Web browser over the Internet or an intranet. This enables nonprogrammers to create wiki applications and add new features without having to be familiar with the code base.

Wikis use various mechanisms to track the history of contributed content so that users can see who made what changes and when. [...]

Knowledge management

Over the years, researchers have offered many proposals to facilitate knowledge management, particularly at the enterprise level.[1] However, the promise of various tools and applications to make tacit knowledge explicit remains largely unfulfilled – much tacit knowledge remains inaccessible. Wikis have the potential to gather such knowledge from far-reaching sources.

Wikis satisfy four key knowledge management needs by

- capturing knowledge from those who have it,
- converting knowledge into an explicitly available format,
- connecting those who want knowledge with those who have it, and
- linking knowledge to knowledge.[2]

In classic knowledge management, acquisition experts are responsible for capturing knowledge from domain experts. Wikis offer a nonintrusive means of capturing information by removing the intermediary and letting people share knowledge directly. Wikis also make information or sources exclusively available to the contributor generally available; users thus directly influence the knowledge base's structure and content. In addition, by making available information about contributors, wikis facilitate connections between interested parties. Finally, through the use of hypertext, wikis let contributors link appropriate knowledge.

Mass collaboration

Wikis are particularly effective in situations in which a large group of people want to leverage their collective knowledge to achieve some goal. For example, during the 2004 US presidential contest, one campaign used a wiki to compile political news stories for their candidate.[3] This approach enabled some 400 staffers to focus on different areas of coverage – for example, around a given periodical. The resulting database served as the basis of twice-daily briefing documents.

Within an enterprise, the choice of whether to implement a wiki depends on the nature of the information as well as the number of users. If a group wishes to keep information private, then wikis, unless tightly limited, are not appropriate as a means of fostering collaboration.

Transparency

To increase participation, content must be transparent; otherwise, multiple participants will not be able to provide coherent and related contributions. Wikis provide transparency by letting users see what others have contributed, thereby converting individual knowledge into communal knowledge.

Pull versus push

Wikis facilitate the connection between those who have information and those who need it. This "pull" mechanism is useful for organizations that want to continually draw on a dynamic, ordered information set. The alternative is to "push" static, unordered information directly to users, either individually or as a group. E-mail represents the most common form of this approach.

Wiki applications

A broad range of general and enterprise wiki applications is in use today.

General applications

The most well-known general wiki application is Wikipedia, the multilingual online encyclopedia that relies on volunteers from around the world to contribute and edit content on any given topic. Launched in January 2001 by Jimmy Wales, it is one of the 10 most popular websites and currently contains more than 9 million articles in 253 languages (http://en.wikipedia.org/wiki/Wikipedia).

The project's tremendous success spawned numerous siblings now operated, along with Wikipedia, by the nonprofit Wikimedia Foundation. These include Wiktionary, a dictionary of term meanings, synonyms, etymologies, and translations; Wikibooks, a collection of open source textbooks and other learning materials; Wikiquote, a compendium of quotations from prominent people and works; Wikisource, a library of public domain texts and other source documents; Wikimedia Commons, a repository of images, sounds, and video; and Wikinews, a source for reports by citizen journalists.

Tens of thousands of independent wiki applications have sprung up on the Web to serve communities interested in broad topics like computing, travel, and entertainment as well as niche subjects such as the online role-playing game *World of Warcraft*. For example, Wikia, a for-profit company cofounded by Jimmy Wales, alone hosts more than 4,700 wiki communities (www.wikia.com/wiki/About_Wikia).

Although some wikis impose restrictions on contributions, all rely on the community at large rather than an elite group to advance knowledge, education, and discussion. The power of wikis to reach a broad constituency has not been lost on technology-minded political candidates, who are beginning to incorporate them into their campaigns (http://vote.peteashdown.org/wiki/index.php/Main_Page).

Enterprise applications

Wikis have many applications within businesses and other organizations.

Wikipedia imitations

The high visibility of Wikipedia has led many companies to replicate this type of application internally.[3] These internal wikis are typically designed to support particular functions by letting employees input information as appropriate in an encyclopedia-like setting. For example, a business might employ a wiki-type product directory to record changes and new offerings.

Meeting setup

Wikis can help mitigate information overload.[4] For example, they can facilitate meetings by gathering input in advance from attendees and making it generally available. This saves time, particularly in the case of multiday meetings with much to assimilate, by enabling participants to review what others have to contribute prior to the meeting so that they can concentrate on areas that need attention.

Project management

Companies can use wikis to capture information about projects. Participants can post documents and progress reports or generate and massage information related to a project on the wiki. For example, CommSecure, an Australian provider of e-billing and e-payment solutions, employs a wiki to help track the implementation status and related documentation of different projects.[5] This can facilitate buy-in by letting participants help construct key inputs and making constraints transparent.

Best practices

Employees can use wikis to describe best practices. For example, the wiki "Library Success" is a "one-stop shop for great ideas and information for all types of librarians" (www.libsuccess.org/index.php?title=Main_Page). Another wiki's expressed goal is to share best practices about the Common Base Event, a fundamental systems management standard (www.ibm.com/developerworks/wikis/display/CBEbestpractice).

Taxonomy development

Wikis can simplify taxonomy development within an enterprise, which generally requires the cooperation of multiple parties. Individual users can propose a portion of the taxonomy and its associated explanation, and others can point out their limitations and suggest changes.

Competitive intelligence

Wikis can be used to gather competitive intelligence, a function traditionally performed by a small group within the organization that acts in relative secrecy. SAP, one of the world's largest business software companies, employs a wiki to monitor how its pricing tactics and sales strategies are working in the field.[3] By making the process open and participatory, the company can get better and more timely collective intelligence and make it available to more people.

Wiki advantages and limitations

In determining whether to implement a wiki, an enterprise or other organization must balance the advantages of the technology with its limitations as well as match the wiki's capabilities to the desired objectives. Figure 9.1 summarizes some of the pluses and minuses of wikis.

Advantages

Wikis offer numerous advantages.

Structure

At the highest level, wikis use a vocabulary or ontology to explicitly organize contributions. However, the use of hypertext to link related concepts and articles within the wiki embeds additional structure. Some wikis, such as Wikipedia, also contain references and external links to other subjects.

Consensus

Wikis can build consensus because many participants often "sign off" on the content. In fact, building consensus is Wikipedia's "fundamental model for

WIKI ADVANTAGES

- Wikis generate a network of knowledge by linking people and content
- Wikis can build consensus
- Wikis collect knowledge from multiple sources
- Wikis engage contributors
- Wikis can be as accurate as traditional published sources
- Wikis delegate control to contributors
- Wikis provide a forum to help users manage their behavior

WIKI LIMITATIONS

- Wikis often do not provide author information, raising questions about content accuracy
- Wikis typically lack referees or peer review, which provide some quality assurance
- Wikis can hinder as well as build consensus focusing on contributors conflicting opinions
- Contributors can easily introduce bias
- Wikis can compromise information security
- Wikis can encourage scope creep
- Contributions can decrease over time
- Wikis can expose an organization to legal problems
- Wikis are subject to vandalism
- Wikis can be contrived to look genuine but have an ulterior motive
- Wiki content is generally not available in a machine-processable format

Figure 9.1 Wikis have both advantages and limitations

editorial decision-making" (http://en.wikipedia.org/wiki/Wikipedia:Consensus). Wikis typically encourage a neutral point of view and have mechanisms to resolve disputes among contributors.

Collective wisdom

Because wikis are generally open, democratic environments, they harness the "wisdom of the crowd." Ideally, content draws on a wide range of contributors with varying perspectives and expertise. Everyone in the community has an opportunity to evaluate the quality of contributions, and those who have an interest in or are knowledgeable about a topic can add to or modify content.

User engagement

Wikis engage users by letting them express themselves freely and for all to see. Although most wikis have etiquette guidelines and codes of conduct prohibiting, for example, hateful content or personal attacks, individuals generally have tremendous flexibility in what they post. Users derive satisfaction from being part of a communal effort as well as seeing their creativity on display.

Accuracy

Contrary to the claims of some critics, wiki accuracy can be comparable to published sources. For example, one recent study found that Wikipedia had roughly four inaccuracies per entry, only one more than *Encyclopedia Britannica.*[6] Some wikis have verifiability guidelines that encourage contributors to cite reliable sources.

Delegation of control

Wikis delegate control of content to potential contributors. This is an advantage in organizations where management seeks bottom-up input on particular issues or processes.

User management

Wikis can help manage users as well as contributors by providing widespread access to equivalent standards for actions and behaviors, whether implicitly or explicitly.

Wiki limitations

Wikis also have several limitations.

Lack of authority

Users might want assurance that material they obtain online is backed by some authority or level of expertise. Unfortunately, in many cases there is limited information about authors of wiki material. For example, a Wikibooks contributor named "Psychofarm" has written books on both Mac OS and Asian honey chicken salad, while another has offered works on both physics and accounting. Such broad interests naturally raise doubts as to whether these authors have the necessary expertise.

No referees

Few wikis referee content to any appreciable extent, if at all, because that violates the open wiki spirit. Consequently, there is no guarantee that information in wikis is accurate or even reasonable. Wikipedia, for example, has had well-documented problems with users submitting invalid information.[7] In contrast, published research is typically peer-reviewed and edited, providing some quality assurance.

"Too many cooks in the kitchen"

Wikis can hinder as well as build consensus. If multiple contributors express conflicting points of view or alternative solutions, the resulting content might be incoherent or focus on differences rather than similarities. Wikis can also misleadingly give the appearance of consensus if only one or a small group of contributors dominate the process early on, thereby thwarting further discussion.

Bias

Although many wikis have policies advocating a neutral point of view, their open nature makes it easy to introduce biased information. For example, a former MTV veejay and podcasting pioneer was caught anonymously editing the Wikipedia entry on podcasting to take credit for its development away from others and inflate his own role.[8]

Information insecurity

Wikis can compromise information security. Organizations often compartmentalize data, giving different pieces of information to different users, but wiki users could inadvertently share data that should not be available to all who have access to the wiki. For example, Microsoft purposely separates product and market information, and users able to intermingle data through a wiki could gain deep insights into the company's revenue stream.[9]

Scope creep

Because wiki contributors can range from amateurs to professionals, from beginners to experts, the resulting content might be too amorphous to be of use to any particular group. Scope creep is a common problem on complex projects, and wikis can encourage it by facilitating changes in team composition.

Decreased contributions

Wikis, particularly discretionary ones, can suffer a slow death. In some cases, contributions are initially heavy but subsequently decrease as participants turn to other activities. In other cases, contributions are light to begin with, increase as users familiarize themselves with the technology, and then decline as the uniqueness of the technology wears off. Unfortunately, both scenarios result in a similar outcome: decreased contributions over time.

Legal problems

Enterprise applications such as project management rely on contributors being frank and honest, but openness in company e-mail has led to expensive lawsuits – even in instances with only one recipient of a message. It is easy to imagine how a wiki could, by disseminating sensitive or private data to numerous people, expose an organization to all sorts of legal problems.

Vandalism

Wikis are only as good as their contributors, and these can include users who submit obscenities, personal attacks, and deliberate nonsense. Vandalism has actually forced some organizations to cancel wiki applications. For example, the *Los Angeles Times* closed down its "Wikitorial" feature because of contributors' repeated use of foul language.[10]

Contrived wikis

Because wikis facilitate consensus, some use them to try to generate consensus within an enterprise or the general public. Contrived wikis are implemented by some anonymous source to look like a standard wiki, with open contributions, but are actually not open and designed to influence public opinion.

Human consumption

In general, wikis are generated by and for humans. However, many knowledge management systems, such as rule-based systems, attempt to put information in a machine-consumable format, intermediary to human consumption. Such machine-based consumption is generally beyond the scope of wikis.

Implementing wikis

Some organizations that implement a wiki might expect to simply "build it and they will come" (and use it). However, the open nature of wikis raises several issues that are often ignored.

Author information

Enterprise wikis usually keep data about wiki authors. [...], capturing such information can be critical to achieving user acceptance of content. It can also foster connections between users and authors. Google recognizes this and is implementing its own competitor to Wikipedia, Knol, that prominently displays authors' names (http://blogo-scoped.com/archive/2007-12-14-n19.html).

Incentives to participate

Wikis should provide potential contributors with incentives to participate. [...] [O]ne way to do this within an enterprise is to issue "points" to employees, with some reward upon reaching a certain threshold, for their efforts. In addition to displaying authors' names, Google's Knol will let authors include advertisements and make money from their contributions.

Administration

Ideally, wikis should have an administrator who referees and manages the changing content. However, if the wiki is substantial, such as Wikipedia, no one person or even group can monitor all of the changes in real time.

Change alerts

One way to provide control over changes is to alert those who have indicated interest in a particular subject or whose previous contribution has been altered by another user. Participants who know that changes they make to existing content will be broadcast to the original author will likely be more discriminating, while those whose contributions have been edited will have a chance to quickly review the changes for inaccuracies or other issues.

Access and registration

The original philosophy of wikis was to let all users contribute and change content. However, such openness can lead to vandalism, tampering, compromised data, and other problems, particularly in noncorporate settings where there is little recourse for destructive acts.

In corporate environments, it is important to determine whether wiki access should be open to outsiders or limited to employees, managers, or a select group of users within the company. Does the wiki contain information – for example, about product faults – or controversial content that, if made available to the wrong people, could negatively impact sales, compromise proprietary secrets, or lead to costly litigation?

Perhaps the least intrusive way to control access is to notify potential contributors that their IP address is being captured. Another method is to require that users register with a valid e-mail address and log in with a username and password. Although the effectiveness of these steps can be mitigated, they at least provide some potential control over users.

Contributor capabilities

One way to manage users is to categorize them according to their capabilities. Wikibooks distinguishes contributors according to their fluency in English and other languages. For example, User en-N connotes a native English speaker, while User en-0, -1, -2, and -3 represent users with zero, basic, intermediate, and advanced levels of English, respectively. To limit wiki access in enterprise settings, contributors can be assigned "roles" based on their responsibilities or level of expertise.

User practice

Although most wikis are relatively simple, they can be intimidating to first-time users. Many sites therefore provide a "sandbox" that lets contributors learn the wiki's various features and practice, thereby limiting potential mistakes. Sandboxes might also facilitate user buy-in.

Policies and guidelines

Wiki contributors should clearly understand what they can and cannot do. The site should therefore offer a list of mandatory policies and advisory guidelines, subject to community approval. For example, Wikipedia users must respect other contributors, respect copyrights, avoid bias, and include only verifiable information (http://en.wikipedia.org/wiki/Wikipedia:Key_policies_and_guidelines).

Copyrighted material

In many settings, wiki-based materials cannot be copyrighted. For example, Wikibooks considers all contributions to fall under the terms of the GNU Free Documentation License (http://www. gnu.org/licenses/fdl.html). Wikibooks warns potential violators that "the posting of copyrighted material without the express permission of the copyright holder(s) is possibly illegal and is a violation of our copyright policy" (http://en.wikibooks.org/wiki/Wikibooks:Copyrights).

Project completion estimates

Although wikis are typically open ended, some projects can have a completed format. In these cases, providing users with an estimate of how much work has been done can be helpful. For example, Wikibooks indicates whether text for any given project is "sparse" (0 percent), "developing" (25 percent), "maturing" (50 percent), "developed" (75 percent), or "comprehensive" (100 percent). Because there are likely to be multiple contributors, and completeness is in the eye of the beholder, estimates can be highly subjective.

Design for participation

Because wikis depend on contributors, any implementation should be designed to facilitate participation. Ross Mayfield, cofounder of Socialtext, the leading enterprise wiki company, suggests starting small with a pilot project that applies a wiki solution to a single process or application.[3] Once the project participants have evaluated the tool through a forum or discussion group, they can "take it public" by each inviting five others in the organization to use the wiki. This can be repeated with successively larger waves of contributors, gradually building a community, adding content, and evolving norms.

Personalization

Many wiki applications let users personalize some aspects such as privacy settings, link formats, image size, editing options, browser appearances, date format, and time zone.

Emerging AI applications in wikis

In simple terms, artificial intelligence aims to incorporate human intelligence into computer-based applications or analysis. There are numerous potential applications of AI in the area of wikis.

Wikis provide substantial structured material about particular subjects, and researchers have used them to generate and maintain ontologies[11] and taxonomies.[12] Similarly, group input could be used in a wiki to generate rule-based knowledge to capture insights and identify conceptual relationships. Systems designed to improve knowledge by intelligent questioning and answering could also leverage wiki content.

Just as electronic auction sites generate reliability or quality estimates about buyers and sellers, AI systems could search the Internet and other wikis to find out what particular authors have contributed on various topics and generate trust or expertise indices. Researchers also could develop intelligent agents to search multiple wikis and assemble material for a comprehensive article on a subject.

Wikis such as Wikipedia address the same topics in numerous languages. Researchers could use this multilingual data to disambiguate topics, terms, or words; generate translations; or analyze structure in a subject area.

Researchers also could use AI systems to help secure wikis, whose open nature makes them particularly vulnerable. For example, concept-based systems could identify vandalism and exclude such contributions prior to posting, while intrusion-detection systems could leverage information gathered about contributors to unmask illegitimate users.

Wikis can be used as a training ground to search for knowledge obtained through machine-learning approaches. Further, annotating wikis with machine-readable content would make them both human and machine-friendly.

Wikis offer tremendous potential to capture knowledge from large groups of people, making tacit, hidden content explicit and widely available. They also efficiently connect those with information to those seeking it: "from each according to his knowledge, to each according to his need." Although wikis have inherent limitations that make them inappropriate in certain settings and for some applications, they are likely to replace existing processes and technologies, providing organizations with a wide range of additional capabilities.

Acknowledgment

The author thanks the anonymous referees for their comments on an earlier version and extends appreciation to the editors for their efforts to help make this a better article.

Author note

Daniel E. O'Leary is a professor in the Marshall School of Business at the University of Southern California. His research focuses on information systems, including enterprise resource planning systems and knowledge management systems. O'Leary received a PhD in information systems and systems engineering from Case Western Reserve University. He is a member of the IEEE, the ACM, the Institute for Operations Research and the Management Sciences, and the Decision Sciences Institute. Contact him at oleary@usc.edu.

References

1 D.E. O'Leary, "Enterprise Knowledge Management," *Computer*, Mar. 1998, pp. 54–61.
2 D.E. O'Leary, "Knowledge-Management Systems: Converting and Connecting," *IEEE Intelligent Systems,* May/June 1998, pp. 30–33.
3 R. Mayfield, "How to Start a Wiki;" podcast, www.veotag.com/player/?u=rivtyskosd.
4 J. Spira, "Information Overload – A Growing Problem," *Collaboration Loop*, 1 Feb. 2007; www.collaborationloop.com/index.php?option=com_content&task=view&id=1945&Itemid=39.
5 L. Wood, "Blogs & Wikis: Technologies for Enterprise Applications?," *The Gilbane Report,* Mar. 2005, pp. 2–9; http:// gilbane.com/artpdf/GR12.10.pdf.
6 J. Giles, "Internet Encyclopedias Go Head to Head," *Nature*, 15 Dec. 2005, pp. 900–901.
7 D. Terdiman, "Growing Pains for Wikipedia," CNET News.com, 5 Dec. 2005; http://news.com.com/Growing%20pains%20for%20Wikipedia/2100-1025_3-5981119.html?tag=st.prev.
8 R. Cadenhead, "Adam Curry Caught in Sticky Wiki," *Workbench,* 1 Dec. 2005; www.cadenhead.org/workbench/news/2818/adam-curry-caught-sticky-wiki.
9 D.E. O'Leary and M.L. Markus, "Microsoft's Management Reporting: SAP, Data Warehousing, and Reporting Tools," *J. Emerging Technologies*, vol. 3, no. 1, 2006, pp. 129–141.
10 P. Naughton, "Foul Language Forces LA Times to Pull the Plug on 'Wikitorial,' " *Times Online*, 21 June 2005; http://technology.timesonline.co.uk/tol/news/tech_and_web/article535749.ece.
11 M. Hepp, D. Bachlechner, and K. Siorpaes, "OntoWiki: Community-Driven Ontology Engineering and Ontology Usage Based on Wikis," *Proc. 2006 Int'l Symp. Wikis*, ACM Press, 2006, pp. 143–144; www.heppnetz.de/files/ontowikiDemo-short-camera-ready.pdf.
12 A.L. Burrow, "Negotiating Access within Wiki: A System to Construct and Maintain a Taxonomy of Access Rules," *Proc. 15th ACM Conf. Hypertext and Hypermedia*, ACM Press, 2004, pp. 77–86.

Interaction and outeraction

Instant messaging in action

Bonnie A. Nardi, Steve Whittaker and Erin Bradner

Abstract We discuss findings from an ethnographic study of instant messaging (IM) in the workplace and its implications for media theory. We describe how instant messaging supports a variety of informal communication tasks. We document the affordances of IM that support flexible, expressive communication. We describe some unexpected uses of IM that highlight aspects of communication which are not part of current media theorizing. They pertain to communicative processes people use to connect with each other and to manage communication, rather than to information exchange. We call these processes "outeraction." We discuss how outeractional aspects of communication affect media choice and patterns of media use.

Keywords: Instant messaging, media theory, informal communication, computer-mediated communication, outeraction.

Introduction

Recent empirical work has shown the importance of informal workplace communication for effective collaboration. By informal we mean interactions that are generally impromptu, brief, context-rich and dyadic [16, 34, 35, 36]. These interactions support joint problem solving, coordination, social bonding, and social learning – all of which are essential for complex collaboration [16, 17, 19, 20, 23, 24, 34, 35]. This research demonstrates that face to face interaction is the primary means of informal communication in the workplace, though email is also gaining ground [18]. In this paper, we document the utility of a technology which is relatively new to the workplace – instant messaging – for effectively supporting informal communication.

In the first part of the paper, we describe the informal communication tasks that IM supports: quick questions and clarifications, coordination and scheduling,

Nardi, B. A., Whittaker, S. and Bradner, E. (2000) 'Interaction and outeraction: instant messaging in action', *Proceedings of the 2000 ACM conference on computer supported cooperative work*, Philadelphia, PA: pp. 78–88.

organizing impromptu social meetings, and keeping in touch with friends and family. These tasks usually involve rapid exchange of information or affect. We also document how the affordances of IM, in particular its immediacy, make it successful in supporting these tasks.

But IM does more than support quickfire informal communication. It facilitates some of the processes that make informal communication possible. In the second part of the paper, we explore unexpected uses of IM for what we call *outeraction*. Outeraction is a set of communicative processes *outside of* information exchange, in which people *reach out* to others in patently social ways to enable information exchange.

Current media theories describe processes by which people ground the content and process of communication [4, 5], initiate interaction [28], or choose an appropriate medium for the task at hand [7, 29]. These theories make a number of assumptions about the nature of communication: (a) that communication is primarily about information exchange; (b) that communication is best studied one interaction at time, rather than in a temporal sequence spanning multiple discrete interactions; (c) that participants are unproblematically available for communication; and (d) that a single medium is used throughout a communication event.

We document uses of IM that challenge these assumptions. First, we describe a distinct stage of communication prior to information exchange in which IM is used to *negotiate the availability* of others to initiate conversation, where the problem of interruptiveness is a major concern. Second, we document that some IM conversations take place in *intermittent* episodes, involving periods of time where no information is exchanged. Here IM is used to *maintain a sense of connection* with others within an active *communication zone*. Finally, we show that IM can be used to *switch media* in the course of a single communication event.

Other recent empirical and systems work on informal communication [16, 26, 35], awareness [8, 13, 14], and media spaces [2, 10, 11, 21, 22, 30, 36] has drawn attention to phenomena that relate to outeraction. One particular focus of this work has been conversational initiation. However, such work has yet to be systematically integrated with media theory. Drawing from our examination of IM use in the workplace, we illustrate that some of the conversational processes reported in other empirical studies also occur in IM. We report new conversational processes, and integrate this work with media theory. We contrast the outeraction approach with other communication theories, such as ethnomethodology [28] and accounts of conversational grounding [4, 5].

Instant messaging system features

Instant messaging is near-synchronous computer-based one-on-one communication. With a fast network, transmission times are fractions of a second and the experience is of near-synchronous interaction. Like chat, IM allows users to type messages into a window, but like the phone, it is based on a dyadic "call" model.

Users do not go into "rooms" to converse with whomever is there; instead there is a single individual with whom they communicate (although they may have several concurrent dyadic conversations with different individuals in progress at a given time). Some IM systems support multiparty chat but our data concern the more typical dyadic communications. As with the phone, the intended recipient of an instant message may or may not "answer."

Most IM systems also provide awareness information about the presence of others. In AOL's Instant Messenger (AIM), the user creates a "buddy list" of people to monitor. A buddy list window shows whether buddies are currently logged into AIM, how long they have been logged in, and whether they are active or idle (and if idle, for how long). Other systems also provide "buddy lists" but show only whether a buddy is logged in. Most systems also have audio alerts signaling when buddies come "online" and "offline." Users can control whether they appear on someone else's "online" buddy list; a "blocking" mechanism allows them to remove themselves from that list. The buddy list is also a convenient way to initiate IMs. Users double-click on the relevant name in the buddy list and a message is automatically initiated and addressed.

IM has ancient roots in Unix utilities such as "talk" and "write," but it has found a wide audience only in the last few years via AOL's Instant Messenger product, available free on the Internet. AOL claims to have 50 million AIM users [1]. Other IM products include Yahoo! Messenger, Excite Messenger, Activerse Ding! and ICQ.

Research questions and methods

We investigated the IM usage of 20 people. Seven study participants worked at a large telecommunications company ("TelCo"). Twelve worked at an Internet company of about 700 employees ("Insight"). An additional participant was an independent contractor. People in our sample included executives in charge of technology transfer, a marketing specialist, graphic artists, software developers, Web designers, secretaries, and others. Usage of IM included colocated workers (often only a cubicle or two away); workers separated by as much as a nine hour time difference; and family members on opposite sides of the International Dateline. All the people we talked to were experienced users of a variety of technologies, including email, voicemail, PC and Web applications.

We asked informants about their jobs and their use of IM, as well as other communication technologies. We asked them to talk about the advantages and disadvantages of using IM, and how it compared with other communication media such as telephone, voicemail, email and face to face interaction. We audiotaped interviews conducted in informants' workplaces. We observed them at work in some cases, and videotaped some sessions. We were able to observe incoming instant messages as we conducted the interviews or observations. Users often received them while we were talking. They would sometimes pause and let us see a message, and show us their response if they chose to respond.

The bulk of our data is from interviews and observations supplemented with logs of a few IM sessions. These logs are drawn from one site only – at the other site the legal department prohibited the collection of logs. All informant names have been changed as have identifying details.

Informal lightweight communication

We present an example log to give a flavor of how IM was used for informal communication. The log shows a session between a secretary and her manager. Although names are changed, the timestamps, spelling, and punctuation are unaltered. The secretary, Melissa, and the manager, Alan, sat within earshot of one another, with Melissa in an open cubicle and Alan in an adjacent office. Melissa shared the cubicle with a secretary, Jackie, who worked for Alan's manager, Sam Jones.

> MELISSA (8:33:32 AM): The fire is out???????? [there has been an embarrassing public relations problem]
>
> AUTO RESPONSE FROM ALAN (8:33:32 AM): I'm idle ... may be asleep. [Alan was there but working on another computer. The message was a personalized automatic response.]
>
> ALAN (8:33:45 AM): not quite ... still putting it out
>
> MELISSA (8:37:13 AM): I can send some water. Just talked with Georgina .... Marsha is running around with her head cut off!!!!!
>
> ALAN (8:37:29 AM): just put Carl on my calendar at 10 am, for half-hour. [Carl was able to help solve the problem.]
>
> MELISSA (8:37:45 AM): You got it!!!!!
>
> MELISSA (8:38:43 AM): By the way .... I can go to lunch if I can catch a ride with you ... Beth has the car for lunch.
>
> ALAN (8:38:56 AM): fine with me!
>
> ALAN (8:39:12 AM): also, do you know when will sam jones be back?
>
> [Melissa turned to Jackie who kept Sam's calendar and asked her about Sam's schedule.]
>
> MELISSA (8:40:39 AM): Sam will be coming in on June 1 as of this moment
>
> ALAN (8:40:56 AM): oh ... not here this fri, eh?
>
> MELISSA (8:41:11 AM): NO .... He is in Hawaii at the moment.
>
> ALAN (8:41:24 AM): right ... for the shareholders meeting.
>
> MELISSA (8:42:09 AM): You got it ... Making Gail crazy needing paperwork from Stan's group yesterday at 4pm and they are out on an Offsite ....
>
> ALAN (8:42:34 AM): :-)

In the last exchange "Making Gail crazy," Melissa was telling Alan that Stan was infuriating Gail regarding the late paperwork. This exchange updated Alan on the emotional atmosphere of the office since he had been away the previous day. Alan returned a smiley face to acknowledge the joke that he knew that the paperwork was long overdue.

In this session, which spanned roughly ten minutes with fifteen brief exchanges, considerable work was accomplished. Alan and Melissa established context about "the fire," arranged a meeting with Carl, coordinated lunch, exchanged information about Alan's manager's schedule and the atmosphere in the office. This was done while other activities occurred, such as Alan taking a phone call and reading email. The conversation involved office jokes, expression of concern over a problem, simple patter ("oh . . . not here this fri, eh?"), and the asking and granting of a small favor.

As the log shows, the general tenor of instant messages is typically casual, informal, and friendly. One user contrasted it with email: "It's more casual so you can be more quirky." Relaxed grammar and spelling are the norm. Standard capitalization is often ignored though caps may be used for emphasis. Multiple exclamation points and question marks are sprinkled liberally throughout Instant messages. This informality lends Instant messages a kind of intimacy that is often absent from other types of mediated communication. In Melissa's exchange with Alan, she used multiple exclamation points to signal a friendly responsiveness ("You got it!!!!!"). Alan returned her query about lunch with a more subdued but still genial "fine with me!" In the interviews, Alan noted, "I use email more like the adult thing. IM is more the fun thing."

In a discussion comparing IM with email, Rick, a software researcher at TelCo, remarked on the informal, conversational flavor of many IM exchanges. He suggested that a key reason for this informality lies in the near-synchronous nature of IM. Conversations can be more interactive because the rapid and evolving nature of IM means that there is immediate context for the current interaction. This context seems to reduce misunderstandings and promote humor. "The give and take of a conversation in IM is much more immediate [than email] and you can tell by the way it's evolving what people's intentions are or what they probably mean because you have context. That helps to shape a context be it light and bantering or certain statements that are meant to be tongue-in-cheek."

Another reason IM interactions tend to be informal is that users typically interact with a small set of people they know well, or plan to get to know well. The buddy lists in our sample averaged twenty-two people, with six friends/family and sixteen coworkers. In practice, participants in our study usually interacted with only four or five of their buddies on a frequent basis. (Teen practice appears to vary in that buddy lists are much larger.) The fact that participants are familiar with each other may contribute to this relaxed and informal conversational style.

Communicative functions of instant messaging

A central use of IM was to support *quick questions and clarifications* about ongoing work tasks. Helen, a web page designer at Insight, characterized this use of IM: "Say I'm working on a project and I want a quick response. [I use IM] rather than waiting for an email or try to contact them by phone and get into the process of having a lengthy conversation when you just want a two second response. I do that really often." At Insight it was common for workers developing Web pages to send each other instant messages to inquire about matters such as the placement of a logo on a page, or a small change in wording. Terry, a programmer at Insight described this process of getting IM requests for small changes to web pages, quickly making the changes, making it possible to get immediate feedback on the results: "Often we can do stuff in real time. So, I'll get a request, I'll fire up the code, make a change...I'll say, 'Hang on a second,' and then make the change and I have a development server and so I'll cut and paste the URL back into [IM] and say, 'Here, check this out'." An important reason for choosing IM over other media for this activity is its efficiency: IM allowed more rapid exchanges than is possible with email but without the overhead of a full-blown face to face conversation.

IM was also used frequently for *coordination and scheduling*. Again a key reason for using IM was its *immediacy*: when scheduling, it is important to know the details of someone's calendar as soon as possible. Sending an email that may not be read for an hour or more may mean that a previously open schedule slot has disappeared and the entire scheduling interaction has to be reinitiated. Laura, an administrative assistant at Insight, described it this way: "You have to [IM] an admin and ask if that person has this time open. They [IM] back and say 'yes,' and then you schedule it right then. Otherwise someone may come in the meantime. An email would be too slow because of lag time. Most of the admins have [IM] and it's faster than calling, although that works sometimes too."

Some users commented that they were able to carry out efficient exchanges because IM enabled them to eliminate certain formalities of address associated with phone and email. Laura from Insight said: "There are all the formalities that are bypassed on [IM] because it's not necessary. Because [IM]'ing them is the same as calling and part of the 'hi, how are you?' is trying to figure out who it is but with the name coming up in IM, you know who it is. Automatically you've identified who it is and what they want in the first line. It's a lot faster."

The visibility of IM also contributes to greater efficiency for tasks requiring rapid responsiveness. This visibility served as an important alerting mechanism making recipients more aware of instant messages, than messages sent in email and voicemail. They were likely to respond more quickly in consequence. Diane, a marketing specialist at Telco, said of her IM interactions with her secretary: "She'd respond faster. When I call her, she's not there and I'll leave a voicemail and she might not get to the voicemail as quickly. Or she's on the phone and I'll have to leave her a voicemail. When she sits down, the IM will be on her screen and it's more likely she'll do something with that before she does other stuff at her computer. Emailing would be a waste because she might check her email only once a day." While visible alerting was considered by most of our users to be a useful affordance, several users complained that it could be distracting when they were working to important deadlines. On these occasions they sometimes resorted to shutting IM down.

IM was also used to *coordinate impromptu social meetings* that took place face to face. The pressures of work in today's world make socializing at work more difficult, but no less important. People still like to go to lunch with one another, and one of the key uses of IM at both our sites was trolling for lunch partners and coordinating lunch plans. In a previous log we saw how Melissa inserted a discussion about lunch into the middle of more serious matters. People would also use IM to arrange to meet others for coffee breaks during the day. Many of these arrangements were made on the spur of the moment. The immediacy of IM meant that participants could determine each others' availability at very short notice. IM was preferred to email and voicemail for making such arrangements because these media may not be accessed immediately.

Another frequent use of IM was to *keep in touch with friends and family* while at work. Most IM users in our study had at least some friends and family they connected with online during the course of the workday. These interactions were often very brief, like, "Hi Hon!" Such interactions seemed to provide a moment of respite in a busy day, a sort of "pat on the shoulder" as one participant said. Users had exchanges with friends about coordinating social activities, such as organizing a camping trip, or a visit to a restaurant. Mike explained, "My room-mate just came online and she can say 'hi.' She can also say what her plans are or if she needs something." IM injected playfulness and intimacy, easing workers' labor by allowing them to connect to loved ones in quick but meaningful ways. Mike observed, "[IM] is a nice break from the work that can be mundane." We are all aware of the way work continues to cross boundaries into the home, but the reverse is true too, with home (and friends) making their own inroads into the workplace.

To summarize, we observed people using IM for short questions and clarifications, coordination and scheduling, arranging impromptu social meetings, and keeping in touch with friends and family. Two things are striking about all these interactions. First is the *flexibility* of IM in terms of the work that it supports. It is used here for clarifications, coordination, task delegation, asking and granting social favors, and tracking others' schedules and arranging social meetings. Second, IM is *expressive*, allowing for affective communication about a work crisis, the general ambiance of the office, jokes and bantering, as well as intimate communication with friends and family. It is interesting that a lightweight technology consisting of no more than typing text into a window succeeds in providing enough context to make a variety of social exchanges vivid, pleasurable, capable of conveying humor and emotional nuance.

IM interactions share many of the characteristics of informal face to face communication, being opportunistic, brief, context-rich and dyadic [16, 35]. Further support for this view is provided by the fact that IM and certain types of face to face interaction were sometimes seen as interchangeable. For example, in the early morning before others arrived in the office Melissa and Alan would often call back and forth to each other out loud, holding the same types of conversations we have documented here. When the office started filling up, they switched to IM, not wanting to disturb others in the work environment with audible informal conversation.

Most people in our study were enthusiastic about IM, but three were "resistors." Two refused to use IM at all. One felt she needed a record for all her communications so she preferred email. Another was a user interface designer who found the interface of her IM tool distasteful (she referred to herself as "a user interface snob"). A third user did not like to use IM when working at home, preferring to work without interruption there. Further work would be necessary to develop general statistics on preferences for IM in the workplace.

We now turn to an entirely different and unexpected set of uses of IM, namely to support *outeraction*. Because informal conversations are not scheduled, *negotiating conversational availability* is problematic [9, 10, 16, 30, 34, 35]. *Establishing social connection* is a critical prelude to interaction. Often informal conversations are comprised of intermittent interactions, so effort must be expended to create and maintain connection with others, and to *preserve a sense of conversational context* between interactions [16, 35, 36]. Once in an interaction, participants must *manage the communication situation* as it unfolds. Together these outeraction processes form the superstructure that facilitates informal communication.

Negotiating conversational availability

How do conversational participants get themselves into a situation where they are available for information exchange? Given the impromptu nature of informal communication, a key problem is to locate and get the attention of the person with whom one wishes to converse. About 60% of workplace phone calls fail to reach intended recipients because they aren't there, or they are already talking to someone else [25, 27, 30, 35].

A second recurring difficulty with initiating an informal conversation is *interruptiveness*. Since informal conversations are normally opportunistic, the recipient may well be present, but the request to talk occurs at an inconvenient time because the recipient is engaged in another task or conversation. This gives rise to a fundamental asymmetry in conversation: the time and topic are convenient for the initiator, but not necessarily the recipient [25, 34]. This asymmetry arises because while initiators benefit from rapid feedback about their pressing issue, recipients are forced to respond to the initiator's agenda, suffering interruption. Our participants were emphatic about the problems of interruptiveness, particularly with respect to the phone. Face to face communication was also mentioned as potentially interruptive – characterized by one informant as "in your face."

IM helped people negotiate availability by allowing conversational initiators to judge whether recipients were on-line by consulting the buddy list. More importantly, IM provided recipients with greater control in deciding whether and when to respond to a message.

Several informants talked about checking the buddy list to see whether recipients were active before sending a message. Helen from Insight said, "First thing this morning I opened it up [the buddy list] and looked to see who was online. My boss was online and I saw that people in Commerce were online. Other designers were online and I knew that there was a certain person that I wanted to contact and she wasn't there so I knew that I could check later." This type of availability information was also useful when trying to track down people who were difficult to find by other means. Keith, a marketing manager at TelCo, described how he used IM availability information to get in touch with Stan, an elusive coworker on the opposite coast: "Last Friday I was on and left two messages for Stan saying I wanted to come out and talk with his people and got no response. Stan is one of my people on here [on his buddy list] and I saw his "Stannies" come up and said: 'Hey Stan. Got time to talk?' And he said, 'Darn. When you turn these things on, people actually find you.' He had turned it on to get a message from his daughter who was having a track meet and he was hoping she would reach him. When he did, I caught him and I asked if we could talk and he said he was busy for five minutes and he'd call me back. He called me and we accomplished what I needed to do for my visit here today." This use of IM is similar to instances to "waylaying" observed in media spaces where initiators with a pressing question leave open a video link so that they can determine the minute the recipient returns to their office [10, 11].

Preambles

The buddy list helped conversation initiators judge when recipients were likely to be available and thus partially addressed the problem of connection failure. A more significant benefit of IM accrued to the *recipient*: IM reduced interruptivity by allowing recipients to negotiate availability. One user noted that with IM it is possible to contact others in a way that "interrupt[s] them without interrupting them too much" (see also [3]). And unlike the phone, instant messages were easily screened and responded to, even when users were engaged in face to face conversation with others in their offices. Initiators of instant messages often checked to see whether recipients were active before sending a message. If an initiating message arrived at an inconvenient time, recipients would often ignore it until they were ready to converse. Many IM conversations therefore took the form of *preambles* where initiators attempted to determine the preparedness of recipients for IM interaction. Often people would send simple instant messages like, "Suzi?" to see if someone was available for an IM exchange. If the recipient responded, an "attentional contract" was established in which both parties explicitly agreed that the communication could proceed.

The usefulness of IM as a technique for negotiating availability is shown by the fact that instant messages were often used to negotiate availability for conversations *in media other than IM*. For example, many informants used instant messages as preambles for phone conversations. While in informants' offices, we observed preambles such as "Is this a good time to call?" and "Are you there?" Rick of TelCo noted, "... a typical [IM] conversation would be talking about 'is X a good time [for a phone conversation]'? [If yes,] we'll upgrade to a phone conversation." Another TelCo informant noted that for him IM was often "a preamble to a more formal conversation" that took place on the phone. These transitions from IM to the phone happened sufficiently frequently that at Insight they were incorporated into the system: people edited their buddy lists to include phone extensions.

IM was also used to negotiate when to have face to face conversations. "Colocated" workers are often distributed on large campuses across many buildings. IM made face to face communication more efficient by allowing people to quickly establish whether a face to face meeting was feasible. IM was considered less intrusive than calling on the phone or dropping by.

Negotiating availability may involve use of multiple media in parallel. Instant messaging is often monitored *while other communications are taking place* such as phone calls or face to face conversations. This lets people prioritize communications and maintain awareness of events while they are attending to other tasks. Such monitoring is more difficult with other media; for example, it is not easy to respond to a phone call and carry on a face to face conversation simultaneously (though sometimes this happens). Likewise, it is difficult to read email and carry on a face to face conversation. In contrast, monitoring IM while conversing in other media is reasonably easy. Laura noted, "If you're talking to somebody and picking up the phone, that's a lot more destructive than seeing the IM and not answering it ... you still know what's going on."

Most of the workers we studied felt they could ignore incoming instant messages without offending the sender. People may feel able to do this because the sender generally doesn't know for certain whether the intended recipient is there or not. As a result, failing to respond is not necessarily interpreted as rude or unresponsive. IM therefore provides *plausible deniability* about one's presence. Ryan, a software developer at Insight, commented, "One thing I like about [IM] is that I'll see a message but I won't have to acknowledge my presence. So I'll respond to them later when I have time."

Informants reported that there were fewer costs associated with delaying a response to an IM, compared with other media. If the message is temporarily ignored, it stays up on the user's computer screen as a reminder (see also [30, 36]). It can be responded to later by simply typing into the window. Responding to an instant message is consequently extremely lightweight compared to the effort of dialing in to retrieve and respond to a voicemail message or finding someone face to face at just the right moment for a conversation. Helen, at Insight said: "You can choose if you want to respond. It's like voicemail but more accessible. I can choose not to respond for a while. It [the message] is still sitting there. I don't have to go in, get my messages ... It's a nice, clean, easy way to communicate."

In contrast, people often feel compelled to answer the phone because they do not know the identity of the caller or their reason for calling (although this is mitigated somewhat by caller-ID). Alan observed, "So the phone can be a very intrusive thing, whereas IM is a lot friendlier because it's just a quick thing of, 'Are you there and available' or very short questions. I don't mind that interruption. With a phone call, you don't know if it's really urgent because there's no way to know who's calling, whether it's urgent and what the topic is." An IM is also typically from someone on the user's buddy list. It is therefore already partially screened and less likely to be an irrelevant distraction.

Together, ease of screening, delayed responding, and plausible deniability of presence allow recipients much more control over responding than with face to face interaction or the phone. This greater control redresses the fundamental communication asymmetry in informal communication. Instead of conversations taking place at the convenience of the initiator, IM allows genuine social negotiation about whether and when to talk. The attentional contract can be negotiated on a more equal footing between initiator and recipient than with face to face or phone interaction. This may explain why IM is often used to negotiate availability for phone calls and face to face conversations.

Communication zones in intermittent conversations

In addition to the rapid exchanges characteristic of IM usage, we also observed that IM was often used in a completely different way to hold *intermittent conversations* over longer periods of time. The fact that recipients can choose when to respond gave rise to an intermittent, slower paced style of IM conversation. Some IM conversations took place over several minutes or even hours as recipients had the freedom to choose when to respond. "I find IM allows it to be a longer period of time, more topics, more ability to formulate the whole discussion as opposed to with a phone call . . . . I never feel on IM that I've got to find something to say back. It's okay if it sits there and we don't talk for awhile or if I head back to my email for awhile."

IM participants seemed to establish longer term "communication zones" within which they could move in and out of informal conversations. IM was used to create a virtual environment similar to a shared physical office, where people engaged in work related tasks, interspersing sporadic interchanges throughout their individual work [3, 6, 9, 14, 15, 26]. IMs are persistent and visible which helps preserve ongoing conversational context. This makes intermittent exchanges more straightforward, allowing participants to attend to other tasks and then return to an IM ("It's okay if it just sits there").

Study participants contrasted the intermittent nature of these IM conversations with phone calls which were seen to be more circumscribed and lacking in IM's emergent, more discursive character. Keith put it this way: "You [IM] for five minutes and then you do something and communicate again. It doesn't have to be a continuous, make sure you've got everything thought through [conversation]. I very often like it more than a phone call because a phone call is like: 'Okay.

We've got five or ten minutes to talk.' But if we're both on Instant Messenger in the evening, when anything comes up we can sort of ding the other person with it." Our participants also contrasted intermittent instant messages with the exchange of emails over similar periods of time. Intermittent instant messages were thought to be more immersive and to give more of a sense of a shared space and context than such email exchanges.

These observations are similar to the "virtual shared office" that is characteristic of open video links [9, 10, 11, 21]. However, key differences between IM and video are that IM supplies contextual information by providing a record of conversation, and allows plausible deniability of presence affording greater participant privacy. This style of conversation, with extended periods of time when no information is exchanged, contrasts with the focus on discrete bounded communication events in current media theory.

Awareness moments

Another process of outeraction is creating and maintaining a sense of social connection to others. While not involved in direct information exchange, participants often used IM in indirect ways to create and maintain a sense of connection to others by monitoring the buddy list. Somewhat to our surprise, we found that people found value in simply knowing who else was "around" as they checked the buddy list, without necessarily wanting to interact with buddies. Other research into technologies to support generalized awareness reports similar observations [8, 13]. These *awareness moments* produced a certain *feeling* in people, rather than accomplishing information exchange. For example, Alan discussed monitoring his buddy list for this reason: "You feel like you know where other people are, so you feel like you're not the only one working on a weekend. To me it's just fascinating to know that someone else is somewhere else doing something while you're doing something. You feel like you're in this world together so this creates a little universe." Alan's discourse employed a spatial metaphor, denoting a sense of occupying a "world," a "little universe," and "knowing where people are." He used the word "feel" three times in this short segment underscoring that he was not talking about accomplishing a specific task, but about how he felt.

Rick also talked about how awareness information helped him form a closer bond with his coworkers: "You can see when people log in and out and when they're off to lunch. It's kind of neat to watch people's comings and goings and it's not so much tracking it but you hear the sound of the door clicking and notice that somebody that everybody's looking for is back ... you get a visual image in your mind of that person and I feel closer to the people I work with as a result of that." Again, Rick reported a feeling. The mere sound of a simulated door opening and closing led to a "visual image in [his] mind" that fostered closeness.

Colocated workers maintain a sense of others as they are opportunistically encountered in shared spaces such as coffee rooms or hallways [2, 8, 10, 16,

20, 30, 34, 35]. But for people collaborating at distance, such encounters are rare. Rick, with colleagues on the opposite coast of the US, made the argument that IM can partially address this problem: "I tell people about [IM] because it helps overcome some social problems you experience when you're a thousand miles away from your coworkers. Things like forgetting that they're there."

Some participants also achieved similar effects of social connection through brief social greetings sent in IM. For example, some people sent "Good morning" messages in IM. They noted that it would be considered lunacy to deliver a "Good morning" message in email, but that people appreciated a quick IM greeting. Mike, a graphic artist at Insight, said, "Lana is two cubes away but she messages me all the time. It's a nice way of saying 'hi' without being too intrusive." Note that the exchange of greetings does not involve substantive information exchange. The aim of greeting exchanges was not to inform others about a fact or a task but to engender a sense of closeness and connection. Alan described his weekend use of IM:

ALAN: On weekends I occasionally log on from home and Rick is working and I say hi.
INTERVIEWER: What's the purpose of that?
ALAN: Just to say hi. There's no purpose and nothing to say.

Of course the purpose was to have a quick social moment with a valued coworker.

People also used IM as a parallel communication channel to establish an affective atmosphere that contributed to a feeling of social connection. During phone conferences, colocated participants often had "sidebar conversations" in which they sent messages such as, "I can't believe he said that!" They would also use IM during phone conferences to do things like place orders for lunch (with a designated lunch gofer), while conference participants in other time zones were far past lunch. This private subgroup activity lent an atmosphere of bonhomie for the colocated participants while also accomplishing the instrumental task of getting the lunch ordered. Two participants likened this style of instant messaging during phone conferences to "passing notes in school."

Awareness moments argue for a richer notion of communication than current media theories allow. Even when no direct information exchange is taking place, people want to maintain connection with others, outside the context of specific events of information exchange.

Managing conversational progress

A final manifestation of outeraction realized in IM was managing conversational progress in the form of deciding to change communication media during an interaction. Often participants would begin an IM interaction and then elect to change the communication medium to phone, face to face or even email. We call this phenomenon *media switching*. The following exchange (drawn from a log of our own use) is characteristic of many of the exchanges we observed while in people's offices:

> BONNINARDI (3:43:37 PM): John,
> JOHNATSUN (3:50:19 PM): Hi, I'm back [a seven minute gap before he replies to Bonnie's message]
> BONNINARDI (3:50:34 PM): Hey, I'm getting my system reconfigured and lost Sally's AIM name.
> JOHNATSUN (3:50:57 PM): Her name (surprisingly) is Sally Smith (with a space between).
> BONNINARDI (3:51:07 PM): Duh. Well, thanks. How are things going?
> JOHNATSUN (3:51:27 PM): Umm, a little hectic, not for work stuff, but hey, I have a question, can I call you?
> BONNINARDI (3:51:31 PM): sure.
> JOHNATSUN (3:51:35 PM): at work?
> BONNINARDI (3:51:39 PM): yes.
> JOHNATSUN (3:51:51 PM): can you save the trouble of looking up the #
> BONNINARDI (3:52:00 PM): 463-7064

In this interaction, a preamble ("John,") is followed (several minutes later) by the exchange of a small bit of information (Sally Smith's AIM name), and then the proposal of a media switch, an opportunistic request for a telephone call. The phone was judged to be more suitable for the longer conversation that John had in mind. Note that John asked for the phone call after Bonnie provided an opening for a longer conversation with the question, "How are things going?" John judged the moment to be a reasonable time to request a longer conversation, using a different medium.

Why do people feel the need to switch media? People talked about switching when they felt that "interaction" was needed, if the conversation was "complicated," or if there was a misunderstanding in the IM. On other occasions they felt it was just more efficient to talk than type. Alan at Telco was asked when he switched: "When it takes me more than three lines to type. Part of it is when it's too complex because it would take more time typing it than talking about it – I remember occasions when I was in New York and Rick was here and we were just talking back and forth even though it was simple things. At some point in time, we were doing this for five minutes and we thought maybe we should just talk. So when it becomes too lengthy. I really see this more for short messages. Almost like single line answers would probably work best."

Other times the inefficiency of typing was associated with the need to have access to the same visual shared workspace. Helen from Insight described it this way: "Let's say that I'm [IM]ing someone I'm working on a project with and it gets to the point where we have to talk. I'll write that I would rather come over and sketch it out or talk in person – it's getting too hard to type so fast and it's getting too detailed." Media switching reveals another element of conversation outside of information exchange. When IMing, participants were constantly monitoring the progress of an interaction and making corrective suggestions to switch media where necessary. The outeractional work of managing conversational progress shows how participants "step outside" ongoing information exchanges to monitor and transform interaction via media switching.

Discussion

Our findings on the importance of negotiating availability, sustaining social connections, switching media, and retaining context in workplace conversation suggest areas of expansion for communication and media theories. Current theories orient to information exchange. We believe that information exchange must be located within a wider scope of outeraction, that is, processes outside of information exchange in which people reach out to others in social rather than informational ways. Information exchange is only made possible through outeractional processes including delicate negotiations about availability, finding ways to establish connection by inhabiting and maintaining a shared communication zone, and the continual work of managing the progress of an interaction, including switching media.

We can think of outeraction as a series of *linked processes* that interleave and feed back on one another. Awareness moments create personal connections that lay the groundwork for interactions, drawing people into a common communicative arena. The process of negotiating availability binds people more tightly together for a specific interaction as they establish an attentional contract. The management of conversational progress during a specific conversational event enables people to direct conversations in ways they deem appropriate as the conversation unfolds. Communication zones delimit a virtual "space" in which a series of conversations can take place. These processes describe dynamically changing looser and tighter links that scaffold information exchange.

Our work overlaps somewhat with research on grounding conversational processes [4, 5] and ethnomethodological analyses of opening and closing conversations [12, 14, 28]. These accounts, however, do not address key aspects of outeraction – the phenomena of media switching and awareness moments, and the creation of communication zones stretching across individual interactions, as we saw in the intermittent conversations in IM.

Our description of negotiating availability is concerned with the same problem of starting a conversation taken up by these theories [5, 12, 14, 28]. In grounding and ethnomethodological accounts, as people enter conversations they follow well-known rules to coordinate the entry smoothly. Joint commitments are established as participants agree that they will converse on a particular topic [5]. While rules of conversation and joint commitments are certainly important, these constructs tend to privilege unproblematic conversational entry through the smooth function of mechanisms such as the summons-answer adjacency pair [5, 28]. With few exceptions [12, 14], this work assumes that initiators already know that the recipient is present and will acknowledge the initiation attempt. We have shown, however, that in IM such acknowledgments are not guaranteed: recipients may be absent or exploit plausible deniability of presence to ignore the summons to converse. These accounts do not consider the problem of participant asymmetry; on the phone or face to face, people may feel compelled to accept conversational offers even when they do not wish to, while in IM this problem is eased. Our work characterizes a distinct stage and set of problems prior to information exchange by which participants establish and negotiate the presence of the recipient, using careful strategies to manage tensions and problems of conversational initiation.

The symbolic interaction perspective of Trevino et al. [31] discusses some of the social aspects of outeraction in positing symbolic reasons for media choice. These reasons include, for example, showing "a desire for teamwork, to build trust, or convey informality ... urgency, ... personal concern ... or [deference]." However, the language of this perspective still emphasizes information transfer rather than relational and affective aspects of communication. The authors observe, "Managers apparently pick face to face to signal a desire for teamwork, to build trust, [etc.]." Managers are "sending signals" to recipients rather than creating and activating conversational linkages and flows in communication zones, as in outeraction.

As well as these theoretical observations, there are a number of important technology implications to our work. IM was highly versatile in supporting awareness, negotiating availability, intermittent conversations, and flexible informal communications. This argues strongly for the integration of text-based messaging into technologies such as media spaces which aim to support informal communication for people collaborating at distance. With some exceptions [30, 33, 36], most media spaces do not have integrated text-messaging.

More specifically, IM might facilitate the initiation of conversation. In many media spaces initiation is supported by video. Using IM to negotiate availability may address major problems observed with using video to initiate informal communications between remote collaborators [10, 14, 21, 30, 34, 35]. In these studies, initiators used video to "glance at" recipients to determine their availability. If accepted by recipients, glances could be converted to full-blown audio/video conversations. However, with video there was no chance for plausible deniability of presence and these systems failed to provide more successful initiation than phone only communication [30, 34]. Paradoxically, an interface that provides *less* awareness information may be more successful because it addresses the problem of participant asymmetry. A second benefit of IM over video systems is the persistence of textual conversation which maintains conversational context and facilitates intermittent interaction, leading to a more robust communication zone.

Another promising area for technical innovation is phone and IM integration. Given the utility of IM for negotiating availability, IM could be integrated with the phone allowing participants to negotiate availability so as to provide less interruptive initiations of phone calls. This may reduce the current high failure rates in initiating work phone calls [25, 27, 30, 34, 35]. The use of IM for creating

parallel channels during audio conferences also suggests a separate new application that automatically creates a parallel IM link between people already engaged
in a phone call or audio conference. An IM link such as this could be used for private "off-line" conversations, or for the exchange of information (such as URLs)
more suited to textual transmission.

In conclusion, we have documented the flexibility and expressivity of IM for
various informal communication tasks. We have described the unexpected use
of IM for outeraction processes that are distinct from but essential for information exchange. Our work suggests that we broaden theoretical accounts to include
multiple facets of communication: interaction, information exchange, symbolic
signals, and outeraction. More research is needed to document processes of outeraction in other media. Future work will provide a more integrated view of these
multiple facets of communication.

Acknowledgments

We thank David Frohlich, Ellen Isaacs and John Tang for helpful comments on
earlier versions of the paper.

References

1 AOL Instant Messenger Home Page http://www.aol.com/aim/home.html
2 Bly, S., Harrison, S., & Irwin, S. (1993). Media spaces: Bringing people together in a
  video, audio and computing environment, *Communications of the ACM*, 36, 28–45.
3 Bradner, E., Kellogg, W., & Erickson, T. The adoption and use of BABBLE. *Proceedings ECSCW'99, European Conference on Computer Supported Cooperative Work*,
  139–158. Dordrecht, The Netherlands: Kluwer Academic Publishers.
4 Clark H., & Brennan, S. (1991). Grounding in communication. In L.B. Resnick,
  J. Levine & S. Teasley, Eds. *Perspectives on socially shared cognition*. Washington
  DC.: APA Press.
5 Clark, H. (1996). *Using Language*. Cambridge: Cambridge University Press.
6 Churchill E., & Bly, S. (1999). "It's all in the words": Supporting activities with
  lightweight tools. *Proceedings of GROUP99*, 40–49, New York: ACM Press.
7 Daft, R., & Lengel, R. (1984). Information richness: a new approach to managerial
  behavior and organizational design. In B. Straw and L. Cummings (Eds)., Research in
  Organizational Behavior, 6, Connecticut: JAI Press.
8 Dourish, P., & Bly, S. (1993). Portholes: Supporting awareness in a distributed work
  group. *Proceedings of CHI'93 Human Factors in Computing Systems*, 541–547,
  New York: ACM Press.
9 Dourish, P., Adler, A., Bellotti, V., & Henderson, A. (1996). Your Place or Mine:
  Learning from long-term use of audio-video communication. *Computer Supported
  Cooperative Work*, 5(1), 33–62.
10 Fish, R., Kraut, R., Root, R., & Rice, R. (1992). Evaluating video as a technology
  for informal communication, In *Proceedings of CHI'92 Human Factors in Computing
  Systems*, 37–48, New York: ACM Press.

11 Gaver, W., Moran, T., MacLean, A., Lovstrand, L., Dourish, P., Carter, K., & Buxton, W. (1992). Realizing a video environment: EuroParc's RAVE system. In *Proceedings of CHI'92 Human Factors in Computing Systems*, 27–35, New York: ACM Press.

12 Goodwin, C. (1981). *Conversational organization: Interaction between speakers and hearers.* New York: Academic Press.

13 Gutwin, C., & Greenberg, S. (1998). Design for individuals, design for groups: Trade-offs between power and workspace awareness. In *Proceedings of CSCW96 Conference on Computer Supported Cooperative Work,* 207–216, New York: ACM Press.

14 Heath, C., & Luff, P. (1991). Disembodied conduct: communication through video in a multimedia environment. In *Proceedings of CHI'91 Human Factors in Computing Systems*, 99–103, New York: ACM Press.

15 Heath, C., & Luff, P. (1992). Collaboration and control, *Computer Supported Cooperative Work*, 1, 65–80, Amsterdam: Kluwer.

16 Kraut, R., Fish, R., Root, R. & Chalfonte, B. Informal Communication in Organizations. (1990). In S. Oskamp and S. Spacapan, (Eds). *People's Reactions to Technology in Factories, Offices and Aerospace*. New York: Sage.

17 Kraut, R., & Streeter, L. (1996). Co-ordination in software development. *Communications of the ACM*, 38, 69–81.

18 Kraut, R. E. & Attewell, P. (1997). Media use and organizational knowledge: Electronic mail in a global corporation. In S. Kiesler (ed.) *Research Milestones on the Information Highway*. Mahwah, N.J.: Erlbaum.

19 Markus, L. (1994). Finding a happy medium: Explaining the negative effects of electronic communication on social life at work. *ACM Transactions on Information Systems,* 12, 119–149.

20 McGrath, J. Time Matters in Groups. (1990). In J. Galegher, R. E. Kraut, & C. Egido (Eds.), *Intellectual teamwork: Social & technological foundations of cooperative work.* Mahwah, N.J.: Lawrence Erlbaum.

21 Mantei, M., Baecker, R., Sellen, A., Buxton, W., Milligan, T., & Wellman, B. (1991). Experiences in the use of a media space. In *Proceedings of CHI'91 Human Factors in Computing Systems*, 203–209, New York: ACM Press.

22 Nardi, B., Kuchinsky, A., Whittaker, S., Leichner, R. & Schwarz, H. (1996). Video-as-data: Technical and social aspects of a collaborative multimedia application. *Computer Supported Cooperative Work*, **4**(1), 73–100.

23 Nardi, B. & Engeström, Y. (1999): A Web on the Wind: The Structure of Invisible Work. In *Computer-supported Cooperative Work*, **8**, 1–2. Special issue, Nardi, B. and Engeström, Y., guest eds.

24 Nardi, B., Whittaker, S. & Schwarz, H. (in press). A Networker's Work is Never Done: Joint Work in Intensional Networks. *Journal of Computer-supported Cooperative Work.*

25 O'Conaill, B., & Frohlich, D. (1995). Timespace in the workplace: Dealing with interruptions. *Proceedings of CHI'95 Human Factors in Computing Systems*, 262–263, New York: ACM Press.

26 Olson, G.M., & Olson, J.S. (in press). Distance matters. *Human-Computer Interaction.*

27 Rice, R. & Shook, D. (1990). Voice messaging, co-ordination and communication. In J. Galegher, R. Kraut & C. Egido Eds. *Intellectual Teamwork: Social & technological foundations of cooperative work.* Mahwah, N.J.: Lawrence Erlbaum Press.

28 Schegloff, E. (1972). Sequencing in conversational openings. In J. Gumperz and D. Hymes (Eds.), *Directions in Sociolinguistics: The Ethnomethodology of Communication,* 346–380, New York: Holt Rinehart and Winston.

29 Short, J., Williams, E., & Christie, B. (1976). *The Social Psychology of Telecommunications.* New York: Wiley.

30 Tang, J., Isaacs, E., & Rua, M. (1994). Supporting distributed groups with a Montage of lightweight interactions. *Proceedings of CSCW '94 Conference on Computer Supported Cooperative Work*, 23–34, New York: ACM Press.

31 Trevino, L., Lengel, R. & Daft, R. (1987). Media Symbolism, Media Richness, and Media Choice in Organizations. *Communication Research* 14, 5: 553–574.

32 Walther, J. Interpersonal effects in computer mediated communication (1992). *Communication Research,* 19, 50–88.

33 White, S. A., Gupta, A., Grudin, J., Chesley, H., Kimberly, G., Sanocki, E. (1999). Evolving Use of A System for Education at a Distance, *Proceedings of CHI99 Conference on Human Factors in Computing Systems,* 274–275, New York: ACM Press.

34 Whittaker, S. (1995). Rethinking video as a technology for interpersonal communication, *International Journal of Human Computer Studies,* **42**, 501–529.

35 Whittaker, S., Frohlich, D. & Daly-Jones, W. (1994). Informal Workplace Communication: What is it Like and How Might We Support It? *Proceedings of CHI'94 Conference on Human Factors in Computing Systems,* 131–137, ACM Press: New York.

36 Whittaker, S., Swanson, G., Kucan, J., & Sidner, C., (1997). Telenotes: managing lightweight interactions in the desktop. *Transactions on Computer Human Interaction*, 4, 137–168.

Part IV

Online collaboration
in action

Introduction to Part IV

Part IV of the Reader will change pace a little, drawing together the threads from the first three parts and preparing for the later parts. We will do this by presenting a single case study of people working together in ways that would not be possible without the use of collaborative technologies: the ongoing development of the Linux operating system.

Linux is a very large project of open-source software development (open source projects are those where the source code of the software is publicly available, rather than restricted to employees of a particular company). Although begun by a single individual, Linus Torvalds, Linux has been collaboratively built by many thousands of individuals over almost twenty years. Linux is very widely used as an operating system on servers, and to a lesser extent on personal computers, across the world. This is partly because of its cost (free), partly because it is seen by some as more secure or more flexible than its main alternative, Microsoft Windows, and partly because the open-source and collaborative principles of the project are highly attractive to some computer users. There are many similar open-source software projects in existence, such as the Firefox web browser, the OpenOffice office suite, and the Apache web server. Of these open-source projects, we have chosen to discuss Linux because it is particularly large, long-standing and has been widely discussed.

A particularly interesting aspect of Linux is that the bulk of the development work has been carried out by people who have never met face-to-face. All their collaborative work has been conducted online, through email and various shared software development tools. Indeed, many of the developers have only contributed a small amount of the code, in their spare time. Yet the product they have collectively produced is highly robust and usable, by some standards more so than commercial alternatives.

An early analysis of Linux was carried out by Eric Raymond (2000), who contrasted two models of software development: the cathedral (monolithic, highly planned from the start, constructed in a strict hierarchy) and the bazaar (distributed, evolving, organised by many different people). His essay, 'The Cathedral and the Bazaar', first published online in 1997, had a big influence upon the development of open-source software. It is often credited as one of the major influences on the (then) Netscape Corporation, encouraging them to make their web browser open-source. This resulted in the development of a number of open-source browsers, most notably Firefox. Raymond wrote the following about the development of Linux:

> Linus Torvalds's style of development – release early and often, delegate everything you can, be open to the point of promiscuity – came as a surprise. No quiet, reverent cathedral-building here – rather, the Linux community seemed to resemble a great babbling bazaar of differing agendas and approaches (aptly symbolized by the Linux archive sites, who'd take submissions from anyone) out of which a coherent and stable system could seemingly emerge only by a succession of miracles. (Raymond 2000)

The case study that comprises Part IV is derived from a book of articles on collaborative working, by Moon and Sproull (2002). It examines the ways in which Linux developed, focusing on critical success factors (the key reasons why it was successful) at three levels: individual, group and community.

Linux is an interesting example of collaborative technologies in action, being used to create a piece of software that is very widespread and influential. Since the events described in the case study, collaborative technologies have moved on considerably, and the development of Linux and other open-source software projects now make great use of these technologies. Nonetheless, the lessons in this case study still remain valuable. These are: the importance of good communication within distributed groups; the value of good leadership and organisational structure in organising large groups; and the many different sources of motivation that exist for involvement within a large-scale project.

References

Moon, J.Y. and Sproull, L. (2002) 'Essence of distributed work: the case of the Linux kernel', in Hinds, P. and Kiesler, S. (eds.), *Distributed Work,* Cambridge, MA, MIT Press, pp. 381–404.

Raymond, E.S. (2000) 'The cathedral and the bazaar', [online], http://www.catb.org/~esr/writings/cathedral-bazaar/cathedral-bazaar/index.html (Accessed 20 May 2009).

Essence of distributed work

The case of the Linux kernel

Jae Yun Moon and Lee Sproull

This chapter provides a historical account from three different perspectives of how the Linux operating system kernel was developed. Each focuses on different critical factors in its success at the individual, group, and community levels. The technical and management decisions of Linus Torvalds were critical in laying the groundwork for a collaborative software development project that has lasted almost a decade. The contributions of volunteer programmers distributed world-wide enabled the development of an operating system on a par with proprietary operating systems. The Linux electronic community was the organizing structure that coordinated the efforts of the individual programmers. The chapter concludes by summarizing the factors important in the successful distributed development of the Linux kernel and the implications for organizationally managed distributed work arrangements.

Complex tasks plus a global economy have impelled the creation of many distributed engineering and development groups supported by information and communication technologies. Distributed groups range in duration from weeks to years, they range in size from fewer than ten people to more than a thousand, and they may have members located in two locations or many locations. Distributed engineering and development depends on careful planning, coordination, and supervision. *Careful* does not necessarily imply micromanagement. Contributors who are geographically distant from one another inevitably operate under some degree of autonomy. The management challenge is to ensure that members of geographically distributed engineering and development teams stay focused on shared goals, schedules, and quality. This challenge grows as the number of employees and sites increases. There have been some notable successes in large-scale distributed engineering and development. For example, the Boeing 777 marshaled 4,500 engineers working on three continents (Committee on Advanced Engineering Environments 1999). Nevertheless, successful large-scale distributed engineering and development projects are rare.

Moon, J. Y. and Sproull, L. (2002) 'Essence of Distributed Work: The Case of the Linux Kernel', in Hinds, P. J. and Kiesler, S. (eds.), *Distributed Work*, Cambridge, MA: MIT Press, pp. 381–404. By permission of The MIT Press.

That in part explains the business and media fascination with Linux. Linux is a PC-based operating system (OS) that has been produced through a software development effort consisting of more than 3,000 developers and countless other contributors distributed over ninety countries on five continents. It is difficult to provide a precise estimate of the number of programmers who have contributed to it. Published estimates range from several hundred to more than 40,000 (Shankland 1998, Raymond 1999). In its first three and a half years of development (November 1991–July 1995), more than 15,000 people submitted code or comments to the three main Linux related newsgroups and mailing lists. In the next three and a half years, thousands continued to contribute code, and hundreds of thousands of people joined electronic discussions about Linux philosophy, applications, competitors, business models, and so forth. In this chapter, we focus narrowly on people writing code for the operating system kernel.

As of December 1998, more than 8 million users were running Linux on a wide variety of platforms. Linux was estimated to have 17 percent of server operating systems sales in 1998 and was projected to have a compound annual growth rate of 25 percent, two and a half times greater than the rest of the market (Shankland 1998, Berinato 1999). It was widely regarded as being of very high quality and reliability, with a failure rate two to five times lower than that of commercial versions of Unix (Valloppillil 1998). In both 1997 and 1998, Linux won the Info World Product of the Year award for best operating system; in 1997 it won the Info World Best Technical Support award. Such a successful large-scale distributed project would make any organization proud and its shareholders happy.

But the real fascination with Linux stems from the fact that it is *not* an organizational project. No architecture group developed the design; no management team approved the plan, budget, and schedule; no human resource group hired the programmers; no facilities group assigned the office space. Instead, volunteers from all over the world contributed code, documentation, and technical support over the Internet just because they wanted to. This chapter analyzes factors contributing to the Linux kernel story and explores how those factors could be brought into play in formal organizations that are managing distributed work.

A 1971 book about the Cuban missile crisis, *Essence of Decision*, suggested the title and rhetorical structure for this chapter. That book's author, Graham Allison, observed that no single perspective could provide an entirely satisfactory explanation of a complex social phenomenon. Thus, in the book, he told the story of the missile crisis three times, each time from a different explanatory perspective. In this chapter, after a brief description of Linux and its enabling conditions, we tell the Linux kernel story three times. (See Table 11.1 for the time line.) First we tell the story from a "great man" perspective, emphasizing the technical and management abilities of Linus Torvalds. We then tell the story a second time from a hacker culture perspective, emphasizing what motivates individual hackers to work on this project. We then tell the story a third time from an electronic community perspective, emphasizing communication forums and role differentiation. We conclude with suggestions for how the factors

Table 11.1 Timeline of key events

Enabling conditions

1960s: MIT AI Lab, ITS
1969: ARPANET, UNIX (Bell Labs)
1976: Unix-to-Unix copy (UUCP)
1979: Usenet
1984: Gnu's Not Unix
1989: GNU General Public License V.1

Linux kernel development

July and August 1991: Torvalds asked Minix newsgroup for help.
October 1991: Torvalds announces Linux v.0.02. First Linux mailing list.
March 1992: First comp.* hierarchy Linux newsgroup
March 1994: Linux v.1.0. Parallel release structure. Credits File.
February 1996: Maintainers File
June 1996: Linux v.2.0

emphasized in these three perspectives could pertain to distributed work within organizations.

What is Linux?

An operating system is a computer's central program that oversees resource allocation, program execution, and the control of input, output, file management, and peripheral devices. The kernel is the central module of the operating system – the part of the operating system that loads first, remains in the main memory of the system, and controls memory management, process and task management, and disk management. Common operating systems in use today are Microsoft Windows and Unix-based systems such as Sun Solaris and IBM AIX.

Linux version 1.0, released in March 1994, offered most features of a typical Unix operating system, including multitasking, virtual memory, and TCP/IP networking. It had about 175,000 lines of code. Linux version 2.0, released in June 1996, offered 64-bit processing; symmetric multiprocessing, which allows the simultaneous deployment of several chips in a system; and advanced networking capabilities. It had about 780,000 lines of code. Version 2.1.110, released in July 1998, had about 1.5 million lines of code: 17 percent in architecture-specific code, 54 percent in platform-independent drivers, and 29 percent in core kernel and file systems.

Linux is now much more than an operating system. By July 2000, there were more than 400 Linux user groups in seventy-one countries (Linux User Groups Worldwide, lugww.counter.li.org/). More Linux users meant more interest in applications to run on the operating system. The August 1999 Linux Software Map database lists about 2,500 people who have contributed over 3,500 applications, which range from word processors and mathematical applications to games (Dempsey, Weiss, Jones, and Greenberg 1999). Approximately 300 people have also contributed over 20 megabytes of Linux documentation ranging from information sheets to full-scale manuals.

Anyone can download all Linux files from the Internet for free. Thus, anyone can install a Linux OS, applications, and documentation on his or her PC without going through (or paying) any commercial organization. For people who do not have the time or skill for a do-it-yourself installation, several commercial firms, such as RedHat, Suse, and Caldera, as well as nonprofit organizations such as Debian, sell and support low-cost CD-ROM distribution versions of Linux.

Enabling conditions: open source and internet

Two enabling factors underlie the Linux development as well as that of similar volunteer distributed software development projects.[1] The first is the social and legal conventions of open source, a means for sharing software code. The second is the information and communications infrastructure of the Internet.

Open sharing of software code was a common practice in the MIT Artificial Intelligence Laboratory in the early 1960s and in similar laboratories at universities such as Stanford and Carnegie Mellon (Levy 1984). Because there were very few computers at that time, people would start a program and leave it available for others using the machine after them to admire and improve upon. By the late 1960s, the scarcity of computers and the growing number of programmers and users led MIT to develop the Incompatible Timesharing System (ITS) for the Digital PDP-10, the large computer in use at the AI Lab. The system had no passwords and gave users the ability to browse both the source code of the system itself, as well as the personal programs and documents created by other users.[2] In essence, the ITS facilitated open sharing of software code.

Also in the late 1960s, a small group of people within AT&T's Bell Laboratories led by Ken Thompson and Dennis Ritchie developed the Unix operating system (Lerner and Tirole 2000, Salus 1994). After Thompson presented the ideas represented in the system at the ACM Symposium on Operating Systems Principles in 1973, Unix began to spread throughout the research and academic community (Salus 1994). AT&T licensed the Unix operating system to academic institutions for a nominal fee and distributed the system in source, but maintained a policy of no official support. Due to the lack of official support, users of the Unix operating system began to share their bug fixes and improvements with one another informally. In 1975, many users met at the first USENIX meeting, designed to bring together various people to share their experiences. In the late 1970s, the Unix user-developers developed a new feature, known as the UUCP (Unix-to-Unix-Copy), that enabled them to exchange files and data over phone lines (Gaffin and Heitkotter 1994). The feature was used to distribute information to the Unix community and led to the beginning of Usenet.[3] In addition to the institutionalization of this open sharing culture, Unix embodied various innovative principles that made the system portable and simple in design.

Advances in computing architecture by the early 1980s saw the demise of the PDP-10 series machines for which MIT's ITS had been developed (Stallman 1998). New machines in the AI Lab were now equipped with proprietary operating systems, which, unlike the ITS, came in binary code wrapped with nondisclosure agreements that forbade sharing with other people. Richard Stallman, who had used ITS at the AI Lab, started the GNU (GNU's Not Unix) project in 1984 to develop a free operating system like ITS to support open sharing and collaboration. However, free access to source code for everyone meant that commercial software developers could exploit the free software to develop proprietary programs. Stallman instituted the Copyleft software license to guarantee sustained easy sharing of code by decreeing that all users of the program have the right to use it, copy it, modify it, and distribute their modifications. Additionally, Copyleft explicitly forbids privatization of derivations from software distributed under Copyleft; derived works must also be distributed under the Copyleft license. The canonical Copyleft license is the GNU General Public License (GPL), which also forbids packaging of proprietary software with GPL-licensed software (Free Software Foundation [FSF] 1991). Copyleft codified the open sharing practices of the early closely knit group of programmers; software distributed under a Copyleft license is known as open source software.

Whereas Copyleft codified the social and legal norms of open sharing,[4] the Internet provided a ubiquitous technology infrastructure that made it easy for programmers to communicate and share their code. While its predecessor, the Advanced Research Projects Agency Network (ARPANET), was a network of research laboratories in academia and industry funded by the U.S. Department of Defense (King, Grinter, and Pickering 1997), the Internet broadened the scope of connectivity through widespread emergence of commercial Internet service providers. It was no longer only the few privileged members of places like the AI Lab at MIT or Bell Labs who could share code and collaborate with others on improving their systems. The standard, robust communication system of the Internet made possible the exchange of both messages and source code among programmers worldwide. People could learn about a project and participate in open discussions about it through Usenet bulletin board discussions and electronic mailing lists. They could also download source code from the Internet and upload their modifications for others to critique and improve. In the early days, the ITS facilitated sharing of code among programmers at the AI Lab; the ARPANET enabled collaboration and open sharing of code among programmers in select geographically dispersed research institutions; and finally the Internet made it possible for people anywhere to share their code and ideas.

Linus Torvalds

In October 1991, Linus Torvalds, a computer science graduate student at the University of Helsinki, announced on the Internet that he had written a "free version of a minix-lookalike for AT-386 computers" and would make it available to anyone who was interested. (See Figure 11.1 for Torvalds's announcement

Date: Sat, 5 Oct 1991 05:41:06 GMT
Reply-To: INFO-MINIX@UDEL.EDU
Sender: INFO-MINIX-ERRORS@PLAINS.NODAK.EDU
Comments: Warning - original Sender: tag was
info-minix-request@UDEL.EDU
From: Linus Benedict Torvalds <torvalds@KLAAVA.HELSINKI.FI>
Subject: Free minix-like kernel sources for 386-AT

Do you pine for the nice days of minix-1.1, when men were men
and wrote their own device drivers? Are you without a nice
project and just dying to cut your teeth on a OS you can try
to modify for your needs? Are you finding it frustrating when
everything works on minix? No more all-nighters to get a nifty
program working? Then this post might be just for you :-)

As I mentioned a month (?) ago, I'm working on a free version
of a minix-lookalike for AT-386 computers. It has finally
reached the stage where it's even usable (though may not
be depending on what you want), and I am willing to put out
the sources for wider distribution. It is just version 0.02
(+1 (very small) patch already), but I've successfully run
bash/gcc/gnu-make/gnu-sed/compress etc under it.

Sources for this pet project of mine can be found at
nic.funet.fi (128.214.6.100) in the directory /pub/OS/Linux.
The directory also contains some README-file and a couple of
binaries to work under linux (bash, update and gcc, what more
can you ask for :-). Full kernel source is provided, as no
minix code has been used. Library sources are only partially
free, so that cannot be distributed currently. The system
is able to compile "as-is" and has been known to work. Heh.
Sources to the binaries (bash and gcc) can be found at the same
place in /pub/gnu.

ALERT! WARNING! NOTE! These sources still need minix-386 to be
compiled (and gcc-1.40, possibly 1.37.1, haven't tested), and
you need minix to set it up if you want to run it, so it is
not yet a standalone system for those of you without minix. I'm
working on it. You also need to be something of a hacker to set
it up (?), so for those hoping for an alternative to minix-386,
please ignore me. It is currently meant for hackers interested
in operating systems and 386's with access to minix.

The system needs an AT-compatible harddisk (IDE is fine)
and EGA/VGA. If you are still interested, please ftp the
README/RELNOTES, and/or mail me for additional info.

I can (well, almost) hear you asking yourselves "why?". Hurd
will be out in a year (or two, or next month, who knows), and
I've already got minix. This is a program for hackers by

Figure 11.1 Announcement of Linux v.0.02, October 1991

```
a hacker. I've enjouyed doing it, and somebody might enjoy
looking at it and even modifying it for their own needs. It
is still small enough to understand, use and modify, and I'm
looking forward to any comments you might have.

I'm also interested in hearing from anybody who has written
any of the utilities/library functions for minix. If your
efforts are freely distributable (under copyright or even
public domain), I'd like to hear from you, so I can add them
to the system. I'm using Earl Chews estdio right now (thanks
for a nice and working system Earl), and similar works will be
very wellcome. Your (C)'s will of course be left intact. Drop
me a line if you are willing to let me use your code.

    Linus

PS. to PHIL NELSON! I'm unable to get through to you, and
keep getting "forward error - strawberry unknown domain" or
something.
```

Figure 11.1 Continued

message.) Minix was a simplified version of Unix written and maintained largely as a teaching tool by a European computer science professor, Andrew Tanenbaum. It was widely used in computer science courses, even though its license cost $79.95 and restricted its redistribution. As a result of Minix use by computer science students, the professor was bombarded with requests and suggestions for improvement. He was reluctant to implement many of them, however, and some students were frustrated with his unresponsiveness.[5] Torvalds, a frustrated Minix user, noted in his announcement message that all of the code in his operating system was freely available to be copied by others. He also volunteered to add functions written by others if they were also freely distributable. In the next thirty months, Torvalds released ninety additional versions of his OS, culminating on March 14, 1994, with the release of version 1.0.

Torvalds certainly did not set out to create a worldwide distributed OS development project. But he exhibited both technical and management capabilities and decisions without which Linux would not have grown. He makes it easy to build a "great man theory" of the success of Linux. Known as a "damn fine programmer" (Raymond 1999) and an "arch hacker" (Moody 1997), Torvalds's programming skills are widely admired. Even today, up to half the code in key parts of the kernel has been written by Linus (Yamagata 1997). And in the early days, if he did not write the code himself, he edited other people's code so heavily "as to be totally unrecognizable" by its original authors (Torvalds 1992, March 8).

Beyond programming skill, Torvalds's chief technical contribution lay in designing a portable, modular architecture for the kernel. Torvalds wrote the initial Linux for his own PC, which had an Intel 386 architecture. By 1993, Linux had been completely rewritten once to run on a Motorola 68K architecture, and it was about to be rewritten yet again to run on a DEC alpha architecture. The prospect of having to maintain a completely separate code base for every new machine architecture was unacceptable to Torvalds. Thus, he redesigned the Linux kernel architecture to have one common code base that could simultaneously support a separate specific tree for any number of different machine architectures (Torvalds 1999b). The architecture greatly improved the Linux kernel portability through establishing systematic modularity. A modular system minimized the need for communication among different components of the kernel and made it possible to write code in parallel on different portions of the kernel (Torvalds 1999a, 1999b). Modularity decreased the total need for coordination and meant that necessary remaining coordination could be deferred.

In creating a worldwide distributed OS development project, Torvalds's management decisions and skills were just as important as his technical ones. Perhaps his most important management decision was establishing in 1994 a parallel release structure for Linux (1994, March 15). Even-numbered releases were reserved for relatively stable systems and focused only on fixing bugs; odd-numbered releases were the development versions on which people could experiment with new features. Once an odd-numbered release series incorporated sufficient new features and became sufficiently stable through bug fixes and patches, it would be renamed and released as the next higher even-numbered release series, and the process would begin again.[6] The parallel release structure allowed Torvalds simultaneously to please two audiences often in conflict with one another. Users who rely on a Linux OS to support their production computing want a stable, reliable system in which new releases introduce only well-tested new functionality, no new bugs, and no backward compatibility problems. Developers, by contrast, want to try out new ideas and get feedback on them as rapidly as possible. The parallel structure offered both relative stability and certainty to users and rapid development and testing to programmers. Table 11.2, which displays the release history of Linux, illustrates the disparate release rate between the two release trees.

Despite his position of importance, there is little that is imperious or dictatorial in Torvalds's communication style. Initially he was (appropriately) quite deprecatory about his project – "just a hobby, won't be big and professional like gnu" (Torvalds 1991, August 25). He never orders anyone to do anything, and even his suggestions are mild mannered. Typical suggestions are of the form: "hint, hint, Linus wants to get out of doing it himself;^)" (Torvalds 1995, June 29) or "my personal priority is not that kind of behaviour, so it would be up to somebody else to implement this . . . (hint hint)" (Torvalds 1996, April 16). Yet there is no confusion about who has decision authority in this project. Torvalds manages and announces all releases – all 569 of them up to May 2000. He acts as a filter on all patches and new features – rejecting, accepting, or revising as he chooses. He can single-handedly decide to redo something completely if he wishes. In the early days he personally reviewed every contribution and communicated by

Table 11.2 Linux release history

Release series	Date of initial release	Number of release	Time to final release in series (months)	Duration of series (months)
0.01	9/17/91	2	2	2
0.1	12/3/91	85	27	27
1.0	3/13/94	9	1	12
1.1	4/6/94	96	11	11
1.2	3/7/95	13	6	14
1.3	6/12/95	115	12	12
2.0	6/9/96	34	24	32
2.1	9/30/96	141	29	29
2.2	1/26/99	14	9	–
2.3	5/11/99	60	12	–

Note: Versions 2.2.x and 2.3.x were still current as of May 2000.

personal e-mail with every contributor. As Torvalds says, "[There is] one person who everybody agrees is in charge (me)" (Yamagata 1997).

Hackers

In October 1991, Linus Torvalds announced on the Internet that he had written a "program for hackers by a hacker." (See Figure 11.1 for the October 1991 announcement message.) Hackers are people who enjoy "exploring the details of programmable systems and how to stretch their capabilities" and appreciate programming over theorizing (*Jargon Dictionary* 2000). Torvalds encouraged people to look at his program, modify it for their own needs, and send him their code to add to the system. People who had been frustrated with the restricted features of Minix accepted the invitation. By the end of the month, ten people had the system working on their machines (Torvalds 1991, October 31). Some offered to work on different features of the program and began sending contributions.

Within two months of the October 1991 announcement, about thirty people had contributed close to 200 reports of errors and problems in running Linux, contributions of utilities to run under Linux, and drivers and features to add to Linux. When Torvalds released version 0.11 in December 1991, he credited contributions by three people in addition to himself (Torvalds 1991, December 3). In version 0.13, released in February 1992, the majority of patches were written by people other than Torvalds. By July 1995, more than 15,000 people from ninety countries on five continents had contributed comments, bug reports, patches, and features.[7] Why did these people accept the invitation to test and modify Linux?

One motivation for working on the Linux project is that hackers by nature enjoy solving interesting technical problems and building new programs (Raymond 1999). Torvalds labeled himself a hacker and said that he "enjoyed" developing the operating system in his October 1991 message and suggested that "somebody else might enjoy looking at it." (See Figure 16.1.) To hackers, who are generally interested in "sexy" and "technically sweet" problems (Raymond 1999, 72), an operating system represents an alluring challenge. Programming an operating system means a hacker has tamed the computer hardware and stretched its functionality. In his October announcement, Torvalds appealed to the hacker's need for such challenges when he asked if they were "without a nice project and just dying to cut [their] teeth on a OS."

People also wrote code to solve particular personal problems. Torvalds himself developed Linux so that he could run a Unix-like operating system on his own PC. In his October announcement, Torvalds noted that Linux was available for anybody "to modify for [their] needs." When people accepted his invitation to try the first Linux release, they wrote their own device drivers to support their choice of hardware and peripherals. For instance, a German programmer using Linux developed the German keyboard driver that was included in the December 1991 release (Thiel 1991). To this day, people work on areas that they know and care about (Raymond 1999). No one tells people what to work on.[8]

Intrinsic pleasure and personal problem solving may be enough to motivate people to write Linux code for their own use, but they do not satisfactorily explain why people contributed that code to a larger effort. People might contribute because they expect others will do so in return (Kollock 1999, Raymond 1999). When Torvalds announced his free operating system, he was also "interested in hearing from anybody who has written any of the utilities/library functions for minix" to add to his system. People posted bug reports hoping others would fix them; people contributed patches expecting that others would post patches to other problems with the system. The Gnu GPL ensured both that their contributions would be made accessible to everyone else and that everyone else's contributions would be accessible to them. This ensured the establishment of a stable generalized exchange system (Kollock 1999) in which people could expect returns to their contributions.

This generalized exchange system, however, could have broken down if everyone waited for someone else to contribute (Kollock 1998). In the Linux case, programmers also contributed because they wanted to be known for writing good code (Raymond 1999). Ackerman and Palen (1996) offer a similar explanation when they suggest that MIT undergraduates contribute to a voluntary on-line help system to develop their reputation as "clueful." An economic explanation suggested that accrued reputation has a positive impact on the programmers' careers (Lerner and Tirole 2000). However, this account fails to explain the motivation of early hackers of the Linux operating system. The potential career opportunities to be gained from building up a reputation as a skilled programmer in the Linux operating system project were not present from the start.

Good code was acknowledged in a variety of ways. The separate management of production and development kernels meant that people contributing good code received rapid positive feedback as their contributions were incorporated in the development kernel in a short period of time. Some programmers left personal signatures within the source code so that others looking at the source code could recognize their work. The GPL ensured that freely contributed code would not be exploited by others. Torvalds also frequently acknowledged the contributions of others. In his original October 1991 announcement message, he credited another programmer for code he had used in the first release ("thanks for a nice and working system Earl ⟨Chews⟩"). In his January 1992 release, he acknowledged the significant contributions of three other programmers (Torvalds 1992, January 9). As the number of contributors grew, it became impossible for Torvalds to acknowledge all those who had contributed code with each release. With the official release of version 1.0 in 1994, Torvalds acknowledged and thanked more than 80 people by name (Torvalds 1994, March 14). Version 1.0 was also the first version to include a credits file that listed the various contributors and their role in developing and maintaining the Linux kernel. The programmers themselves were responsible for requesting to be added to the credits file if they considered themselves to be "worth mentioning" (Torvalds 1993, December 21). In the early days, Torvalds credited programmers personally. The credits file marked a transition to a process in which programmers could credit themselves according to a shared understanding of what constituted creditable contributions.

Whereas reputation as a skilled programmer was the most important motivation for contributing code, it was not the only way of gaining reputation. Credit could also come from significant contributions of documentation and other information useful to developers and users of Linux. In fact, in an early message, Torvalds acknowledged a contributor for compiling the Linux information sheet (Torvalds 1992, January 9) and stated that one did not "need to be a *kernel* developer to be on the credits list" (Torvalds 1993, December 21).

Community

Several months before his October 1991 announcement, Torvalds posted messages to a Usenet group to which he belonged asking the group for help on a project. He asked where to find a particular set of operating system standards, what things group members liked and disliked about Minix, and what features they would want in a free Minix look-alike. (See Figure 11.2 for one of these messages.) Torvalds did not create his original project in social isolation. He was a member of an ongoing active community of programmers, electronically organized in a Usenet group, comp.os.minix, with thousands of members.[9] It was to this group that Torvalds turned for advice, suggestions, and code and to which he announced his initial project. It was from this group that early Linux contributors were drawn. And it was out of this group that the first Linux group was created.

Writing code is a solitary activity. Some people may have written Linux code for the joy of it or to solve a personal problem with no thought of contributing to a larger endeavor. But the hackers already described did not upload code to the Internet randomly. Their code was motivated, organized, and aggregated by

```
Date: Sun, 25 Aug 1991 20:57:08 GMT
Reply-To: INFO-MINIX@UDEL.EDU
Sender: INFO-MINIX-ERRORS@PLAINS.NODAK.EDU
Comments: Warning - - original Sender: tag was
info-minix-request@UDEL.EDU
From: Linus Benedict Torvalds <torvalds@KLAAVA.HELSINKI.FI>
Subject: What would you like to see most in minix?
Hello everybody out there using minix -

I'm doing a (free) operating system (just a hobby, won't be
big and professional like gnu) for 386 (486) AT clones. This
has been brewing since april, and is starting to get ready.
I'd like any feedback on things people like/dislike in minix,
as my OS resembles it somewhat (same physical layout of the
file-system (due to practical reasons) among other things).

I've currently ported bash (1.08) and gcc (1.40), and things
seem to work. This implies that I'll get something practical
within a few months, and I'd like to know what features most
people would want. Any suggestions are welcome, but I won't
promise I'll implement them :-)

Linus (torvalds@kruuna.helsinki.fi)

PS. Yes - it's free of any minix code, and it has a
multi-threaded fs. It is NOT protable (uses 386 task switching
etc), and it probably never will support anything other than
AT-harddisks, as that's all I have :-(.
```

Figure 11.2 Announcement of Torvalds's project, August 1991

and through features of the Linux electronic community. Two attributes of this community have been particularly important: its group communication structure and its role structure.[10]

Linux mailing lists and Usenet groups provided a map of the growing and changing Linux territory so that people could know what new code had been written, where to send their code or comments, and where to find information that interested them. The first Linux mailing list, Linux-activists, was created in October 1991, and had about 400 subscribers by January 1992. Today there are more than 700 Linux mailing lists. Comp.os.linux was formed in March 1992, the first of fourteen comp.os.linux.* Usenet groups devoted to Linux formed in the next two years. Beginning in 1994, an additional hierarchy of Linux groups, linux.* was formed, which by 1998 had 369 groups.[11]

The linux-kernel mailing list organizes the behavior of kernel programmers.[12] Feature freezes, code freezes, and new releases are announced on this list. Bug reports are submitted to it. Programmers who want their code to be included in the kernel submit it to this list. Other programmers can then download it, test it within their own environment, suggest changes back to the author, or endorse it.[13] From June 1995 to April 2000, about 13,000 contributors posted almost 175,000 messages to the linux-kernel list. This is how individual behavior is organized into a product with social utility. Coordination of the individual programmers is achieved through the modular structure of the Linux kernel.

The previous two sections might convey the impression that the Linux development project consisted of Linus Torvalds and an undifferentiated band of happy hackers. In fact, the community has developed a differentiated role structure that both reflects and supports its activities. The two most important roles within this community are credited developer and maintainer. Beginning with the v1.0 release in 1994, new releases of the kernel were accompanied by a credits file that publicly acknowledges people who have contributed substantial code to the kernel. The initial credits file listed eighty contributors. By the release of Linux 2.0 in June 1996, there were 190 acknowledged contributors. By July 2000, the list had grown to approximately 350 contributors from over thirty countries worldwide. People who have contributed extensively to the Linux kernel but do not add themselves to the credits file are also recognized by the community.

The maintainer role was first formally acknowledged in February 1996, when the maintainers' file was announced (Cox 1996). The first maintainers' file contained 3 names; today it contains 147 names. Designated maintainers are responsible for particular modules of the kernel. They review linux-kernel mailing list submissions (bug reports, bug fixes, new features) relevant to their modules, build them into larger patches, and submit the larger patches back to the list and to Torvalds directly.[14] Over the years, Torvalds and the community have come to know and trust the technical competence of these maintainers, most of whom still "work on Linux for free and in their spare time" (Linux-kernel mailing list FAQ, www.tux.org/lkml). Indeed, one maintainer, Alan Cox, has complete responsibility for overseeing the stable tree. Torvalds still announces major stable tree releases, but this is a pro forma gesture.[15]

Table 11.3 displays the message contribution profile for the linux-kernel mailing list. Note that approximately 2 percent of the contributors contributed more than 50 percent of the messages, an indicator of the differentiated role structure and contribution profile of the community. Of these 254 contributors, 30 percent are credited developers, and 19 percent are designated maintainers.

Because the linux-kernel mailing list is the central organizing forum for kernel developers and supports a very heavy volume of message traffic, people need a clear understanding of how to contribute to the list. Maintainers of the linux-kernel mailing list FAQ create that understanding. The FAQ is the document that explains the rules of the road for kernel development to newcomers ("How do I make a patch?" "How do I get my patch into the kernel?"). It also reiterates the norms and values of the community ("A line of code is worth a thousand words. If you think of a new feature, implement it first, then post to the list for comments.") In addition to learning through the FAQ, newcomers can learn directly from the more experienced and skilled developers on the list through direct observation and

Table 11.3 Message contribution profile

Messages	Number of contributors	Percentage of total contributors	Unique messages contributed	Cumulative message count	Percentage of total (messages)
10 or fewer	10,925	84.07%	27,861	27,861	15.99%
11–100	1,816	13.97	53,186	81,047	30.52
100+	134	1.03	18,999	100,946	10.90
200+	46	0.35	11,334	111,380	6.50
300+	16	0.12	5,563	116,943	3.19
400+	15	0.12	6,608	123,551	3.79
500+	10	0.08	5,483	129,034	3.15
600+	5	0.04	3,266	132,300	1.87
700+	5	0.04	3,750	136,050	2.15
800+	3	0.02	2,490	138,540	1.43
900+	2	0.02	1,837	140,377	1.05
1,000+	18	0.14	33,880	174,257	19.44

Note: The source is the linux-kernel mailing list, June 1995 to April 2000

questions posted to the list. Newcomers can develop into skilled Linux kernel programmers through such informal training (Brown and Duguid 1991, Cox 1998). Twelve people maintain the FAQ, all of them credited developers or maintainers. The mailing list, with its thousands of contributors, differentiated role structure, dedicated role incumbents, and rules of the road, is more than just a list. As the FAQ explains, "Remember the list is a community."

Lessons for organizations

Others have written about lessons from Linux for commercial software development projects (Raymond 1999). Here we consider how factors important in the Linux case might apply more generally to distributed work in and across organizations (Markus, Manville, and Agres 2000). It might seem odd to derive lessons for formal organizations from a self-organizing volunteer activity. After all, the employment contract, should ensure that people will fulfill their role obligations and act in the best interest of the organization. Yet, particularly in distributed work, employees must go beyond the letter of their job description to exhibit qualities found in the Linux developers: initiative, persistence, and activism. We suggest that the enabling conditions for Linux (the Internet and open source) usefully support these conditions. We then consider how factors emphasized in each of the three versions of the Linux story (great man and task structure, incentives for contributors, and communities of practice) can facilitate organizational distributed work.

Clearly, easy access to the Internet or its equivalent is a necessary precondition for the kind of distributed work represented by Linux. Developers used the Internet both for easy access to work products (to upload and download files) and easy communication with other developers (to ask and answer questions, have discussions, and share community lore). Both capabilities are surely important, and they are simple. It is noteworthy that despite the technical prowess of Linux developers, they relied on the simplest and oldest of Internet tools: file transfer, e-mail distribution lists, and Usenet discussion groups. Even with today's wider variety of more sophisticated Web-based tools, Linux developers continue to rely on these tools for coordinating their efforts. These tools are simple, they are available worldwide, and they are reliable.

The organizational equivalent of Copyleft is a second precondition for the kind of distributed work represented by Linux. Both the formal and informal reward and incentive systems must reward sharing and discourage hoarding. (See Constant, Kiesler, and Sproull 1996 and Orlikowski 1992 for discussions of incentives for information sharing in organizations.) Moreover, work products should be transparently accessible so that anyone can use and build on good features and anyone can find and fix problems. We do not underestimate the difficulty of creating the equivalent of Copyleft for organizational work products. Failing to do so, however, can hobble distributed work.

Does every successful large-scale distributed project require one great person to be in charge? Clearly this was important in the Linux case. Yet other successful open source development projects have had different leadership models (Fielding 1999, Wall 1999). The capabilities that a singular leader brings to a project – clear locus of decision making, singular vision, consistent voice – are important. But in principle, they can be achieved through a variety of leadership models.

Task decomposition has been an important organizational principle for at least the past forty years (March and Simon 1958). Modularity is an extreme form of task decomposition, one that may be particularly suited to distributed work. Modular task decomposition reduces coordination costs to an irreducible minimum. Moreover, it allows for redundant development, which can increase the probability of timely, high-quality solutions. That is, multiple groups can work on the same module independent of one another. The first (or best) solution is selected for adoption.

Parallel release structures that support both stability and rapid development are not commonly deployed in organizational development projects. More typical are linear structures or phased structures that hand off a project from developers to clients or maintainers. Organizations are typically viewed as having to manage a trade-off between exploration and exploitation (March 1991). Ongoing parallel release structures could generate both more innovation and more continuous improvement.

In the Linux case, people were motivated to work for pleasure and improve their personal work situation. They were motivated to contribute their work to others for the same reasons: for reputational credit and to contribute to the community. Careful attention to motivation and incentive structures are extremely important in distributed work projects. "Careful" need not mean "heavy-handed," however. Encouraging people to sign their work can be a low-cost, high-payoff motivator.

Publicly naming contributors can be another. This approach is analogous to one employed in the Xerox system for technical service representatives in which they are encouraged to submit their fixes to machine problems that are not adequately handled by their formal documentation (Bell et al. 1997).

Finally, Linux developers were members of and supported by vigorous electronic communities of practice. Creating and sustaining such communities can importantly contribute to distributed work. Electronic communities require both (simple) computer tools and social tools. We discussed computer tools under enabling conditions. The social tools include differentiated roles and norms. It is not enough to enable electronic communication among people working on a distributed project. In a project of any size, people must understand and take on differentiated electronic roles. These roles, with their corresponding obligations and responsibilities, should be explicitly designated and understood by all. Indeed, one category of community norms is the expectations associated with role behaviors. More generally, norms are the rules of the road for the particular electronic community. Because distributed projects cannot rely on the tacit reinforcements that occur in face-to-face communications, persistent explicit reminders of norms are necessary in the electronic context. (See Sproull and Patterson 2000 for more on this topic.)

The scope of computer-supported distributed work will continue to increase in organizations. The lessons of open source software development are surely not applicable to all distributed work. Indeed one fruitful avenue for further work will be to delineate features of projects for which these lessons are more or less applicable. Still, Linux and its kin will continue to offer fascinating cases of distributed work in their own right and fruitful sources of lessons for organizational distributed work.

Notes

A version of this chapter was presented at the Distributed Work Workshop, Carmel, California, August 2000. A longer version was published in *First Monday*, November 2000 firstmonday.org/issues/issue5_11/moon/index.html). We thank participants in the Electronic Communities seminar at Stern (spring 2000), participants at the NSF Distributed Work Workshop (August 2000), Sara Kiesler, Gloria Mark, Wanda Orlikowski, and Bob Sproull for their valuable comments. We also thank members of the Linux community, in particular John A. Martin and Matti Aarnio, for their help in understanding the community.

  1 Other software projects developed by volunteer programmers distributed geographically include the Apache Web server (Fielding 1999), Perl programming language (Wall 1999), GNU Emacs editor (Stallman 1999), the fetchmail e-mail client program (Raymond 1999), and the Tcl/tk scripting language (Ousterhout 1999). A large part of Internet infrastructure also is the product of such collaborations. Sendmail, which enables people to send and receive e-mail, and BIND (Berkeley Internet Name Domain), the technology that makes it possible to navigate Web pages using natural language addresses instead of numbers, are among these (O'Reilly 1999). Several commercial programs adopted an open source collaborative development style. These

include but are not limited to Netscape Mozilla, Sun Microsystems Star Office, and Microsoft Virtual Worlds (DuBois 2000, Netscape Press Relations 1998, Virtual Worlds Group 2000).

2 The source code of a software program is a set of instructions that can be understood and modified by programmers. Compiling the source code produces binary code that is executable on the platform for which it was compiled. However, such code is not readily comprehended by people and thus cannot be usefully modified by them.

3 Usenet is a system of interconnected computer networks in which people form newsgroups to discuss topics of common interest. Newsgroups act as a selective broadcasting system: people post to newsgroups, hoping to find interested readers.

4 The enforceability of the GPL has not yet been determined in the courts. However, the GPL as a statement of informal norms and good practices carries power even with companies, which tend to honor the GPL (Powell 2000). The FSF also polices the proper use of software code distributed under GPL license. Detailed exposition of the debate surrounding the legal enforceability of the Copyleft licenses is beyond the scope of this chapter. For a view that GPL is not legally enforceable, see Merges 1997; for an opposing view see Moglen 1999.

5 In response to "most requested features in Minix," replies from the professor included "never." "No. too much hair. Mucks up kernel and MM too much." "Ha, ha" (Tanenbaum 1991).

6 Torvalds did not invent the concept of parallel release series, but he was the first to open his development series to the entire world.

7 We identified the contributors by extracting headers of archived mail and newsgroup messages. Although multiple e-mail addresses were resolved manually, some duplications might have been missed.

8 In the early days, contributors were mostly hackers interested in working on an operating system for fun. Although commercial firms today also develop drivers and products for the Linux system, only 6 percent of maintained kernel modules and drivers (8 of 129) are maintained by people whose job requires it as indicated for Linux version 2.3, released in May 1999. An interview study of developers found that only 10 percent of those interviewed reported that their job in some way involved Linux (Kuwabara 2000, and personal communications).

9 In 1992, there were 43,000 readers of the newsgroup (Tanenbaum 1992). By 1995 that number had fallen to 25,000 (Minix information sheet, www.cs.vu.nl/~ast/minix. html).

10 Other important attributes and practices, which we omit because of space constraints, are norms, boundary maintenance, generational reproduction, and socialization.

11 The first Linux Usenet group was alt.os.linux, which was formed in January 1992 to move the growing Linux discussion off of the Minix group. The number of newsgroups and lists is based on information retrieved on April 25, 2000, from various sources including the Liszt Newsgroups site (www.liszt.com/news) and the Linux Portal Site (www.linuxlinks.com/Newsgroups/Miscellaneous). It is assumed that other Linux-related firms also have forums for discussion, but that these do not take the form of a newsgroup. A search on the Liszt Newsgroup page yielded 143 groups that contained the word *linux* as part of the newsgroup name. A similar search of Liszt listed mailing lists and IRC channels resulted in 128 hits for lists and 192 hits for IRC channels.

12 Prior to the creation of the linux-kernel mailing list, the first Linux kernel mailing list, Linux activists, served this organizing function.

13 Programmers are cautioned not to send code via e-mail directly to Torvalds because he will be unlikely to see it (Linux-kernel mailing list FAQ, www.tux.org/lkml/#s1–14).

14 As Torvalds explained, "What happens is that if I get a patch against something where I'm not the primary developer (against a device driver or a filesystem I have nothing to do with, for example), I am less likely to react to that patch if it doesn't come from the person who is responsible for that particular piece of code. If I get a networking patch, for example, it's a _lot_ more likely to get a reaction if it is from Alan Cox, and then it usually goes in with no questions asked. Similarly . . . , if it is a patch against the SCSI subsystem, I much prefer to have it from somebody I know works on SCSI (Eric, Drew, Leonard)" (Torvalds 1996, February 19).

15 Red Hat, a Linux distribution firm, funds Cox in addition to other key Linux developers (Shankland 1999). Thus, Cox's role in the Linux community is in large measure subsidized by Red Hat.

References

Ackerman, M. S., and Palen, L. (1996). The Zephyr help instance: Promoting ongoing activity in a CSCW system. In *Proceedings of the ACM Conference on Human Factors in Computing Systems CHI '96* (268–275). New York: ACM Press.

Allison, G. T. (1971). *Essence of decision: Explaining the Cuban missile crisis.* Boston: Little, Brown.

Bell, D. G., Bobrow, D. G., Raiman, O., and Shirley, M. H. (1997). Dynamic documents and situated processes: Building on local knowledge in field service. In T. Wakayama, S. Kannapan, C. M. Khoong, S. Navathe, and J. Yates (eds.), *Information and process integration in enterprises: Rethinking documents* (261–276). Norwell, MA: Kluwer Academic Publishers.

Berinato, S. (1999, April 1). Linux shows 25% annual growth rate. *ZdNet: eWeek.* Available at: www.zdnet.com/zdnn/stories/news/0,4586,1014254,00.html.

Brown, J. S., and Duguid, P. (1991). Organizational learning and communities-of-practice: Toward a unified view of working, learning, and innovation. *Organization Science, 2,* 40–57.

Committee on Advanced Engineering Environments, National Research Council. (1999). *Advanced engineering environments: Achieving the vision, phase 1.* Washington DC: National Academy Press.

Constant, D., Kiesler, S., and Sproull, L. (1996). The kindness of strangers: On the usefulness of weak ties for technical advice. *Organization Science, 7,* 119–135.

Cox, A. (1996, February 21). Maintainers and source submission procedures. Linux kernel source code (v.1.3.68). Available at: ftp://tsx-11.mit.edu/pub/linux.

Cox, A. (1998, October 13). Cathedrals, bazaars and the town council. *Slashdot.* Available at: slashdot.org/features/98/10/13/1423253.shtml.

Dempsey, B. J., Weiss, D., Jones, P., and Greenberg, J. (1999, October 6). *A quantitative profile of a community of open source Linux developers.* Available at: metalab. unc.edu/osrt/develpro.html.

DuBois, G. (2000, July 20). Open-source StarOffice earns early praise. *Zdnet: cWeek.* Available at: www.zdnet.com/eweek/stories/general/0,11011,2605874,00.html.

Fielding, R. T. (1999). Shared leadership in the Apache project. *Communications of the ACM, 42,* 42–43.

Free Software Foundation (1991). *GNU General Public License.* Available at: www.gnu.org/copyleft/gpl.html.

Gaffin, A., and Heitkotter, J. (1994, September). Usenet History. *EFF's extended guide to the Internet: A round trip through global networks, life in cyberspace, and everything...* Available at: www.eff.org/papers/eegtti/eeg_toc.html#SEC88.

King, J. L., Grinter, R. E., and Pickering, J. M. (1997). The rise and fall of Nerville: The saga of a cyberspace construction boomtown in the great divide. In S. Kiesler (ed.), *Culture of the Internet* (3–34). Hillside, NJ: Erlbaum.

Kollock, P. (1998). Social dilemmas: The anatomy of cooperation. *Annual Review of Sociology, 24,* 183–214.

Kollock, P. (1999). The economies of online cooperation: Gifts and public goods in cyberspace. In M. A. Smith and P. Kollock (eds.), *Communities in cyberspace* (220–239). London: Routledge.

Kuwabara, K. (2000). Linux: A bazaar at the end of chaos. *First Monday, 5* (3). Available at: www.firstmonday.dk/issues/issue5_3/kuwabara/index.html.

Lerner, J., and Tirole, J. (2000, February 25). *The simple economics of open source.* Available at: www.people.hbs.edu/jlerner/simple.pdf.

Levy, S. (1984). *Hackers: Heroes of the computer revolution.* Garden City, NY: Anchor Press/Doubleday.

March, J. G. (1991). Exploration and exploitation in organizational learning. *Organization Science, 2,* 71–87.

March, J. G., and Simon, H. A. (1958). *Organizations.* New York: Wiley.

Markus, M. L., Manville, B., and Agres, C. E. (2000). What makes a virtual organization work? *Sloan Management Review, 42,* 13–26.

Merges, R. P. (1997). The end of friction? Property rights and contract in the "Newtonian" world of on-line commerce. *Berkeley Technology Law Journal, 12*(1). Available at: www.law.berkeley.edu/journals/btlj/articles/12_1/Merges/html/reader.html.

Moglen, E. (1999). Anarchism triumphant: Free software and the death of copyright. *First-Monday, 4* (8). Available at: www.firstmonday.dk/issues/issue4_8/moglen/.

Moody, G. (1997, August). The greatest OS that (n)ever was. *Wired.* Available at: www.wired.com/wired/5.08/linux_pr.html.

Netscape Press Relations (1998, January 22). *Netscape announces plans to make next-generation communicator source code available free on the net.* Available at: www.netscape.com/newsref/pr/newsrelease558.html.

O'Reilly, T. (1999). Lessons from open-source software development. *Communications of the ACM, 42*(4), 32–37.

Orlikowski, W. (1992). Learning from Notes: Organizational issues in groupware implementation. In *Proceedings of the 1992 Computer Supported Cooperative Work,* ACM Digital Library. Available at: www.acm.org/pubs/citations/proceedings/cscw/143457/p362-orlikowski/.

Ousterhout, J. (1999). Free software needs profit. *Communications of the ACM, 42*(4), 44–45.

Powell, D. E. (2000, June 26). Comment: Judgment day for the GPL? *LinuxPlanet.* Available at: www.linuxplanet.com/linuxplanet/reports/2000/1/.

Raymond, E. S. (1999). *The cathedral and the bazaar: Musings on Linux and open source by an accidental revolutionary.* Sebastopol, CA: O'Reilly & Associates.

Salus, P. H. (1994). *A quarter century of UNIX.* Reading, MA: Addison-Wesley.

Shankland, S. (1998, December 16). Linux shipments up 212 percent. *CNET News.com*. Available at: news.cnet.com/category/0–1003–200–336510.html.

Shankland, S. (1999, August 11). Red Hat shares triple in IPO. *CNET News.com*. Available at: www.canada.cnet.com/news/0–1003–200–345929.html.

Sproull, L., and Patterson, J. (2000). *Computer support for local community*. New York: New York University, Center for Information Intensive Organizations.

Stallman, R. (1998). *The GNU project*. Available at: www.gnu.org/gnu/thegnuproject.html.

Stallman, R. (1999). The GNU operating system and the free software movement. In C. DiBona, S. Ockman, and M. Stone (eds.), *Open sources: Voices from the open source revolution* (53–70). Sebastopol, CA: O'Reilly & Associates.

Tanenbaum, A. (1991, February 4). Re: Most requested features in MINIX. *comp.os.minix*. Available at: listserv.nodak.edu/archives/minix-l.html.

Tanenbaum, A. (1992, February 3). Unhappy campers. *comp.os.minix*. Available at: listserv.nodak.edu/archives/minix-l.html.

The Jargon Dictionary. (2000). Available at: info.astrian.net/jargon.

Thiel, W. (1991, November 21). Keyboard.S with German keyboard. *Linux-activists*. Available at: ftp://tsx-11.mit.edu/pub/linus.

Torvalds, L. (1991, August 25). What would you like to see most in minix. *comp.os.minix*. Available at: listserv.nodak.edu/archives/minix-1.html.

Torvalds, L. (1991, October 31). Re: [comp.os.minix] Free minix-like kernel sources for 386-AT. *comp.os.minix*. Available at: listserv.nodak.edu/archives/minix-1.html.

Torvalds, L. (1991, December 3). Last call for diffs for 0.11. *Linux-activists*. Available at: ftp://tsx-11.mit.edu/pub.linux.

Torvalds, L. (1992, January 9). Linux information sheet (non monthly posting). *comp.os.minix*. Available at: listserv.nodak.edu/archives/minix-1.html.

Torvalds, L. (1992, March 8). Linux 0.95. *Linux-activists*. Available at: ftp://tsx-11.mit.edu/pub.linux.

Torvalds, L. (1992, May 5). Re: Writing an OS – questions!!. *Linux-activists*. Available at: www.li.org/linuxhistory.php.

Torvalds, L. (1993, December 21). Re: Credits file. *Linux-activists*. Available at: ftp://tsx-11.mit.edu/pub.linux.

Torvalds, L. (1994, March 14). Linux 1.0 – A better UNIX than Windows NT. comp.os.linux.announce. Available at: www.cs.helsinki.fi/u/mjrauhal/linux/cola.html.

Torvalds, L. (1994, March 15). New order. *Linux-activists*. Available at: ftp://tsx-11.mit.edu/pub.linux.

Torvalds, L. (1994, May). Linux code freeze. *Linux journal*. Available at: www2.linuxjournal.com/lj-issues/issue1/2733.html.

Torvalds, L. (1995, June 29). Re: Shared interrupts – PCI. *Linux-kernel*. Available at: www.uwsg.iu.edu/hypermail/linux/kernel/9506/0194.html.

Torvalds, L. (1996, February 19). Re: torvalds@cs.helsinki.fi==/dev/null??? *Linux-kernel*. Available at: www.uwsg.iu.edu/hypermail/linux/kernel/9602/0529.html.

Torvalds, L. (1996, April 16). Re: Unices are created equal, but . . . *Linux-kernel*. Available at: www.uwsg.iu.edu/hypermail/linux/kernel/9604.1/0771.html.

Torvalds, L. (1999a). The Linux edge. *Communications of the ACM, 42*(4), 38–39.

Torvalds, L. (1999b). The Linux edge. In C. DiBona, S. Ockman, and M. Stone (eds.), *Open sources: Voices from the open source revolution* (101–111). Sebastopol, CA: O'Reilly & Associates.

Vallopillil, V. (1998, August 11). *Open source software: A (new?) development methodology*. Available at: www.opensource.org/halloween/halloween1.html.

Virtual Worlds Group. (2000, August 24). *Virtual Worlds Web Site FAQ*. Available at: www.vworlds.org/faq.asp.

Wall, L. (1999). The origin of the camel lot in the breakdown of the bilingual Unix. *Communications of the ACM*, 40–41.

Yamagata, H. (1997, September 30). *The pragmatist of free software: Linus Torvalds interview*. Available at: www.tlug.gr.jp/linus.html.

Part V

Online communities

Introduction to Part V

In Part V we consider the concept of a community, and how this might (or might not) apply in an online context. The Internet is a rich source of online groups, where people share ideas, thoughts and knowledge. These groups can be spread over different geographical areas: local, national or global. People join online groups to take part in discussions, to help each other or simply to socialise. These groups are often described as online communities, but there is much debate about the concept of an online (or 'virtual') community. Some people question whether it is possible to have a true community whose members have never met. Others feel that communities are defined by common understanding and purpose, and need not be restricted to a particular geographic area.

The global nature of the Internet has led to suggestions that it could create online communities focused on human needs and interests. Attempts have been made to create these alternative communities via computers and networks, typically using text-based communication tools such as discussion forums. The development of these online environments has often been based on 'utopian' ideas of an ideal community, where human values take priority over commercial interests.

The most well-known proponent of online communities is Howard Rheingold. The community on which Rheingold originally focused was a discussion environment called The WELL. The first reading in Part V is an extract from Rheingold's book 'The Virtual Community' (Rheingold, 2000). Rheingold identified several aspects that he felt were characteristic of a virtual community, such as emotional support and shared interests. He also argued that an online community can feel like a real place where you meet people and socialise with them.

There are a number of theories that can help our understanding of online communities. Some of these are explored in the second reading, which is a chapter from the book 'Online Communities' (Preece, 2000). The reading discusses the concepts of social presence, media richness and common ground. Social presence relates to whether people feel each other to be 'really there' when communicating online (whether synchronously or asynchronously). Media richness (which was also discussed in Part III) focuses on the capabilities of the communication medium (for example, can it convey tone of voice or facial expression?). Common ground expresses the idea that effective communication must be based on shared knowledge and understanding.

The idea of a community has been extended, primarily by Etienne Wenger and Jean Lave, to form the concept of a 'community of practice' (Lave & Wenger, 1991; Wenger, 1998). This is a community with a shared purpose and shared practices and activities, where people develop their skills and knowledge together. In their field study research, Lave and Wenger observed that informal learning was a key part of the practices of people who regularly worked together. The third and final reading in Part V (Ramage, 2010) discusses the concept of a community of practice. It then goes on to introduce the idea of a virtual community of practice – where the community is supported by communication technologies.

Part V explores the concept of community, and the extent to which this can apply in an online setting. Some commentators are very positive about online communities, while others claim that face-to-face contact is essential for developing a sense of community. The readings in Part V contribute to this ongoing debate.

References

Lave and Wenger, E. (1991) *Situated Learning: Legitimate Peripheral Participation*, Cambridge: Cambridge University Press.

Preece, J. (2000) *Online Communities: Designing Usability, Supporting Sociability*, Chichester: John Wiley, pp. 147–167.

Ramage, M. (2010) 'Communities of practice – real and virtual' in Donelan, H., Kear, K. and Ramage, M. (eds.) *Online Communication and Collaboration: A Reader*, London: Routledge, pp. 176–178.

Rheingold, H. (2000) *The Virtual Community*, Cambridge, MA: MIT Press (originally published in 1993), pp. 1–12.

Wenger, E. (1998), *Communities of Practice: Learning, Meaning and Identity*, Cambridge: Cambridge University Press.

Reading 12

The heart of the WELL

Howard Rheingold

In the summer of 1986, my then-two-year-old daughter picked up a tick. There was this blood-bloated *thing* sucking on our baby's scalp, and we weren't quite sure how to go about getting it off. My wife, Judy, called the pediatrician. It was eleven o'clock in the evening. I logged onto the WELL. I got my answer online within minutes from a fellow with the improbable but genuine name of Flash Gordon, M.D. I had removed the tick by the time Judy got the callback from the pediatrician's office.

What amazed me wasn't just the speed with which we obtained precisely the information we needed to know, right when we needed to know it. It was also the immense inner sense of security that comes with discovering that real people – most of them parents, some of them nurses, doctors, and midwives – are available, around the clock, if you need them. There is a magic protective circle around the atmosphere of this particular conference. We're talking about our sons and daughters in this forum, not about our computers or our opinions about philosophy, and many of us feel that this tacit understanding sanctifies the virtual space.

The atmosphere of the Parenting conference – the attitudes people exhibit to each other in the tone of what they say in public – is part of what continues to attract me. People who never have much to contribute in political debate, technical argument, or intellectual gamesmanship turn out to have a lot to say about raising children. People you knew as fierce, even nasty, intellectual opponents in other contexts give you emotional support on a deeper level, parent to parent, within the boundaries of Parenting, a small but warmly human corner of cyberspace.

Here is a short list of examples from the hundreds of separate topics available for discussion in the Parenting conference. Each of these entries is the name of a conversation that includes scores or hundreds of individual contributions spread over a period of days or years, like a long, topical cocktail party you can rewind back to the beginning to find out who said what before you got there.

From Rheingold, H. (2000) *The Virtual Community*, Cambridge, MA: MIT Press (originally published in 1993), pp. 1–12. By permission of The MIT Press.

Great Expectations: You're Pregnant: Now What? Part III
What's Bad About Children's TV?
Movies: The Good, the Bad, and the Ugly
Initiations and Rites of Passage
Brand New Well Baby!!
How Does Being a Parent Change Your Life?
Tall Teenage Tales (cont.)
Guilt
MOTHERS
Vasectomy – Did It Hurt?
Introductions! Who Are We?
Fathers (Continued)
Books for Kids, Section Two
Gay and Lesbian Teenagers
Children and Spirituality
Great Parks for Kids
Quality Toys
Parenting in an Often-Violent World
Children's Radio Programming
New WELL Baby
Home Schooling
Newly Separated/Divorced Fathers
Another Well Baby – Carson Arrives in Seattle!
Single Parenting
Uncle Philcat's Back Fence: Gossip Here!
Embarrassing Moments
Kids and Death
All the Poop on Diapers
Pediatric Problems – Little Sicknesses and Sick Little Ones
Talking with Kids About the Prospect of War
Dealing with Incest and Abuse
Other People's Children
When They're Crying
Pets for Kids

People who talk about a shared interest, albeit a deep one such as being a parent, don't often disclose enough about themselves as whole individuals online to inspire real trust in others. In the case of the sub-community of the Parenting conference, a few dozen of us, scattered across the country, few of whom rarely if ever saw the others face-to-face, had a few years of minor crises to knit us together and prepare us for serious business when it came our way. Another several dozen read the conference regularly but contribute only when they have something important to add. Hundreds more every week read the conference without comment, except when something extraordinary happens.

Jay Allison and his family live in Massachusetts. He and his wife are public-radio producers. I've never met any of them face-to-face, although I feel I know something powerful and intimate about the Allisons and have strong emotional ties to them. What follows are some of Jay's postings on the WELL:

Woods Hole. Midnight. I am sitting in the dark of my daughter's room. Her monitor lights blink at me. The lights used to blink too brightly so I covered them with bits of bandage adhesive and now they flash faintly underneath, a persistent red and green, Lillie's heart and lungs.

Above the monitor is her portable suction unit. In the glow of the flashlight I'm writing by, it looks like the plastic guts of a science-class human model, the tubes coiled around the power supply, the reservoir, the pump.

Tina is upstairs trying to get some sleep. A baby monitor links our bedroom to Lillie's. It links our sleep to Lillie's too, and because our souls are linked to hers, we do not sleep well.

I am naked. My stomach is full of beer. The flashlight rests on it, and the beam rises and falls with my breath. My daughter breathes through a white plastic tube inserted into a hole in her throat. She's fourteen months old.

Sitting in front of our computers with our hearts racing and tears in our eyes, in Tokyo and Sacramento and Austin, we read about Lillie's croup, her tracheostomy, the days and nights at Massachusetts General Hospital, and now the vigil over Lillie's breathing and the watchful attention to the mechanical apparatus that kept her alive. It went on for days. Weeks. Lillie recovered, and relieved our anxieties about her vocal capabilities after all that time with a hole in her throat by saying the most extraordinary things, duly reported online by Jay.

Later, writing in *Whole Earth Review*, Jay described the experience:

Before this time, my computer screen had never been a place to go for solace. Far from it. But there it was. Those nights sitting up late with my daughter, I'd go to my computer, dial up the WELL, and ramble. I wrote about what was happening that night or that year. I didn't know anyone I was "talking" to. I had never laid eyes on them. At 3:00 a.m. my "real" friends were asleep, so I turned to this foreign, invisible community for support. The WELL was always awake.

Any difficulty is harder to bear in isolation. There is nothing to measure against, to lean against. Typing out my journal entries into the computer and over the phone lines, I found fellowship and comfort in this unlikely medium.

Over the years, despite the distances, those of us who made heart-to-heart contact via the Parenting conference began to meet face-to-face. The WELL's annual summer picnic in the San Francisco Bay area grew out of a face-to-face gathering that was originally organized in the Parenting conference. We had been involved in intense online conversations in this conference all year. When summer rolled around we started talking about doing something relaxing together, like bringing our kids somewhere for a barbecue. In typical WELL fashion, it quickly amplified to a WELLwide party hosted by the Parenting conference. Phil Catalfo reserved a picnic site and the use of a softball field in a public park.

Parents talk about their kids online – what else? – and therefore we all already knew about my daughter Mamie and Philcat's son Gabe and Busy's son, the banjo player, but we had not seen many of them before. I remember that when I arrived at the park, Mamie and I recognized one particular group, out of the first half-dozen large parties of picnickers we saw in the distance. There was just something about the way they were all standing, talking with each other in knots of two or three, while the kids ran around the eucalyptus grove and found their way to the softball diamond. I remember playing on the same team with a fellow who never ceases to annoy me when he wrenches every conversation online around to a debate about libertarianism; I remember thinking, after we had darn near accomplished a double play together, that he wasn't such a bad guy.

It was a normal American community picnic – people who value each other's company, getting together with their kids for softball and barbecue on a sum-mer Sunday. It could have been any church group or PTA. In this case, it was the indisputably real-life part of a virtual community. The first Parenting con-ference picnic was such a success that it became an annual event, taking place around the summer solstice. And kids became a fixture at all the other WELL parties.

Another ritual for parents and kids and friends of parents and kids started in the winter, not long after the picnic tradition began. For the past four or five years, in December, most of the conference participants within a hundred miles, and their little ones, show up in San Francisco for the annual Pickle Family Circus benefit and potluck. One of the directors of this small circus is a beloved and funny member of the WELL community; he arranges a special block of seats each year. After the circus is over and the rest of the audience has left, we treat the performers, the stagehands, and ourselves to a potluck feast.

Albert Mitchell is an uncommonly fierce and stubborn fellow – many would say pugnacious – who argues his deeply felt principles in no uncertain terms. He can be abrasive, even frightening, in his intensity. He gets particularly riled up by certain topics – organized religion, taxation, and circumcision – but there are other ways to cross him and earn some public or private vituperation. I discov-ered that I could never again really be too frightened by Albert's fierce online persona – the widely known and sometimes feared "sofia" – after seeing him and his sweet daughter, Sofia, in her clown suit, at a Pickle potluck. He gave me a jar of honey from his own hive at that event, even though we had been shouting at each other online in ways that probably would have degenerated into fisticuffs face-to-face. At the Pickle Family Circus or the summer picnic, we were meet-ing in the sacred space of Parenting, not the bloody arenas of WELL policy or politics.

The Parenting conference had been crisis-tested along with the Allisons, and had undergone months of the little ups and downs with the kids that make up the normal daily history of any parent, when one of our most regular, most dear, most loquacious participants, Phil Catalfo, dropped a bombshell on us.

Topic 349: Leukemia
By: Phil Catalfo (philcat) on Wed, Jan 16, '91
404 responses so far
<linked topic>
I'd like to use this topic for discussing leukemia, the disease, both as it affects my family and what is known about it generally.

We learned early last week that our son Gabriel, 7 (our middle child), has acute lymphocytic leukemia, aka ALL. I will be opening one or more additional topics to discuss the chronology of events, emotions and experiences stirred up by this newly central fact of our lives, and so on. (I'm also thinking of opening a topic expressly for everyone to send him get-well wishes.) I intend for this topic to focus on the disease itself – his diagnosis and progress, but also other cases we know about, resources (of all types) available, etc. etc.

If Tina has no objection, I'd like to ask the hosts of the Health conf. to link any/all of these topics to their conf. I can't think offhand of where else might be appropriate, but I'm sure you'll all suggest away.

The first thing I want to say, regardless of how it does or doesn't pertain to this particular topic, is that the support and love my family and I, and especially Gabe, have been receiving from the WELL, have been invaluable. This turns out to have a medical impact, which we'll discuss in good time, but I want to say out loud how much it's appreciated: infinitely.

With that, I'll enter this, and return as soon as I can to say more about Gabe's case and what I've learned in the past week about this disease and what to do about it.

404 responses total.

1: Nancy A. Pietrafesa (lapeche) Wed, Jan 16, '91 (17:21)

Philcat, we're here and we're listening. We share your hope and a small part of your pain. Hang on.

2: Tina Loney (onezie) Wed, Jan 16, '91 (19:09)

Phil, I took the liberty of writing to flash (host of the Health conf) and telling him to link whichever of the three topics he feels appropriate. I very much look forward to you telling us all that you can/are able about Gabe. In the meanwhile, I'm thinking about Gabriel and your entire family. Seems I remember Gabe has quite a good Catalfic sense of humor, and I hope you're able to aid him in keeping that in top form.... Virtual hugs are *streaming* in his direction....

The Parenting regulars, who had spent hours in this conference trading quips and commiserating over the little ups and downs of life with children, chimed in with messages of support. One of them was a nurse. Individuals who had never contributed to the Parenting conference before entered the conversation, including a couple of doctors who helped Phil and the rest of us understand the daily reports about blood counts and other diagnostics and two other people who had firsthand knowledge, as patients suffering from blood disorders themselves.

Over the weeks, we all became experts on blood disorders. We also understood how the blood donation system works, what Danny Thomas and his St. Jude Hospital had to do with Phil and Gabe, and how parents learn to be advocates for their children in the medical system without alienating the caregivers. Best of all, we learned that Gabe's illness went into remission after about a week of chemotherapy.

With Gabe's remission, the community that had gathered around the leukemia topic redirected its attention to another part of the groupmind. Lhary, one of the people from outside the Parenting conference who had joined the discussion of leukemia because of the special knowledge he had to contribute, moved from the San Francisco area to Houston in order to have a months-long bone-marrow transplant procedure in an attempt to abate his own leukemia. He continued to log onto the WELL from his hospital room. The Catalfos and others got together and personally tie-dyed regulation lab coats and hospital gowns for Lhary to wear around the hospital corridors.

Many people are alarmed by the very idea of a virtual community, fearing that it is another step in the wrong direction, substituting more technological ersatz for yet another natural resource or human freedom. These critics often voice their sadness at what people have been reduced to doing in a civilization that worships technology, decrying the circumstances that lead some people into such pathetically disconnected lives that they prefer to find their companions on the other side of a computer screen. There is a seed of truth in this fear, for virtual communities require more than words on a screen at some point if they intend to be other than ersatz.

Some people – many people – don't do well in spontaneous spoken interaction, but turn out to have valuable contributions to make in a conversation in which they have time to think about what to say. These people, who might constitute a significant proportion of the population, can find written communication more authentic than the face-to-face kind. Who is to say that this preference for one mode of communication – informal written text – is somehow less authentically human than audible speech? Those who critique CMC because some people use it obsessively hit an important target, but miss a great deal more when they don't take into consideration people who use the medium for genuine human interaction. Those who find virtual communities cold places point at the limits of the technology, its most dangerous pitfalls, and we need to pay attention to those boundaries. But these critiques don't tell us how Philcat and Lhary and the Allisons and my own family could have found the community of support and information we found in the WELL when we needed it. And those of us who do find communion in cyberspace might do well to pay attention to the way the medium we love can be abused.

Although dramatic incidents are what bring people together and stick in their memories, most of what goes on in the Parenting conference and most virtual communities is informal conversation and downright chitchat. The model of the WELL and other social clusters in cyberspace as "places" is one that naturally emerges whenever people who use this medium discuss the nature of the medium. In 1987, Stewart Brand quoted me in his book *The Media Lab* about what tempted me to log onto the WELL as often as I did: "There's always another mind there. It's like having the corner bar, complete with old buddies and delightful new-comers and new tools waiting to take home and fresh graffiti and letters, except instead of putting on my coat, shutting down the computer, and walking down to the corner, I just invoke my telecom program and there they are. It's a place."

The existence of computer-linked communities was predicted twenty-five years ago by J. C. R. Licklider and Robert Taylor, research directors for the Department of Defense's Advanced Research Projects Agency (ARPA), who set in motion the research that resulted in the creation of the first such community, the ARPANET: "What will on-line interactive communities be like?" Licklider and Taylor wrote in 1968: "In most fields they will consist of geographically separated members, sometimes grouped in small clusters and sometimes working individually. They will be communities not of common location, but of common interest. . . ."

My friends and I sometimes believe we are part of the future that Licklider dreamed about, and we often can attest to the truth of his prediction that "life will be happier for the on-line individual because the people with whom one interacts most strongly will be selected more by commonality of interests and goals than by accidents of proximity." I still believe that, but I also know that life online has been unhappy at times, intensely so in some circumstances, because of words I've read on a screen. Participating in a virtual community has not solved all of life's problems for me, but it has served as an aid, a comfort, and an inspiration at times; at other times, it has been like an endless, ugly, long-simmering family brawl.

I've changed my mind about a lot of aspects of the WELL over the years, but the sense of place is still as strong as ever. As Ray Oldenburg proposed in *The Great Good Place*, there are three essential places in people's lives: the place we live, the place we work, and the place we gather for conviviality. Although the casual conversation that takes place in cafes, beauty shops, pubs, and town squares is universally considered to be trivial, idle talk, Oldenburg makes the case that such places are where communities can come into being and continue to hold together. These are the unacknowledged agorae of modern life. When the auto-mobilecentric, suburban, fast-food, shopping-mall way of life eliminated many of these "third places" from traditional towns and cities around the world, the social fabric of existing communities started shredding.

Oldenburg explicitly put a name and conceptual framework on that phe-nomenon that every virtual communitarian knows instinctively, the power of informal public life:

> Third places exist on neutral ground and serve to level their guests to a con-dition of social equality. Within these places, conversation is the primary activity and the major vehicle for the display and appreciation of human

personality and individuality. Third places are taken for granted and most have a low profile. Since the formal institutions of society make stronger claims on the individual, third places are normally open in the off hours, as well as at other times. The character of a third place is determined most of all by its regular clientele and is marked by a playful mood, which contrasts with people's more serious involvement in other spheres. Though a radically different kind of setting for a home, the third place is remarkably similar to a good home in the psychological comfort and support that it extends.

Such are the characteristics of third places that appear to be universal and essential to a vital informal public life. . . .

The problem of place in America manifests itself in a sorely deficient informal public life. The structure of shared experience beyond that offered by family, job, and passive consumerism is small and dwindling. The essential group experience is being replaced by the exaggerated self-consciousness of individuals. American life-styles, for all the material acquisition and the seeking after comforts and pleasures, are plagued by boredom, loneliness, alienation, and a high price tag. . . .

Unlike many frontiers, that of the informal public life does not remain benign as it awaits development. It does not become easier to tame as technology evolves, as governmental bureaus and agencies multiply, or as population grows. It does not yield to the mere passage of time and a policy of letting the chips fall where they may as development proceeds in other areas of urban life. To the contrary, neglect of the informal public life can make a jungle of what had been a garden while, at the same time, diminishing the ability of people to cultivate it.

It might not be the same kind of place that Oldenburg had in mind, but so many of his descriptions of third places could also describe the WELL. Perhaps cyberspace is one of the informal public places where people can rebuild the aspects of community that were lost when the malt shop became a mall. Or perhaps cyberspace is precisely the *wrong* place to look for the rebirth of community, offering not a tool for conviviality but a life-denying simulacrum of real passion and true commitment to one another. In either case, we need to find out soon.

The feeling of logging into the WELL for just a minute or two, dozens of times a day, is very similar to the feeling of peeking into the café, the pub, the common room, to see who's there, and whether you want to stay around for a chat. As social psychologist Sara Kiesler put it in an article about networks for *Harvard Business Review*: "One of the surprising properties of computing is that it is a social activity. Where I work, the most frequently run computer network program is the one called 'Where' or 'Finger' that finds other people who are logged onto the computer network."

Because we cannot see one another in cyberspace, gender, age, national origin, and physical appearance are not apparent unless a person wants to make such characteristics public. People whose physical handicaps make it difficult to form new friendships find that virtual communities treat them as they always wanted to be treated – as thinkers and transmitters of ideas and feeling beings, not carnal vessels with a certain appearance and way of walking and talking (or not walking and not talking).

One of the few things that enthusiastic members of virtual communities in Japan, England, France, and the United States all agree on is that expanding their circle of friends is one of the most important advantages of computer conferencing. CMC is a way to *meet* people, whether or not you feel the need to affiliate with them on a community level. It's a way of both making contact with and maintaining a distance from others. The way you meet people in cyberspace puts a different spin on affiliation: in traditional kinds of communities, we are accustomed to meeting people, then getting to know them; in virtual communities, you can get to know people and then choose to meet them. Affiliation also can be far more ephemeral in cyberspace because you can get to know people you might never meet on the physical plane.

How does anybody find friends? In the traditional community, we search through our pool of neighbors and professional colleagues, of acquaintances and acquaintances of acquaintances, in order to find people who share our values and interests. We then exchange information about one another, disclose and discuss our mutual interests, and sometimes we become friends. In a virtual community we can go directly to the place where our favorite subjects are being discussed, then get acquainted with people who share our passions or who use words in a way we find attractive. In this sense, the topic is the address: you can't simply pick up a phone and ask to be connected with someone who wants to talk about Islamic art or California wine, or someone with a three-year-old daughter or a forty-year-old Hudson; you can, however, join a computer conference on any of those topics, then open a public or private correspondence with the previously unknown people you find there. Your chances of making friends are magnified by orders of magnitude over the old methods of finding a peer group.

You can be fooled about people in cyberspace, behind the cloak of words. But that can be said about telephones or face-to-face communication as well; computer-mediated communications provide new ways to fool people, and the most obvious identity swindles will die out only when enough people learn to use the medium critically. In some ways, the medium will, by its nature, be forever biased toward certain kinds of obfuscation. It will also be a place that people often end up revealing themselves far more intimately than they would be inclined to do without the intermediation of screens and pseudonyms.

The sense of communion I've experienced on the WELL is exemplified by the Parenting conference but far from limited to it. We began to realize in other conferences, facing other human issues, that we had the power not only to use words to share feelings and exchange helpful information, but to accomplish things in the real world.

[...]

References

Allison, Jay. "Vigil." *Whole Earth Review* 75 (Summer 1992): 4.

Brand, Stewart. *The Media Lab: Inventing the Future at MIT*. New York: Penguin, 1987.

Kiesler, Sara. "The Hidden Messages in Computer Networks." *Harvard Business Review* (January–February 1986).

Licklider, J. C. R. "Man-Computer Symbiosis." *IRE Transactions on Human Factors in Electronics* HFE-1 (March 1960): 4–11.

Licklider, J. C. R., Robert Taylor, and E. Herbert. "The Computer as a Communication Device." *International Science and Technology* (April 1968).

Oldenburg, Ray. *The Great Good Place: Cafés, Coffee Shops, Community Centers, Beauty Parlors, General Stores, Bars, Hangouts, and How They Get You through the Day*. New York: Paragon House, 1991.

Oldenburg, Ray. *The Great Good Place: Cafés, Coffee Shops, Bookstores, Bars, Hair Salons, and Other Hangouts at the Heart of the Community*, 3rd ed. New York: Marlowe & Company, 1999.

Reading 13

Research speaks to practice
Interpersonal communication

Jenny Preece

Everybody gets so much information all day long that they lose their common sense.

– Gertrude Stein (quoted in Sumrall, 1992, p. 13)

Abstract Communities are composed of individuals who can be observed individually, in small groups or in toto. The aim of this chapter is to examine communication within and among pairs and small groups of community participants. Common-ground theory is used as a framework for this discussion, to help to inform online community development by explaining why certain types of social interactions tend to be associated with particular media characteristics. [...]

Theory helps explain, predict, and guide our understanding of physical and social events. The theories that are relevant to online communities could fill several pages. They come from sociology, anthropology, psychology, human–computer interaction (HCI), communications studies, computer-mediated communication (CMC), computer-supported cooperative work (CSCW), and computer science. Because the topic of online communities is relatively new, researchers have to reach out to established fields for theories to help explain the behavior they observe.

We begin this chapter with a brief review of early work in computer-mediated communication, specifically by discussing social presence and media richness, two closely related theories that describe participants' sense of "being – or not being – there" when communicating via computers. Social presence theory provides the background for examining common-ground theory, which helps to explain how pairs and small groups negotiate shared understanding – that is, common ground. Understanding how common ground develops helps to explain why some media support communication better than other media and why certain types of social interaction may occur.

From Preece, J. (2000) *Online Communities: Designing Usability, Supporting Sociability*, London: John Wiley, pp. 147–167.

Early work in computer-supported cooperative work

Early research in computer-supported cooperative work (CSCW) examined the effect of different media on groups working remotely on collaborative tasks. Much of this early research was done in controled laboratory environments (Olson & Olson, 1997), and used face-to-face communication as a benchmark for comparison.

Although email, listservers, Internet Relay Chat (IRC), and bulletin boards were common [...] the spotlight was on video conferencing during the 1980s and early 1990s. However, because of the high demand for bandwidth, video conferencing was expensive. Not only were special computers, cameras, and audio facilities needed, most networks at that time provided insufficient bandwidth for video conferencing to be widely used, except in large companies.

The advantage of broadband video conferencing is that it more closely resembles face-to-face communication, in which voice tone, gestures, body language, and contextual information (where speakers are located) are communicated. Decision making and socially oriented communication are greatly enriched by this array of nonverbal information. Narrow bandwidth (i.e., textual systems), in contrast, is limited, and cannot transmit much nonverbal information. However, for communicating basic factual information, such as a list of names, addresses, and phone numbers, low-bandwidth systems are adequate (Sellen, 1994). Prejudices against low-bandwidth textual communication also tended to over-emphasize reports of negative experiences (Parks & Floyd, 1996). Therefore, knowing which tasks required high bandwidth and which could be done using low bandwidth became important. (See Olson & Olson, 1997, for an excellent review of research in CSCW.)

Researchers working on computer-mediated communication in business reported that consensus building using textual systems is less effective than in face-to-face meetings (e.g., Kiesler, Sproull, & McGuire, 1984; Sproull & Kiesler, 1991). Similar reports came from education (e.g., Hiltz, 1985). This led to an early assumption that textual CMC systems support communication poorly, particularly socioemotional communication. Two closely related theories that help to explain these observations are *social presence theory* (Short, Williams, & Christie, 1976) and *media richness theory* (Daft & Lengel, 1986).

Social presence

Social presence theory (Short et al., 1976) addresses how successfully media convey a sense of the participants being physically present, using face-to-face communication as the standard for the assessment. Social presence depends not only on the words people speak but also on verbal and nonverbal cues, body language, and context (Rice, 1987, 1993). Reduced social cues (i.e., gestures, body language, facial expression, appearance and so on) are caused by low bandwidth, which affects communication (Walther, 1993).

Media richness theory is similar to social presence but takes a media perspective (Daft & Lengel, 1986). It describes the media's capacity for immediate feedback – how well it conveys cues, and how many and in which ways the senses are involved (Daft & Lengel, 1986). As an aside, it is interesting to note that social presence theory originated ten years earlier than media richness theory. Why? Because researchers in one field are not always cognizant of related work in other fields. It seems that Daft's contribution, and Lengel's, though extremely useful because it takes a different perspective, was made without knowledge of Short, Williams, & Christie's work (Short et al., 1976; Rice, 1999).

Reduced cues

Social presence fundamentally affects how participants sense emotion, intimacy, and immediacy (Rice, 1993). Early studies reported fewer personal messages with lower socioemotional content (e.g., Hiltz, Johnson, & Turoff, 1986) that lacked cues about social context (Sproull & Keisler, 1986). The "cues-filtered-out hypothesis" was used to explain these observations (Culnan & Markus, 1987). Bandwidth was insufficient to carry all the communication signals needed for communicating social, emotional, and contextual content. In text-only systems, for example, both task information and social information are carried in the same single verbal/linguistic channel, which, though adequate for most task information, cannot transmit nonverbal information such as body language, voice tone, and so on (Walther, 1994, p. 476).

The consequences of filtering out social, emotional, and contextual information vary depending on their importance to the communication task. There are three main ways that this affects communication. First, signals needed to understand conversation may be missing; for example, when face to face, speakers can check frequently with each other to ensure they understand the conversation as it progresses. This is the aforementioned important concept known as common ground, which will be discussed in detail in the next section. Nonverbal signals such as a nod of the head, a quizzical look, or a wave of the hand can say a lot. Second, conversations proceed by speakers taking turns; various signals such as pauses in speech or a gaze are used to cue the next speaker to take his or her turn. Third, seeing and hearing the speaker enables the listener to infer information regarding the context of the conversation and the speaker's feelings. Olson and Olson succinctly argue that differences in "local physical contexts, time zones, culture, and language all persist in spite of the use of distance technologies," and that these differences take a toll on communication. Furthermore speakers do not get evidence of each other's emotional states. They cannot see if the person is having a bad day or is tired, so they do not know whether or how to temper their comments. Consequently, "distance matters" (Olson & Olson, 2000).

In addition, reduced social cues can encourage unusual behavior that would not occur if people could see each other. Some people feel comfortable behaving aggressively online because they are hidden behind a veil of anonymity. The way participants form impressions of each other and how much personal information they are prepared to disclose are also influenced. In addition, with fewer social cues to monitor, some people find it easier, even fun, to assume different persona[e] or even switch gender. These effects are interrelated in complex ways, therefore separating them is not straightforward.

Misunderstandings

Both speakers and listeners develop mental models of each other (Norman, 1986), as well as of the information content of their discussion, but speakers in low-bandwidth environments have to work extra hard to compensate for missing non-verbal information. Not surprisingly, in these environments misunderstandings and frustration occur widely. Furthermore, relationship development is inhibited, which is sometimes indicated by angry comments; in extreme cases, people launch unwarranted attacks, known as flaming, on others they may not know and have never met (Hiltz et al., 1986; Spears & Lea, 1992; Sproull & Keisler, 1986).

People using low-bandwidth systems also tend to send fewer messages during the same time period, over high-bandwidth systems, and this, too, inhibits relationships developing (Hiltz et al., 1986; Walther, 1993). Nevertheless, given sufficient time, people in closed textual discussion groups do form strong relationships (Walther, 1993). In fact, there is evidence that some people develop extremely rich social relationships this way (Spears & Lea, 1992). It just takes longer to send a comparable number of messages, and correspondingly longer for relationships to develop, than in high-bandwidth environments.

Because of the high potential for misunderstandings to occur online, some developers believe that the best way to prevent the problem is to develop systems that enable participants to represent themselves with icons, photographs, or 3D avatars, to increase social presence. An alternative, low-tech, solution is to educate participants about their online writing style [...] For example, *linguistic softeners*, such as phrasing a comment tentatively, to avoid being thought aggressive, are used by experienced participants to avoid conflict online (Wallace, 1999). When stating an opinion, they commonly preface it with the acronym IMHO, for "in my humble opinion." Emoticons can also be used as softeners; a smiley, for example, may be included to assure the reader that a comment is well meant. [...]

Impression development and self-disclosure

Filtering out social cues impedes normal impression development. The cartoon of a dog sitting at a keyboard with the caption "Nobody knows you're a dog on the Internet," captures the essence of this well. First impressions are developed in face-to-face conversations primarily from nonverbal signs. Physical appearance – how people dress, their physical attractiveness, their race, age and gender – have an enormous impact on the impressions others develop. Furthermore, although those impressions tend to develop very quickly, they can be remarkably powerful and resilient to change, even when evidence suggests they are incorrect (Wallace, 1999). Age and gender in particular are strong *social markers*.

Psychologically, the more people discover that they are similar to each other, thus, the more they tend to like each other, thus, the more they will disclose about themselves. *Self-disclosure* reciprocity is powerful online – if you tell me something about yourself, I'll tell you something about me (Wallace, 1999). Anonymity often encourages people to disclose more about themselves; they even become *hyper-personal* (Lea, O'Shea, Fung, & Spears, 1992; Spears, Russell, & Lee, 1990; Walther, 1996) as in a support group for those suffering from knee injuries (Preece, 1998). Verbal probes are used to find out about another person and it is particularly easy to do this via text. Consequently, it appears that, rather than eliminate social information or blinding participants to it, the limited bandwidth of CMC may retard normal impression development and relational communication (Walther, Anderson, & Park, 1994). CMC seems to affect the time it takes for relationships to develop though this is also influenced by experience (Walther, 1993; Ogan, 1993). Experienced users, for example, are adept at finding ways to deal with the absence of visual cues (Rice & Barnett, 1986).

Online personas and gender

Revealing one's gender online can have startling consequences. For example, it is well known that in some online environments, responses to men are different from those to women (Bruckman, 1993; Herring, 1992; Turkle, 1995, 1999). One of the first questions a newcomer is asked is what his or her gender is. A person identified as female may receive from men excessive, unwanted, attention and be bombarded by questions and sometimes propositions or harassment. Consequently, women frequently disguise their gender so that they can maintain their freedom in the electronic world.

For less practical purposes, some people like to explore changing their persona to see how people treat them in their new guise. Both men and women are known to switch genders, a practice known as *gender bending*, in order to explore what life is like as the other sex. There are also other reasons for assuming a new persona online. The classic book, *Life on* [the] *Screen*, by Sherry Turkle tells how people take on new identities to explore their own personalities, particularly aspects of themselves that they find troubling in the real world (Turkle, 1995). Online, there is little risk for the ultra shy person who decides to be outspoken or become a passionate romantic. If the situation starts to feel threatening, poof! the person can log off and vanish, never to be heard from again. There are, however, risks associated with gender bending. People can and do get hurt, for example, when heterosexuals discover that their online relationship is in fact homosexual or vice versa. Gender bending online, however, is not as easy as it sounds. People reveal themselves without realizing it. For example, women tend to hedge their comments, to be more self-deprecating, and apologetic, and to include more adjectives in their speech (Tannen, 1990, 1994). Hence, linguistic style can betray a person's gender. Research on textual communication suggests that emotions are typically transmitted – both semantically and syntactically (Herring, 1992; Reid, 1993). For example, Susan Herring gives an example of how women avoid criticism in email discussions by phrasing their questions in defensive forms, such as "This may be a naïve question, but . . ." (Herring, 1992).

Likewise, online romances of any sort may fail when real-life meetings result in dashed fantasies. For example, online, no one is overweight, but in reality a person's extra 25 pounds can make a difference. And dishonesty works only as long as the relationship remains online only. A ten-year-old photograph will be revealed as misleading in a face-to-face meeting.

What this research says to online community developers is that they need to look for ways of educating participants about how they are perceived by others online. Moderation may help but it is time-consuming and expensive. [. . .] Lack of social presence also impacts how well people understand each other in conversation.

Common ground

Common-ground theory can be used as a framework for determining how two people or a small group validate that they understand each other. It focuses on how communication process and content are coordinated. Much of this coordination depends upon social presence or appropriate ways of compensating for its absence. In the words of Herb Clark and Susan Brennan, developers of the theory:

> It takes two people working together to play a duet, shake hands, play chess, waltz, teach, or make love. To succeed, the two of them have to coordinate both the content and the process of what they are doing . . . They cannot even begin to coordinate on content without assuming a vast amount of shared information or common ground – that is, mutual knowledge, mutual beliefs, and mutual assumptions. . . . [T]o coordinate on process, they need to update their common ground moment by moment. All collective actions are built on common ground and its accumulation (Clark & Brennan, 1993, p. 222).

If person A speaks to person B about "my dogs," the two of them must understand that person A is referring to the two dogs sleeping in front of the fire in his or her home, and not dogs that live down the street. Common ground is established by a process called *grounding*. Grounding varies from situation to situation. It takes one form in face-to-face conversation, another in computer-mediated communication, still another when calling, for example, directory assistance, chatting with a friend, or engaging in intellectual debate. Grounding is, therefore, influenced both by the *communication medium* and the *communication task*.

Grounding leads participants to a mutual belief that they share a common understanding. Several rounds of verifying that the person has heard and understood a comment may be needed. While this may sound cumbersome, most conversations require a series of twists and turns that move the conversation forward only when the speaker is convinced that he or she has been heard and understood. Usually, conversations have identifiable entry points, "bodies," and exits. Noticing how much attention a partner is paying to his or her comments enables the speaker to judge whether there is shared understanding. Utterances, gazes, nodding, and facial expression are all indicators of attention. Checking, repeating, or rephrasing incomplete or misinterpreted comments encourage common ground.

Generally people try to establish common ground unconsciously, with as little effort as possible. This is where media have an influence. The amount and type of effort changes with the communication medium. Techniques that work in one medium may not in another; and even if available, they may require more effort to achieve grounding. Furthermore, people who are not used to a particular medium will be unfamiliar with good ways of solving problems. For example, a nod may work in a face-to-face conversation, not over the phone, where instead a grunt or other spoken word is needed. Similarly, a word, exclamation mark or some other textual expression is needed in a bulletin board discussion. Establishing common ground has been an issue in video conferencing design, where low bandwidth, poor resolution, and small screens have obscured facial expressions, voice tone and body language, thereby hampering development of common ground and delaying turn-taking.

Different media also offer different opportunities, as the following list of characteristics indicates (Clark & Brennan, 1993, p. 229).

- *Co-presence: A and B share the same physical environment, as in face-to-face conversation.* Compensating for lack of co-presence is an important aim for online community developers. Years of learning the nuances and pleasantries of face-to-face conversational protocol train individuals to expect, if not assume, the same rules apply to other media. Human beings assume face-to-face communication as their standard. Many online community developers strive to find ways of creating a sense of co-presence. Avatars can help to provide partial solutions. (Co-presence can be similar to social presence. (Short, Williams, & Christie, 1976). However, co-presence refers to people having temporal and geographical proximity, which is not always necessary for a social presence.)
- *Visibility: A and B are visible to each other, as in face-to-face communication and video conferencing.* Being able to see one another enables participants to "read" each other's body language, which is important for communicating

emotion. Developers provide emoticons and other techniques to compensate for lack of visibility in textual systems.

- *Audibility: A and B communicate by speaking, which can be very effective for conveying factual information.* Voice tone provides clues about emotional state.
- *Cotemporality: B receives at roughly the same time as A presents, so the message is received immediately.*
- *Simultaneity: A and B can send and receive at once and simultaneously.* The communication comprises rapid, short exchanges as in busy chats, MUDs, and MOOs.
- *Sequentiality: A's and B's turns cannot get out of sequence as in asynchronous communication.* In asynchronous communication, periods of several seconds, minutes, hours, or days may pass between a message being sent and a response being generated.
- *Reviewability: B can review A's message.* For example, text messages can be reviewed, whereas spoken messages are lost when the speaker stops talking.
- *Revisability: A can revise messages for B.* If messages persist, they can be revised – providing they can be accessed.

If one of these opportunities is not present, the communication is constrained by its absence, and ways of overcoming or dealing with it have to be found. Overcoming constraints generally takes time and effort (Clark & Brennan, 1993, pp. 230–231). Interestingly, some circumstances that at first might seem to be disadvantageous turn out to be the opposite. For example, the delay between receiving a message via asynchronous textual conferencing and sending a reply can provide valuable time for reflection. In a study of recovering alcoholics, for example, participants of a listserver community said they liked having time to reflect and compose, which they could not get in face-to-face sessions (King, 1994).

Common ground and different media

Table 13.1 summarizes the communication opportunities offered by different types of media/systems, and comments on their advantages and disadvantages.

Examining each of the media in terms of common ground helps to identify features that support or inhibit grounding, and to make explicit comparisons between the various media and face-to-face communication. Keep in mind, originally the theory was developed to explain grounding face-to-face, and has been drawn on in CMC and CSCW research (Isaacs, Morris, Rodrigues, & Tang, 1995). Interestingly, however, face-to-face communication lacks some opportunities offered by other media. For example, it is difficult to review a face-to-face conversation, and there may be little time to reflect, whereas a text-based interchange is a much better medium for reviewing and reflecting. Of course, no one medium is perfectly suited to all tasks, so none can be considered the "best";

Table 13.1 Media and common ground*

Medium	Opportunities	Comments
Face-to-face	Co-presence, visibility, audibility, cotemporality, simultaneity, sequentiality	*It may be difficult to delay response to reflect. In addition, people may communicate certain feelings unintentionally via body language. An awkward glance, for example, may reveal lack of agreement despite the words being spoken.*
Telephone	Audibility, cotemporality, simultaneity, sequentiality	*No opportunity to "read" body language thereby limiting socioemotional communication. Voice tone helps. Good for conveying factual information.*
Video teleconference	Visibility, audibility, cotemporality, simultaneity, sequentiality (*in some systems*)	*Response capability of technology can adversely influence synchrony and impede turn-taking. Reception of messages may be slow; delays may cause misunderstandings. Small viewing window makes seeing cues and body language difficult. Helpful as introduction among participants, but video often abandoned thereafter unless discussion is about an object that must be seen, such as an architect's model. High bandwidth required to prevent a frustrating experience.*
Terminal teleconference (*textual*)	Cotemporality, sequentiality, reviewability	*Production takes more time, but there is some macro control over timing. Having time to reflect can be very useful, because understanding message content is often heightened. Emotional understanding, however, may suffer from poor social presence; developers need to seek ways to remedy this problem.*
Answering machines	Audibility, reviewability	*Receiving only. Social presence limited.*
Electronic mail	Reviewability, revisability	*Production takes more time, though some macro control gives time to reflect. Turn-taking is often delayed, but understanding of verbal messages is often better; however, emotional understanding can suffer from poor social presence. Alternatives are needed to make up for absence of body language transmission for supporting socioemotional and contextual communication.*

Table 13.1 Continued

Medium	Opportunities	Comments
Letters	Reviewability, revisability	*Very slow turn-taking. Generally the effect is adverse, though understanding may be improved by reflection time.*
Bulletin board messages	Reviewability, revisability, sequentiality	*Production takes time, though macro control offers time to reflect. Understanding verbal messages is better. Threading helps delineate among speakers. Socioemotional communication is often supported by use of icons.*
Chats	Cotemporality, simultaneity	*Often very fast moving, which prohibits long messages. Turn-taking is often chaotic, as there is no time for delay or fault correction. This format can be difficult for poor or slow typists.*
MOOs – text only	Cotemporality, simultaneity	*Learning curve prohibits casual participation. Response time depends on number of participants. Ways of displaying emotion are well developed in some systems.*
MOOs & MUDs – graphical, with avatars	Cotemporality, simultaneity	*As above; but sense of social presence is aided by avatar and graphical world of community action.*
Computer virtual environments	Cotemporality, simultaneity	*Requires high bandwidth. Strong sense of co-presence provided with intention of improving communication.*

*Adapted from Clark & Brennan, 1993, p. 230. Material added by author appears in italics.

different attributes are better for various communication tasks in specific contexts (Rice, 1987a). Consequently, if online community developers focus on the communication task(s) rather than on the media, they are more likely to select media wisely.

Despite the limitations of the various media listed in Table 13.1, many fulfill the tasks for which they are commonly used surprisingly well. For example, chats are very restricted. Participants cannot see each other, and often, at best, they can send only short remarks – if they can type fast enough. There is little time for reflection, no time for fault correction, and speaker turn-taking (i.e., change-over) is chaotic here. Despite these limitations, people who use chats regularly love them, particularly students and other young people. Many switch between chats, instant messaging and the phone with ease.

Online community developers play a key role in identifying the best media for their users' communication tasks. But whatever they are given, as users get to know a medium's limitations, they often develop ingenious ways of getting around them [...] so that it works well for them. For example, chat users speed things up with short acronyms, [...] which are fast to type and easy to remember. Experienced chatters become adept at following the threads from different channels, as though they were in a room listening to several conversations going on at once – they participate in one and eavesdrop on others. Chatters also seem willing to accept lag times of two to three seconds; but at eight or nine seconds, frustration starts to mount (Wallace, 1999).

Only a few attempts have been made to apply common ground theory to mass interaction (Whittaker, Terveen, Hill, & Cherny, 1998); nevertheless, it is useful for identifying constraints in one-to-one and small group communication via different media.

Common ground and empathy

Empathy is defined as "knowing what another person is feeling, feeling what another person is feeling, and responding compassionately to another person" (Levenson & Ruef, 1992). Although empathy has value to all forms of communication, its importance is most pronounced among people who share very similar experiences (Eisenberg & Strayer, 1987; Etchegoyen, 1991; Ickes, 1993, 1997). The more similar people are, the less they have to "go outside themselves" to gather cues; hence the more readily they can respond naturally to their circumstances (Hodges & Wegner, 1997, p. 324). A recent comment from an online support community aptly sums this up: "We're all in this together, which helps!" Empathy can be a powerful force online, especially in support communities (Preece, 1998, 1999a).

Many researchers have observed empathy online. As early as 1993, Howard Rheingold reported how the WELL community in San Francisco supported the parent of a dying child (Rheingold, 1993). Other researchers have commented on how fellow workers (Sproull & Kiesler, 1991) and learners (Hiltz, 1994) understand each other's problems and support each other. Still others analyzed messages from listserver communities for people with chronic and acute illnesses and found that empathy was important in both (Schoch & White, 1997).

There is, however, no research on the relationship between common ground and empathy, though it seems likely that when socioemotional content is involved, establishing common ground is aided by empathy, or vice versa. Empathy, like common ground, depends heavily on nonverbal communication, such as gaze and body language (Eisenberg & Strayer, 1987; Etchegoyen, 1991; Lanzetta & Englis, 1989), so it is likely to be influenced by the properties of different media in a similar way to common-ground development. Empathy is such a fundamental component of human communication (Ickes, 1997) that online community developers need to be aware of its impact, particularly when designing for communities in which trust is important. [...]

Summary

Forms of communication – chatting, discussing, debating, asking and answering questions, consoling, advising, empathizing – are the magic ingredients of a community. Indeed, it is the ability to interact and communicate that draws millions of people into online communities every day. In contrast, Web pages can be fascinating on the first read, maybe even on the second, but unless their content changes readers get bored.

Social presence, or more particularly lack of social presence, can critically influence how people behave online, form impressions of others, and negotiate common ground. Empathy is important in communities in which emotional topics are discussed. Over 80 percent of empathy is conveyed nonverbally (Goleman, 1995). Like common ground, empathy is also affected by how the various media convey social presence. Thus a leading question that online community developers must answer is how to facilitate common ground and empathy online. Emoticons, dictionaries of acronyms, and advice on how to phrase comments are some solutions [...] Developers familiar with these theories and who work to compensate for shortcomings in media will be the most successful at creating good sociability.

[...]

Further reading

"Grounding in Communication" (Clark & Brennan, 1993)
   This seminal paper, which provided a basis for this chapter, explains the theory of common ground, and discusses how it applies to different kinds of computer-mediated communication. It contains a detailed discussion of the constraints and costs of using the different media. It is essential reading for anyone interested in this subject.

Empathic Accuracy (Ickes, 1997)
   This collection contains papers by most of the key researchers in this field. It describes the nature of empathy, and addresses many key questions, such as whether empathy is gender-related. But note, all of the studies covered are concerned with face-to-face communication, which limits the book's value for those working in online communication.

"Research on Computer-Supported Cooperative Work" (Olson & Olson, 1997)
   This chapter in the book by Martin Helander et al. provides an excellent overview of major research and development contributions in CSCW. Many of the concepts discussed in this chapter, such as social presence, are also addressed in this work.

"Distance Matters" (Olson & Olson, 2000)
   This paper is an interesting follow-up to the work cited in the preceding listing. It reviews much of the work by the two authors and others in the field, and provides a compelling justification for the types of communication and situations that are well suited to online transfer. The overall conclusion is that, for many types of interactions, "distance matters."

"Empathic Communities: Reaching out across the Web" (Preece, 1998), and "Empathic Communities: Balancing Emotional and Factual Communication" (Preece, 1999a)

These papers describe studies of empathy in online communities, which is particularly important in health support communities but is also evident in other communities. Online community developers need to seek better ways of supporting empathy, as well as information exchange.

Connections: New Ways of Working in the Networked Organization (Sproull & Kiesler, 1991)

This seminal work describes computer networking within organizations and how it is changing the way people work. It contains many insights about the benefits and problems of electronic discussion groups.

The Psychology of the Internet (Wallace, 1999)

I encourage everyone to read this book. Lucidly written, it provides an excellent and enjoyable account of why people behave as they do on the Internet.

References

Bruckman, A. (1993). Gender swapping on the Internet. Paper presented at the Internet Society (INET '93) Conference, San Francisco, CA.

Clark, H. H. & Brennan, S. E. (1993). Grounding in communication. In R. M. Baecker (Ed.), *Readings in Groupware and Computer-Supported Cooperative Work*. San Mateo, CA: Morgan Kaufmann Publishers.

Culnan, M. J. & Markus, M. L. (1987). Information technologies. In F. M. Jablin, L. L. Putnam, K. H. Roberts, & L. W. Porter (Eds), *Handbook of Organizational Communication: An Interdisciplinary Perspective*. Newbury Park, CA: Sage.

Daft, R. L. & Lengel, R. H. (1986). Organizational information requirements, media richness and structural design. *Management Science, 32*, 554–571.

Eisenberg, N. & Strayer, J. (1987). Critical issues in the study of empathy. In N. Eisenberg & J. Strayer (Eds), *Empathy and Its Development*. Cambridge, UK: Cambridge University Press.

Etchegoyen, R. H. (1991). *The Fundamentals of Psychoanalytic Technique*. New York: Karnac Books.

Goleman, G. (1995). *Emotional Intelligence*. New York: Bantam Books.

Herring, S. (1992). Gender and participation in computer-mediated linguistic discourse: ERIC Clearinghouse on Languages and Linguistics (October).

Hiltz, S. R. (1985). *Online Communities: A Case Study of the Office of the Future*. Norwood, NJ: Ablex Publishing Corp.

Hiltz, S. R., Johnson, K., & Turoff, M. (1986). Experiments in group decision making: Communication process and outcome in face-to-face versus computerized conferencing. *Human Communication Research, 13*, 225–252.

Hiltz, S. R. (1994). *The Virtual Classroom: Learning without Limits via Computer Networks*. Norwood, NJ: Ablex Publishing Corporation.

Hodges, S. D. & Wegner, D. M. (1997). Automatic and controlled empathy. In W. Ickes (Ed.), *Empathic Accuracy*. New York: The Guilford Press.

Ickes, W. (1993). Empathic accuracy. *Journal of Personality, 61*, 587–610.

Ickes, W. (1997). *Empathic Accuracy*. New York: The Guilford Press.

Isaacs, E., Morris, T., Rodrigues, T. K., & Tang, J. C. (1995). A comparison of face-to-face and distributed presentations. Paper presented at the CHI '95 Conference: Human Factors in Computing Systems, Denver.

Kiesler, S., Sproull, J. & McGuire, T. W. (1984). 'Social psychological aspects of computer-mediated communication', *American Psychologist*, 39(10), 1123–1134.

King, S. (1994). Analysis of electronic support groups for recovering addicts. *Interpersonal Computing and Technology: An Electronic Journal for the 21st Century (IPCT)*, 2(3), 47–56.

Lanzetta, J. T. & Englis, B. G. (1989). Expectations of cooperation and competition and their effects on observers' vicarious emotional responses. *Journal of Personality and Social Psychology, 56*, 543–544.

Lea, M., O'Shea, T., Fung, P., & Spears, R. (1992). "Flaming" in computer-mediated communication: Observations, explanations, and implications. In M. Lea (Ed.), *Contexts of Computer-Mediated Communication*. London: Harvester-Wheatsheaf.

Levenson, R. W. & Ruef, A. M. (1992). Empathy: A physiological substrate. *Journal of Personality and Social Psychology, 63*, 234–246.

Norman, D. A. (1986). Cognitive engineering. In D. Norman & S. Draper (Eds), *User-Centered Systems Design*. Hillsdale, NJ: Lawrence Erlbaum.

Ogan, C. (1993). Listserver communication during the Gulf War: What kind of medium is the electronic bulletin board? *Journal of Broadcasting and Electronic Media*, (Spring), 177–195.

Olson, G. M. & Olson, J. S. (1997). Research on computer-supported cooperative work. In M. Helander, T. K. Landauer, & P. Prabhu (Eds), *Handbook of Human-Computer Interaction (2nd Edition)* Amsterdam: Elsevier.

Olson, G. M. & Olson, J. S. (2000). Distance matters. *Transactions on Computer Human Interaction* (TOCHI). In press.

Parks, M. R. & Floyd, K. (1996). Making friends in cyberspace. *Computer-Mediated Communication, 4. ascusc.org/jcmc/roll/issue4/parks.html*

Preece, J. (1998). Empathic Communities: Reaching out across the Web. *Interactions Magazine, 2*(2), 32–43.

Preece, J. (1999a). Empathic communities: Balancing emotional and factual communication. *Interacting with Computers, 12*, 63–77.

Reid, E. (1993). Electronic Chat: Social issues on Internet Relay Chat. *Media Information Australia, 67*, 62–70.

Rheingold, H. (1993). *The Virtual Community: Homesteading on the Electronic Frontier*. Reading, MA: Addison Wesley.

Rice, R. E. & Barnett, G. (1986). Group communication networks in electronic space: Applying metric multidimensional scaling. In M. McLaughlin (Ed.), *Communication Yearbook 9*. Newbury Park, CA: Sage.

Rice, R. E. (1987). Computer-mediated communication and organizational innovations. *Journal of Communication, 37*, 85–108.

Rice, R. E. (1993). Media appropriateness. Using social presence theory to compare traditional and new organizational media. *Human Communication Research, 19*(4), 451–484.

Rice, R. (1999). Personal communication.

Schoch, N. A. & White, M. D. (1997). A study of the communication patterns of participants in consumer health electronic discussion groups. Paper presented at the Proceedings of the 60th ASIS Annual Meeting, Washington, DC.

Sellen, A. (1994). Remote conversations: The effects of mediating talk with technology. *Human-Computer Interaction, 10*(4), 401–444.

Short, J., Williams, E., & Christie, B. (1976). *The Social Psychology of Telecommunications*. London: John Wiley & Sons.

Spears, M., Russell, L., & Lee, S. (1990). De-individuation and group polarization in computer-mediated communication. *British Journal of Social Psychology, 29*, 121–134.

Spears, R. & Lea, M. (1992). Social influence and the influence of "social" in computer-mediated communication. In M. Lea (Ed.), *Contexts of Computer-Mediated Communication*. Hemel Hempstead, UK: Harvester Wheatsheaf.

Sproull, L. & Kiesler, S. (1986). Reducing social context cues: Electronic mail in organizational communication. *Management Science, 32*, 1492–1512.

Sproull, L. & Kiesler, S. (1991). *Connections: New Ways of Working in the Networked Organization*. Cambridge, MA: MIT Press.

Sumrall, A. C. (1992). *Write to the Heart: Wit & Wisdom of Women Writers*. Freedom, CA: The Crossing Press.

Tannen, D. (1990). *You Just Don't Understand. Men and Women in Conversation*. New York: William Morrow & Co. Ltd.

Tannen, D. (1994). *Talking from 9 to 5*. New York: William Morrow and Company, Inc.

Turkle, S. (1995). *Life on the Screen. Identity in the Age of the Internet*. New York: Simon & Schuster.

Turkle, S. (1999, Winter 1999/2000). Tinysex and gender trouble. *IEEE Technology and Society Magazine, 4*, 8–20.

Wallace, P. (1999). *The Psychology of the Internet*. Cambridge: Cambridge University Press.

Walther, J. B. (1993). Impression development in computer-mediated interaction. *Western Journal of Communications, 57*, 381–398.

Walther, J. B., Anderson, J. F., & Park, D. W. (1994). Interpersonal effects in computer-mediated interaction: A meta-analysis of social and antisocial communication. *Communication Research, 21*, 460–487.

Walther, J. B. (1994). Anticipated ongoing interaction versus channel effects on relational communication in computer-mediated interaction. *Human Communication Research, 20*(4), 473–501.

Walther, J. B. (1996). Computer-mediated communication: Impersonal, interpersonal, and hyperpersonal interaction. *Communications Research, 23*(1), 3–43.

Whittaker, S., Terveen, L., Hill, W., & Cherny, L. (1998). The dynamics of mass interaction. Paper presented at the ACM CSCW '98, Seattle, WA.

Communities of practice – real and virtual

Magnus Ramage

The word 'community' is a familiar one, much used by the media and policy-makers. It describes a group of people united by some common characteristic, typically their geographical location (e.g. 'the Milton Keynes community'), some aspect of their identity (e.g. 'the Black community'), or some common interest (e.g. 'the Open University student community'). But how might we think of communities in people's working lives?

An influential theory by the educational theorist Etienne Wenger talks about "communities of practice" – communities of people united by not just a common interest but a common way of working and of understanding the world. As he and his colleagues define it:

> communities of practice are groups of people who share a concern, a set of problems, or a passion about a topic, and who deepen their knowledge and expertise in this area by interacting on an ongoing basis. (Wenger et al. 2002, p. 4)

This definition suggests that there are three basic elements of a community of practice (CoP): a clearly-identifiable group of people, some area of concern or passion as its focus, and a body of knowledge and ways of acting (Wenger refers to these as the community, the domain, and the practice). The definition implies other features of a CoP: it needs to be acknowledged as some sort of explicit community, with members who know each other somewhat and share ideas together; and the members need to be working together to develop their skills and knowledge in their chosen field – that is, they are engaged in some kind of collective learning activity.

Learning, in Wenger's approach, is "not something we do when we do nothing else or stop doing when we do something else" (Wenger 1998, p. 8) – it happens throughout life. He jointly coined the term 'communities of practice' with his colleague Jean Lave in a book entitled *Situated Learning* (Lave and Wenger, 1991), which argues that a great deal of practical learning occurs in a situated way – in the same situation that the learning is used. Their examples included such groups as midwives, tailors, naval quartermasters, butchers and non-drinking alcoholics, in each case examining the way in which the individual learnt (in a form of apprenticeship) how to become an expert practitioner in the field – in other words, how to become part of a community of practice.

Communities of practice don't need to be explicit organisations, like clubs or departments. Part of what makes them interesting is that they are fluid, coming into being as their members need them, changing their shape quickly and then ending. Wenger is keen to stress that there is nothing esoteric or modern about a CoP. They have existed throughout history and only the name is new. The medieval guilds would clearly fit the definition; so would the scientific societies of the eighteenth and nineteenth centuries. Wenger originally intended the concept as a description of communities which had arisen spontaneously. But in the past ten years or so, the concept has become very fashionable in business circles, and many companies have consciously tried to create communities of practice.

A few modern examples of communities of practice might include (based on Wenger (2006)):

- a group of engineers working together on similar problems;
- a group of accounting students based in different companies but sharing experiences of their studies;
- a support group for parents of young children with learning difficulties;
- a group of recently-appointed managers in a company all learning together how to do their new job.

These are very different kinds of people, but in each case they have a common interest or purpose about which they are learning together, in a very practical way.

So how do communities of practice relate to online communities, as discussed for example by Rheingold (2000) and Preece (2001)? This has been the subject of healthy debate in the literature on communities of practice. The sorts of groups that Wenger and his colleagues (including the anthropologist Jean Lave) studied were typically co-located – they worked in fairly close proximity to one another and their collective learning was largely carried out face-to-face.

However, it is clear from the previous readings that it is possible to have an online community – so is it possible to have an online CoP? Undoubtedly, many communities of practice have an online element to them (sometimes the terms 'distributed' or 'virtual' CoP are used instead, which give a slightly different emphasis but amount to the same thing). In many groups today, some element of their communication takes place online, even if they have a significant face-to-face element. An online/distributed/virtual CoP is something beyond this. Wenger et al. (2002) define a distributed CoP as:

> any community of practice that cannot rely on face-to-face meetings and interactions as its primary vehicle for connecting members (p. 115).

They identify many problems with distributed CoPs, including distance, size, affiliation (juggling membership in multiple communities) and cross-cultural issues. Nonetheless, Wenger and his colleagues present a series of ways to form and maintain distributed CoPs.

There are some clear examples of online communities that could be called communities of practice. Many open-source software tools, such as Linux and Firefox, have been developed almost wholly online by a large group who do not know each other face-to-face, but who share a common purpose and are engaged in collectively learning. The same is true for the online encyclopaedia, Wikipedia, written together by a large group of people, few of whom meet face-to-face. As Bryant *et al.* (2005, p. 2) argue:

> observations of members' behaviour in Wikipedia reveals that the three characteristics of CoPs identified by Wenger are strongly present on the site.

The slight distinction is that each of these communities has, at its heart, a project to create and modify an object, rather than the goal of collective learning. While learning undoubtedly occurs, it is slightly peripheral to the main purpose of the community.

Some researchers find the idea of a virtual CoP highly problematic. Kimble and Hildreth (2004), who discuss the different issues involved, conclude that 'wholly virtual CoPs pose significant problems' (p. 5) and note that 'the most common distributed form of a so called "virtual" CoP has a co-located active core'.

However, it seems clear that, as communities of practice evolve, most are becoming a blend of co-located and virtual communities.

References

Bryant, S., Forte, A. and Bruckman, A. (2005) 'Becoming Wikipedian: Transformation of Participation in a Collaborative Online Encyclopaedia' *GROUP '05: Proceedings of the 2005 international ACM SIGGROUP conference on Supporting group work* (Sanibel Island FL, USA), pp. 1–10.

Kimble, C. and Hildreth, P. (2004) 'Communities of practice: going one step too far?' Proceedings of the 9th Colloque de l'AIM, Evry, France, http://papers.ssrn.com/sol3/papers.cfm?abstract_id=634642 [accessed 27 June 2009].

Lave, J. and Wenger, E. (1991) *Situated Learning: Legitimate Peripheral Participation*, Cambridge: Cambridge University Press.

Preece, J. (2001) 'Online communities: designing usability, supporting sociability', in Donelan, H., Kear, K. and Ramage, M. (eds.) (2010), *Online Communication and Collaboration: A Reader*, Abingdon, Routledge, pp. 161–175.

Rheingold, H. (2000) 'The heart of the WELL', in Donelan, H., Kear, K. and Ramage, M. (eds.) (2010), *Online Communication and Collaboration: A Reader*, Abingdon: Routledge, pp. 151–160.

Wenger, E. (1998) *Communities of Practice: Learning, Meaning, and Identity*. Cambridge, UK: Cambridge University Press.

Wenger, E. (2006) 'Communities of practice: a brief introduction', http://www.ewenger.com/theory/. Accessed 27 October 2009.

Wenger, E., McDermott, R. and Snyder, W. (2002) *Cultivating Communities of Practice: A Guide to Managing Knowledge*, Cambridge, MA: Harvard Business School Press.

Part VI

Virtual worlds

Introduction to Part VI

In Part VI we will be looking at online tools that create a 'virtual world' for their users. These synchronous environments allow large numbers of users to communicate and carry out activities online together. The activities might be games, business transactions or simply social interactions. The common thread is the use of textual descriptions or graphics to create a sense of place, presence and identity for participants. For example, in some multi-player online games players carry out 'quests' together, and in the *Second Life* virtual world users build and 'live in' environments of their own choosing.

The very first 'virtual worlds' were text-based online environments, described as MUDs (Multi-User Dungeons). These originated in 'Dungeons and Dragons' fantasy games. People acting in MUDs had virtual identities in the MUD, as well as their identities in real life. Users of MUDs often became engrossed in the virtual world created by the textual descriptions and communications with other users. The first reading in Part VI (Curtis, 1997) was written by the creator of a MUD called LambdaMOO. The author gives his perspective on how people behaved in a MUD, and how this related to social behaviour in real life. Many of the issues discussed in the reading also arise in current virtual worlds.

The development of computer graphics means that virtual worlds are now highly visual environments. The computer games industry has had a major impact, using powerful hardware and sophisticated software to create environments which capture users' imaginations. Increasingly, these gaming environments are online and multi-user. Because of the very large numbers of users, they are often described as Massively Multiplayer Online Role-Playing Games (MMORPGs). The designers of these games, and of other virtual worlds, aim to make users feel that they are really there with others in the online environment – that they are 'immersed'. This idea is discussed in the second reading in Part VI. This is an extract from the book 'Synthetic Worlds' by the economist Edward Castronova (Castronova, 2005).

The third reading considers further the concept of immersion. This reading is a short extract from the book *Designing Virtual Worlds* (Bartle, 2003) by the online game designer and researcher Richard Bartle. It makes connections between the concept of immersion and the concept of identity. To what extent does our identity online correspond to our identity 'in real life'? How does this correspondence relate to the degree of immersion we experience?

At the time of writing, the most prominent example of a virtual world is *Second Life*, developed by Linden Labs, and launched in 2003. In Second Life, as in other graphical online worlds, users have visual representations of themselves. These are usually called 'avatars' (taken from the Hindu word meaning 'incarnation'). Users 'live' in the virtual world through their avatars. They move around within the world, interact with others, and if they wish, build parts of the world themselves. The fourth and final reading in Part VI is from the book *Coming of Age in Second Life* by the anthropologist Tom Boellstorff (Boellstorff, 2008). Boellstorff has had a presence in Second Life since its early days, and has undertaken anthropological research there. The extract describes the kinds of activities that can be carried out in Second Life. It also gives an idea of what it is like to experience the world of Second Life and to interact with other 'inhabitants'.

The readings in Part VI consider the range of online environments described as virtual worlds. Even the early, text-based virtual worlds (MUDs) gave users a sense of place and identity. More recent environments, such as multi-user online games and Second Life, use powerful graphics to create virtual worlds for users to explore and enhance together. Some users can become so involved (immersed) in these worlds that they feel that they are 'really there'.

References

Bartle, R. (2003) *Designing Virtual Worlds,* Indianapolis, IN: New Riders, pp. 154–157.

Boellstorff, T. (2008) *Coming of Age in Second Life: an Anthropologist Explores the Virtually Human*, Princeton: Princeton University Press pp. 8–15.

Castronova, E. (2005) *Synthetic Worlds: the Business and Culture of Online Games*, Chicago: The University of Chicago Press. pp. 1–7.

Curtis, P. (1997) 'Mudding: social phenomena in text-based virtual realities', in Kiesler, S. (ed.) *Culture of the Internet*, Pittsburgh Carnegie Mellon University, pp. 121–142.

Reading 15

Mudding

Social phenomena in text-based virtual realities

Pavel Curtis

Abstract A MUD (Multiuser Dungeon or, sometimes, Multiuser Dimension) is a network-accessible, multiparticipant, user-extensible virtual reality whose user interface is entirely textual. Participants (usually called players) have the appearance of being situated in an artificially constructed place that also contains those other players who are connected at the same time. Players can communicate easily with each other in real time. This virtual gathering place has many of the social attributes of other places, and many of the usual social mechanisms operate there. Certain attributes of this virtual place, however, tend to have significant effects on social phenomena, leading to new mechanisms and modes of behavior not usually seen "IRL" (in real life). In this chapter, I relate my experiences and observations from having created and maintained a MUD for over a year.

A brief introduction to mudding

> *The Machine did not transmit nuances of expression. It only gave a general idea of people – an idea that was good enough for all practical purposes.*
> *– E. M. Forster (1928/1973)*

A MUD is a software program that accepts connections from multiple users across some kind of network (e.g., telephone lines or the Internet) and provides to each user access to a shared database of "rooms," "exits," and other objects. Each user browses and manipulates this database from "inside" one of those rooms, seeing only those objects that are in the same room and moving from room to room mostly via the exits that connect them. A MUD, therefore, is a kind of virtual reality, an electronically represented place that users can visit.

From Curtis, P. (1997) 'Mudding: social phenomena in text-based virtual realities', in Kiesler, S. (ed) *Culture of the Internet*, Mahwah, NJ: Lawrence Erlbaum Associates Inc., pp. 121–142.

Table 15.1 A typical MUD database interaction

---

look
Corridor
The corridor from the west continues to the east here but the way is blocked by a
purple-velvet rope stretched across the hall. There are doorways leading to the north
and south.
You see a sign hanging from the middle of the rope here.
read sign
This point marks the end of the currently-occupied portion of the house. Guests
proceed beyond this point at their own risk.
– The residents
go east
You step disdainfully over the velvet rope and enter the dusty darkness of the unused
portion of the house.

MUDs are not, however, like the kinds of virtual realities that one usually hears about, with fancy graphics and special hardware to sense the position and orientation of the user's real-world body. A MUD user's interface to the database is entirely text based; all commands are typed in by the users and all feedback is printed as unformatted text on their terminal. The typical MUD user interface is most reminiscent of old computer games like "Adventure" and "Zork" (Raymond, 1991); a typical interaction is shown in Table 15.1. Three major factors distinguish a MUD from an "Adventure"-style computer game, though:

1   A MUD is not goal oriented; it has no beginning or end, no score, and no notion of winning or success. In short, even though users of MUDs are commonly called players, a MUD isn't really a game at all.

2   A MUD is extensible from within; a user can add new objects to the database such as rooms, exits, "things," and notes. Certain MUDs, including the one I run, even support an embedded programming language in which a user can describe whole new kinds of behavior for the objects they create.

3   A MUD generally has more than one user connected at a time. All of the connected users are browsing and manipulating the same database and can encounter the new objects created by others. The multiple users on a MUD can communicate with each other in real time.

This last factor has a profound effect on the ways in which users interact with the system, transforming the interaction from a solitary activity into a social activity.

Most interplayer communication on MUDs follows rules that fit within the framework of the virtual reality. If players "say" something (using the say command), then every other player in the same room will "hear" them. For example, suppose that a player named Munchkin typed the command say Can anyone hear me?

Then Munchkin would see the feedback

    You say, "Can anyone hear me?"

and every other player in the same room would see

    Munchkin says, "Can anyone hear me?"

Similarly, the emote command allows players to express various forms of nonverbal communication. If Munchkin types

    emote smiles.

then every player in the same room sees

    Munchkin smiles.

Most interplayer communication relies entirely on these two commands.[1]

There are two circumstances in which the realistic limitations of say and emote have proved sufficiently annoying that new mechanisms were developed. It sometimes happens that one player wishes to speak to another player in the same room, but without anyone else in the room being aware of the communication. If Munchkin uses the whisper command

    whisper "I wish he'd just go away . . ." to Frebble

then only Frebble will see

    Munchkin whispers, "I wish he'd just go away . . ."

The other players in the room see nothing of this at all.

Finally, if one player wishes to say something to another who is connected to the MUD but currently in a different and perhaps "remote" room, the page command is appropriate. It is invoked with a syntax very like that of the whisper command and the recipient sees output like this:

    You sense that Munchkin is looking for you in The Hall.
    He pages, "Come see this clock, it's tres cool!"

Aside from conversation, MUD players can most directly express themselves in three ways: by their choice of player name, by their choice of gender, and by their self-description.

When players first connect to a MUD, they choose a name by which the other players will know them. This choice, like almost all others in MUDs, is not cast in stone; players can rename themselves at any time, though not to a name currently in use by other players. Typically, MUD names are single words, in contrast to the longer full names used in real life.

Initially, MUD players appear to be neuter; automatically generated messages that refer to such a player use the family of pronouns including *it, its,* and so on. Players can choose to appear as a different gender, though, and not only male or female. On many MUDs, players can also choose to be plural (appearing to be a kind of "colony" creature: "ChupChups leave the room, closing the door behind them"), or to use one of several sets of gender-neutral pronouns (e.g., *s/he, him/her* and *his/her,* or *e, em* and *eir*).

Every object in a MUD optionally has a textual description that players can view with the look command. For example, the description of a room is automatically shown to players when they enter that room and can be seen again just by typing "look." To see another player's description, one might type "look Bert." Players can set or change their descriptions at any time. The lengths of player descriptions typically vary from short one-liners to 12-line paragraphs.

Aside from direct communication and responses to player commands, messages are printed to players when other players enter or leave the same room, when others connect or disconnect and are already in the same room, and when objects in the virtual reality have asynchronous behavior (e.g., a cuckoo clock chiming the hours).

MUD players typically spend their connected time socializing with each other, exploring the various rooms and other objects in the database, and adding new such objects of their own design. They vary widely in the amount of time they spend connected on each visit, ranging from only a minute to several hours; some players stay connected (and almost always idle) for days at a time, only occasionally actively participating.

This very brief description of the technical aspects of mudding suffices for the purposes of this chapter. It has been my experience, however, that it is difficult to properly convey the sense of the experience in words. Readers desiring more detailed information are advised to try mudding themselves, as described in the final section of this chapter.

Social phenomena observed on one mud

Man is the measure.

E. M. Forster (1928/1973)

In October of 1990, I began running an Internet-accessible MUD server on my personal workstation here at PARC. Since then, it has been running continuously, with interruptions of only a few hours at most. In January of 1991, the existence of

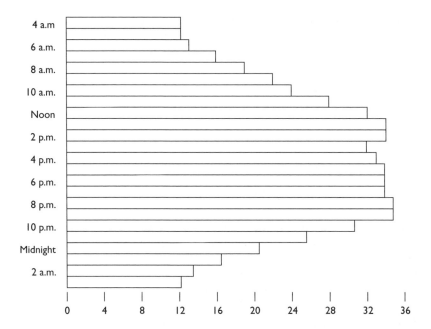

Figure 15.1 Average number of connected players on the LambdaMOO, by time of day

the MUD (called LambdaMOO[2]) was announced publicly, via the Usenet news-group rec.games.mud. As of this writing, well over 3,500 different players have connected to the server from over a dozen countries around the world and, at any given time, over 750 players have connected at least once in the last week. Recent statistics concerning the number of players connected at a given time of day (Pacific Standard Time) appear in Figure 15.1.

LambdaMOO is clearly a reasonably active place, with new and old players coming and going frequently throughout the day. This popularity has provided me with a position from which to observe the social patterns of a fairly large and diverse MUD clientele. I have no formal training in sociology, anthropology, or psychology, however, so I cannot make any claims about methodology. What I relate below are merely my personal observations made over a year of mudding. In most cases, my discussions of the motivations and feelings of individual players are based on in-MUD conversations with them; I have no means of checking the veracity of their statements concerning their real-life genders, identities, or (obvi-ously) feelings. On the other hand, in most cases I have no reason to doubt them.

I have grouped my observations into three categories: phenomena related to the behavior and motivations of individual players, phenomena related to interac-tions between small groups of players (especially observations concerning MUD conversation), and phenomena related to the behavior of a MUD's community as a whole. Cutting across all of these categories is a recurring theme to which

I would like to draw the reader's attention. Social behavior on MUDs is in some ways a direct mirror of behavior in real life, with mechanisms being drawn nearly unchanged from real life, and in some ways very new and different, taking root in the new opportunities that MUDs provide over real life.

Observations about individuals

The mudding population

The people who have an opportunity to connect to LambdaMOO are not a representative sample of the world population; they all read and write English with at least passable proficiency and they have access to the Internet. Based on the names of their network hosts, I believe that well over 90% of them are affiliated with colleges and universities, mostly as students and, to a lesser extent, mostly undergraduates. It appears to me that no more than half (and probably fewer) of them are employed in the computing field; the increasing general availability of computing resources on college campuses and in industry appears to be having an effect, allowing a broader community to participate.

In any case, it appears that the educational background of the mudding community is generally above average and it is likely that the economic background is similarly above the norm. Based on my conversations with people and on the names of those who have asked to join a mailing list about programming in LambdaMOO, I would guess that over 70% of the players are male.

Player presentation

As described in the introduction to mudding, players have a number of choices about how to present themselves in the MUD; the first such decision is the name they will use. Table 15.2 shows some of the names used by players on

Table 15.2 A selection of player names from LambdaMOO

Toon	Gemba	Gary_Severn	Ford	Frand
li'ir	Maya	Rincewind	yduJ	funky
Grump	Foodslave	Arthur	EbbTide	Anathae
yrx	Satan	byte	Booga	tek
chupchups	waffle	Miranda	Gus	Merlin
Moonlight	MrNatural	Winger	Drazz'zt	Kendal
RedJack	Snooze	Shin	lostboy	foobar
Ted_Logan	Xephyr	King_Claudius	Bruce	Puff
Dirque	Coyote	Vastin	Player	Cool
Amy	Thorgeir	Cyberhuman	Gandalf	blip
Jayhirazan	Firefoot	JoeFeedback	ZZZzzz...	Lyssa
Avatar	zipo	Blackwinter	viz	Kilik
Maelstorm	Love	Terryann	Chrystal	arkanoiv

LambdaMOO. One can pick out a few common styles, for names (e.g., names from or inspired by myth, fantasy, or other literature, common names from real life, names of concepts, animals, and everyday objects that have representative connotations, etc.), but it is clear that no such category includes a majority of the names. Note that a significant minority of the names are in lower case; this appears to be a stylistic choice (players with such names describe the practice as "cool") and not, as might be supposed, an indication of a depressed ego.

Players can be possessive about their names, resenting others who choose names that are similarly spelled or pronounced or even that are taken from the same mythology or work of literature. In one case, for example, a player named "ZigZag" complained to me about other players taking the names "ZigZag!" and "Zig."

The choice of a player's gender is, for some, one of great consequence and forethought; for others (mostly males), it is simple and without any questions. For all that this choice involves the fewest options for the players (unlike their names or descriptions, which are limited only by their imagination), it is also the choice that can generate the greatest concern and interest on the part of other players.

The great majority of players who are male generally choose to present themselves as such. Some males, however, taking advantage of the relative rarity of females in MUDs, present themselves as female and thus stand out to some degree. Some use this distinction just for the fun of deceiving others, some of them going so far as to try to entice male-presenting players into sexually explicit discussions and interactions. This is such a widely noticed phenomenon, in fact, that one is advised by the common wisdom to assume that any flirtatious female-presenting players are, in real life, males. Such players are often subject to ostracism based on this assumption.

Some MUD players have suggested to me that such transvestite flirts are perhaps acting out their own (latent or otherwise) homosexual urges or fantasies, taking advantage of the perfect safety of the MUD situation to see how it feels to approach other men. Although I have had no personal experience talking to such players, let alone the opportunity to delve into their motivations, the idea strikes me as plausible given the other ways in which MUD anonymity seems to free people from their inhibitions. (I say more about anonymity later on.)

Other males present themselves as female more out of curiosity than as an attempt at deception; to some degree, they are interested in seeing "how the other half lives," what it feels like to be perceived as female in a community. From what I can tell, they can be successful at this.

Female-presenting players report a number of problems. Many of them have told me that they are frequently subject both to harassment and to special treatment. One reported seeing two newcomers arrive at the same time, one male-presenting and one female-presenting. The other players in the room struck up conversations with the putative female and offered to show her around but completely ignored the putative male, who was left to his own devices.

In addition, probably due mostly to the number of female-presenting males one hears about, many female players report that they are frequently (and sometimes aggressively) challenged to "prove" that they are, in fact, female. To the best of my knowledge, male-presenting players are rarely if ever so challenged. Because of these problems, many players who are female in real life choose to present themselves otherwise, choosing either male, neuter, or gender-neutral pronouns. As one might expect, the neuter and gender-neutral presenters are still subject to demands that they divulge their real gender.

Some players apparently find it difficult to interact with those whose true gender has been called into question; because this phenomenon is rarely manifest in real life, they have grown dependent on "knowing where they stand," on knowing what gender roles are "appropriate." Some players (and not only males) also feel that it is dishonest to present oneself as being a different gender than in real life; they report feeling "mad" and "used" when they discover the deception. I encourage the interested reader to look up Van Gelder's (1991) fascinating article for many more examples and insights, as well as the story of a remarkably successful deception via electronic transvestism.

The final part of a player's self-presentation, and the only part involving prose, is the player's description. This is where players can, and often do, establish the details of a persona or role they wish to play in the virtual reality. It is also a significant factor in other players' first impressions, because new players are commonly looked at soon after entering a common room.

Some players use extremely short descriptions, either intending to be cryptic (e.g., "the possessor of the infinity gems") or straightforward (e.g., "an average-sized dark elf with lavender eyes") or, often, just insufficiently motivated to create a more complex description for themselves. Other players go to great efforts in writing their descriptions; one moderately long example appears in Table 15.3.

A large proportion of player descriptions contain a degree of wish fulfillment; I cannot count the number of "mysterious but unmistakably powerful" figures I have seen wandering around in LambdaMOO. Many players, it seems, are taking advantage of the MUD to emulate various attractive characters from fiction.

Table 15.3 A moderately long player description

You see a quiet, unassuming figure, wreathed in an oversized, dull-green Army jacket which is pulled up to nearly conceal his face. His long, unkempt blond hair blows back from his face as he tosses his head to meet your gaze. Small round gold-rimmed glasses, tinted slightly grey, rest on his nose. On a shoulder strap he carries an acoustic guitar and he lugs a backpack stuffed to overflowing with sheet music, sketches, and computer printouts. Under the coat are faded jeans and a T-Shirt reading 'Paranoid CyberPunks International.' He meets your gaze and smiles faintly, but does not speak with you. As you surmise him, you notice a glint of red at the rims of his blue eyes, and realize that his canine teeth seem to protrude slightly. He recoils from your look of horror and recedes back into himself.

Given the detail and content of so many player descriptions, one might expect to find a significant amount of role playing, players who adopt a coherent character with features distinct from their real-life personalities. Such is rarely the case, however. Most players appear to tire of such an effort quickly and simply interact with the others more-or-less straightforwardly, at least to the degree one does in normal discourse. One factor might be that the roles chosen by players are usually taken from a particular creative work and are not particularly viable as characters outside of the context of that work; in short, the roles don't make sense in the context of the MUD.

A notable exception to this rule is one particular MUD I've heard of, called "PernMUSH." This appears to be a rigidly maintained simulacrum of the world described in Ann McCaffrey's celebrated *Dragon* books. All players there have names that fit the style of the books and all places built there are consistent with what is shown in the series and in various fan materials devoted to it. Pern-MUSH apparently holds frequent "hatchings" and other social events, also derived in great detail from McCaffrey's works. This exception probably succeeds only because of its single-mindedness; with every player providing the correct context for every other, it is easier for everyone to stay more-or-less in character.

Player anonymity

It seems to me that the most significant social factor in MUDs is the perfect anonymity provided to the players. There are no commands available to the players to discover the real-life identity of each other and, indeed, technical considerations make such commands either very difficult or impossible to implement. It is this guarantee of privacy that makes players' self-presentation so important and, in a sense, successful. Players can only be known by what they explicitly project and are not locked into any factors beyond their easy control, such as personal appearance, race, and so forth. In the words of an old military recruiting commercial, MUD players can "be all that you can be."[3]

This also contributes to what might be called a shipboard syndrome, the feeling that because one will likely never meet anyone from the MUD in real life, there is less social risk involved and inhibitions can safely be lowered. For example, many players report that they are much more willing to strike up conversations with strangers they encounter in the MUD than in real life. One obvious factor is that MUD visitors are implicitly assumed to be interested in conversing, unlike visitors in most real-world contexts. A deeper reason, though, is that players do not feel that very much is at risk. At worst, if they feel that they've made an utter fool of themselves, they can always abandon the character and create a new one, losing only the name and the effort invested in socially establishing the old one. In effect, a new lease on life is always a ready option.

Players on most MUDs are also emboldened somewhat by the fact that they are immune from violence, both physical and virtual. The permissions systems of all MUDs (excepting those whose whole purpose revolves around adventuring and the slaying of monsters and other players) generally prevent any player from having any kind of permanent effect on any other player. Players can certainly annoy each other, but not in any lasting or even moderately long-lived manner.

This protective anonymity also encourages some players to behave irresponsibly, rudely, or even obnoxiously. We have had instances of severe and repeated sexual harassment, crudity, and deliberate offensiveness. In general, such cruelty seems to be supported by two causes: The offenders believe (usually correctly) that they cannot be held accountable for their actions in the real world, and the very same anonymity makes it easier for them to treat other players impersonally, as other than real people.

Wizards

Usually, societies cope with offensive behavior by various group mechanisms, such as ostracism, and I discuss this kind of effect later. In certain severe cases, however, it is left to the authorities or police of a society to take direct action, and MUDs are no different in this respect. On MUDs, it is a special class of players, usually called wizards or (less frequently) gods, who fulfill both the authority and police roles. A wizard is a player who has special permissions and commands available, usually for the purpose of maintaining the MUD, much like a system administrator or "superuser" in real-life computing systems. Players can only be transformed into wizards by other wizards, with the maintainer of the actual MUD server computer program acting as the first such.

On most MUDs, the wizards' first approach to solving serious behavior problems is, as in the best real-life situations, to attempt a calm dialogue with the offender. When this fails, as it usually does in the worst cases of irresponsibility, the customary response is to punish the offender with "toading." This involves either (a) severely restricting the kinds of actions the player can take or preventing the player from connecting at all, (b) changing the name and description of the player to present an unpleasant appearance (often literally that of a warty toad), and (c) moving the player to some very public place within the virtual reality. This public humiliation is often sufficient to discourage repeat visits by the player, even in a different guise.

On LambdaMOO, the wizards as a group decided on a more low-key approach to the problem; we have, in the handful of cases where such a severe course was dictated, simply "recycled" the offending players, removing them from the database of the MUD entirely. This is a more permanent solution than toading, but also lacks the public spectacle of toading, a practice none of us was comfortable with.

Wizards, in general, have a very different experience of mudding than other players. Because of their palpable and extensive extra powers over other players, and because of their special role in MUD society, they are frequently treated differently by other players. Most players on LambdaMOO, for example, upon first encountering my wizard player, treat me with almost exaggerated deference and respect. I am frequently called "sir" and players often apologize for "wasting" my time. A significant minority, however, appear to go to great lengths to prove that they are not impressed by my office or power, speaking to me bluntly and making demands that I assist them with their problems using the system, sometimes to the point of rudeness.

Because of other demands on my time, I am almost always connected to the MUD but idle, located in a special room I built (my "den") that players require my permission to enter. This room is useful, for example, as a place in which to hold sensitive conversations without fear of interruption. This constant presence and unapproachability, however, has had significant and unanticipated side-effects. I am told by players who get more circulation than I do that I am widely perceived as a kind of mythic figure, a mysterious wizard in his magical tower. Rumor and hearsay have spread word of my supposed opinions on matters of MUD policy. One effect is that players are often afraid to contact me for fear of capricious retaliation at their presumption.

Although I find this situation disturbing and wish that I had more time to spend out walking among the "mortal" members of the LambdaMOO community, I am told that player fears of wizardly caprice are justified on certain other MUDs. It is certainly easy to believe the stories I hear of MUD wizards who demand deference and severely punish those who transgress; there is a certain ego boost to those who wield even simple administrative power in virtual worlds and it would be remarkable indeed if no one had ever started a MUD for that reason alone. In fact, one player sent me a copy of an article, written by a former MUD wizard, based on Machiavelli's *The Prince*; it details a wide variety of more-or-less creative ways for wizards to make ordinary MUD players miserable. If this wizard actually used these techniques, as he claims, then some players' desires to avoid wizards are understandable.

Observations about small groups

MUD conversation

The majority of players spend the majority of their active time on MUDs in conversation with other players. The mechanisms by which those conversations get started generally mirror those that operate in real life, though sometimes in interesting ways.

Chance encounters between players exploring the same parts of the database are common and almost always cause for conversation. As mentioned earlier, the anonymity of MUDs tends to lower social barriers and to encourage players to be more outgoing than in real life. Strangers on MUDs greet each other with the same kinds of questions as in real life: "Are you new here? I don't think we've met." The very first greetings, however, are usually gestural rather than verbal: "Munchkin waves. Lorelei waves back."

Table 15.4 Sample output from LambdaMOO's @who command

Player name	Connected	Idle time	Location
Haakon (#2)	3 days	a second	Lambda's Den
Lynx (#8910)	a minute	2 seconds	Lynx' Abode
Garin (#23393)	an hour	2 seconds	Carnival Grounds
Gilmore (#19194)	an hour	10 seconds	Heart of Darkness
TamLin (#21864)	an hour	21 seconds	Heart of Darkness
Quimby (#23279)	3 minutes	2 minutes	Quimby's room
koosh (#24639)	50 minutes	5 minutes	Corridor
Nosredna (#2487)	7 hours	36 minutes	Nosredna's Hideaway
yduJ (#68)	7 hours	47 minutes	Hackers' Heaven
Zachary (#4670)	an hour	an hour	Zachary's Workshop
Woodlock (#2520)	2 hours	2 hours	Woodlock's Room

Total: 11 players, 6 of whom have been active recently.

The @who (or WHO) command on MUDs allows players to see who else is currently connected and, on some MUDs, where those people are. An example of the output of this command appears in Table 15.4. This is, in a sense, the MUD analog of scanning the room in a real-life gathering to see who's present.

Players consult the @who list to see if their friends are connected and to see which areas, if any, seem to have a concentration of players in them. If more than a couple of players are in the same room, the presumption is that an interesting conversation may be in progress there; players are thus more attracted to more populated areas. I call this phenomenon "social gravity"; it has a real-world analog in the tendency of people to be attracted to conspicuous crowds, such as two or more people at the door of a colleague's office.

It is sometimes the case on a MUD, as in real life, that one wishes to avoid getting into a conversation, either because of the particular other player involved or because of some other activity one does not wish to interrupt. In the real world, one can refrain from answering the phone, screen calls using an answering machine, or even, in copresent situations, pretend not to have heard the other party. In the latter case, with luck, the person will give up rather than speak up more loudly.

The mechanisms are both similar and interestingly different on MUDs. It is often the case that MUD players are connected but idle, perhaps because they have stepped away from their terminal for a while. Thus, it often happens that one receives no response to an utterance in a MUD simply because the other party wasn't really present to see it. This commonly understood fact of MUD life provides for the MUD equivalent of pretending not to hear. I know of players who take care after such a pretense not to type anything more to the MUD until the would-be conversant has left, thus preserving the apparent validity of their excuse.

Another mechanism for avoiding conversation is available to MUD players but, as far as I can see, not to people in real-life situations. Most MUDs provide a mechanism by which each player can designate a set of other players as "gagged"; the effect is that nothing will be printed to the gagging player if someone they've gagged speaks, moves, emotes, and so on. There is generally no mechanism by which the gagged player can tell a priori that someone is gagging him; indeed, unless the gagged player attempts to address the gagging player directly, the responses from the other players in the room (who may not be gagging the speaker) may cause the speaker never even to suspect that some are not hearing him.

We provide a gagging facility on LambdaMOO, but it is rarely used; a recent check revealed only 45 players out of almost 3,000 who are gagging other players. The general feeling appears to be that gagging is rude and is only appropriate (if ever) when someone persists in annoying you in spite of polite requests to the contrary. It is not clear, though, how universal this feeling is. For example, I know of some players who, on being told that some other players were offended by their speech, suggested that gagging was the solution: "If they don't want to hear me, let them gag me; I won't be offended." Also, I am given to understand that gagging is much more commonly employed on some other MUDs.

The course of a MUD conversation is remarkably like and unlike one in the real world. Participants in MUD conversations commonly use the emote command to make gestures, such as nodding to urge someone to continue, waving at player arrivals and departures, raising eyebrows, hugging to apologize or soothe, and so forth. As in electronic mail (though much more frequently), players employ standard "smiley-face" glyphs, e.g., :-), :-(, and :-|, to clarify the tone with which they say things. Utterances are also frequently addressed to specific participants, as opposed to the room as a whole (e.g., Munchkin nods to Frebble. "You tell 'em!").

The most obvious difference between MUD conversations and those in real life is that the utterances must be typed rather than simply spoken. This introduces significant delays into the interaction and, like nature, MUD society abhors a vacuum.

Even when there are only two participants in a MUD conversation, it is very rare for there to be only one thread of discussion; during the pause while one player is typing a response, the other player commonly thinks of something else to say and does so, introducing at least another level to the conversation, if not a completely new topic. These multitopic conversations are a bit disorienting and bewildering to the uninitiated, but it appears that most players quickly become accustomed to them and handle the multiple levels smoothly. Of course, when more than two players are involved, the opportunities for multiple levels are only increased. It has been pointed out that a suitable punishment for truly heinous social offenders might be to strand them in a room with more than a dozen players actively conversing.

This kind of cognitive time sharing also arises due to the existence of the page command, which allows a player to send a message to another room. It is not uncommon (especially for wizards, whose advice is frequently sought by "distant" players) to be involved in one conversation "face-to-face" and one or two more conducted via page. Again, although this can be overwhelming at first, one can actually come to appreciate the relief from the tedious long pauses waiting for a fellow conversant to type.

Another effect of the typing delay (and of the low bandwidth of the MUD medium) is a tendency for players to abbreviate their communications, sometimes past the point of ambiguity. For example, some players often greet others with "hugs" but the meanings of those hugs vary widely from recipient to recipient. In one case the hug might be a simple friendly greeting, in another it might be intended to convey a very special affection. In both cases, the text typed by the hugger is the same (e.g., "Munchkin hugs Frebble."); it is considered too much trouble for the hugger to type a description of the act sufficient to distinguish the kind of hug intended. This leads to some MUD interactions having much more ambiguity than usually encountered in real life, a fact that some mudders consider useful.

The somewhat disjointed nature of MUD conversations, brought on by the typing pauses, tends to rob them of much of the coherence that makes real-life conversants resent interruptions. The addition of a new conversant to a MUD conversation is much less disruptive; the flow being disrupted was never very strong to begin with. Some players go so far as to say that interruptions are simply impossible on MUDs; I think that this is a minority impression, however. Interruptions do exist on MUDs; they are simply less significant than in real life.

Other small-group interactions

I would not like to give the impression that conversation is the only social activity on MUDs. Indeed, MUD society appears to have most of the same social activities as real life, albeit often in a modified form. PernMUSH holds large-scale, organized social gatherings such as "hatchings" and they are not alone. Most MUDs have at one time or another organized more or less elaborate parties, often to celebrate notable events in the MUD itself, such as an anniversary of its founding. We have so far had only one or two such parties on LambdaMOO, to celebrate the "opening" of some new area built by a player; if there were any other major parties, I certainly wasn't invited!

One of the more impressive examples of MUD social activity is the virtual wedding. There have been many of these on many different MUDs; we are in the process of planning our first on LambdaMOO, with me officiating in my role as archwizard.

I have never been present at such a ceremony, but I have read logs of the conversations at them. As I do not know any of the participants in the ceremonies I've read about, I cannot say much for certain about their emotional content. As in real life, they are usually very happy and celebratory occasions with an intriguing undercurrent of serious feelings. I do not know and cannot even speculate about whether or not the main participants in such ceremonies are usually serious or not, whether or not the MUD ceremony usually (or even ever) mirrors another ceremony in the real world, or even whether or not the bride and groom have ever met outside of virtual reality.

In the specific case of the upcoming LambdaMOO wedding, the participants first met on LambdaMOO, became friendly, and eventually decided to meet in real life. They have subsequently become romantically involved in the real world and are using the MUD wedding as a celebration of that fact. This phenomenon of couples meeting in virtual reality and then pursuing a real-life relationship is not uncommon; in one notable case, one of them lived in Australia and the other in Pittsburgh!

It is interesting to note that the virtual reality wedding is not specific to the kinds of MUDs I've been discussing; Van Gelder (1991) mentioned an online reception on CompuServe and weddings are common on Habitat (Morningstar & Farmer, 1991), a half-graphical, half-textual virtual reality popular in Japan.

The very idea, however, brings up interesting and potentially important questions about the legal standing of commitments made only in virtual reality. Suppose, for example, that two people make a contract in virtual reality. Is the contract binding? Under which state's (or country's) laws? Is it a written or verbal contract? What constitutes proof of signature in such a context? I suspect that our real-world society will have to face and resolve these issues in the not-too-distant future.

Those who frequent MUDs tend also to be interested in games and puzzles, so it is no surprise that many real-world examples have been implemented inside MUDs. What may be surprising, however, is the extent to which this is so.

On LambdaMOO alone, we have machine-mediated Scrabble, Monopoly, Mastermind, Backgammon, Ghost, Chess, Go, and Reversi boards. These attract small groups of players on occasion, with the Go players being the most committed; in fact, there are a number of Go players who come to LambdaMOO only for that purpose. I say more about these more specialized uses of social virtual realities later on. In many ways, though, such games so far have little, if anything, to offer over their real-world counterparts except perhaps a better chance of finding an opponent.

Perhaps more interesting are the other kinds of games imported into MUDs from real life, the ones that might be far less feasible in a nonvirtual reality. A player on LambdaMOO, for example, implemented a facility for holding food fights. Players throw food items at each other, attempt to duck oncoming items, and, if unsuccessful, are "splattered" with messes that cannot easily be removed. After a short interval, a semianimate "Mr. Clean" arrives and one-by-one removes the messes from the participants, turning them back into the food items from which they came, ready for the next fight. Although the game was rather simple to implement, it has remained enormously popular nearly a year later.

Another player on LambdaMOO created a trainable Frisbee, which any player could teach to do tricks when they threw or caught it. Players who used the Frisbee seemed to take great pleasure in trying to outdo each other's trick descriptions. My catching description, for example, reads "Haakon stops the frisbee dead in the air in front of himself and then daintily plucks it, like a flower." I have also heard of MUD versions of paint-ball combat and fantastical games of Capture the Flag.

Observations about the MUD community as a whole

MUD communities tend to be very large in comparison to the number of players actually active at any given time. On LambdaMOO, for example, we have between 700 and 800 players connecting in any week but rarely more than 40 simultaneously. A good real-world analog might be a bar with a large number of "regulars," all of whom are transients without fixed schedules.

The continuity of MUD society is thus somewhat tenuous; many pairs of active players exist who have never met each other. In spite of this, MUDs do become true communities after a time. The participants slowly come to consensus about a common (private) language, about appropriate standards of behavior, and about the social roles of various public areas (e.g., where big discussions usually happen, where certain "crowds" can be found, etc.).

Some people appear to thrive on the constant turnover of MUD players throughout a day, enjoying the novelty of always having someone new to talk to. In some cases, this enjoyment goes so far as to become a serious kind of addiction, with some players spending as many as 35 hours out of 48 constantly connected and conversing on MUDs. I know of many players who have taken more-or-less drastic steps to curtail their participation on MUDs, feeling that their habits had gotten significantly out of control.

One college-student player related to me his own particularly dramatic case of MUD addiction. It seems that he was supposed to go home for the Christmas holidays but missed the train by no less than 5 hours because he had been unable to tear himself away from his MUD conversations. After calling his parents to relieve their worrying by lying about the cause of his delay, he eventually boarded a train for home. However, on arrival there at 12:30 A.M. the next morning, he did not go directly to his parents' house but instead went to an open terminal room in the local university, where he spent another 2½ hours connected before finally going home. His parents, meanwhile, had called the police in fear for their son's safety in traveling.

It should not be supposed that this kind of problem is computer addiction; the fact that there is a computer involved here is more-or-less irrelevant. These people are not addicted to computers, but to communication; the global scope of Internet MUDs implies not only a great variety in potential conversants, but also 24-hour access. As Figure 15.1 shows, the sun never really sets on LambdaMOO's community.

Although it is at the more macroscopic scale of whole MUD communities that I feel least qualified to make reliable observations, I do have one striking example of societal consensus having concrete results on LambdaMOO.

From time to time, we wizards are asked to arbitrate in disputes among players concerning what is or is not appropriate behavior. My approach generally has been to ask a number of other players for their opinions and to present the defendant in the complaint with a precis of the plaintiff's grievance, always looking for the common threads in their responses. After many such episodes, I was approached by a number of players asking that a written statement on LambdaMOO manners be prepared and made available to the community. I wrote up a list of those rules that seemed implied by the set of arbitrations we had performed and published them for public comment. Very little comment has ever been received, but the groups of players I've asked generally agree that the rules reflect their own understandings of the common will. For the curious, I have summarized our rules in Table 15.5; the actual "help manners" document goes into a bit more detail about each of these points.

Table 15.5 The main points of LambdaMOO manners

Be polite. Avoid being rude. The MOO is worth participating in because it is a pleasant place for people to be. When people are rude or nasty to one another, it stops being so pleasant.

"Revenge is ours," sayeth the wizards. If someone is nasty to you, please either ignore it or tell a wizard about it. Please don't try to take revenge on the person; this just escalates the level of rudeness and makes the MOO a less pleasant place for everyone involved.

Respect other players' sensibilities. The participants on the MOO come from a wide range of cultures and backgrounds. Your ideas about what constitutes offensive speech or descriptions are likely to differ from those of other players. Please keep the text that players can casually run across as free of potentially offensive material as you can.

Don't spoof. Spoofing is loosely defined as "causing misleading output to be printed to other players." For example, it would be spoofing for anyone but Munchkin to print out a message like "Munchkin sticks out his tongue at Potrzebie." This makes it look like Munchkin is unhappy with Potrzebie even though that may not be the case at all.

Don't shout. It is easy to write a MOO command that prints a message to every connected player. Please don't.

Only teleport your own things. By default, most objects (including other players) allow themselves to be moved freely from place to place. This fact makes it easier to build certain useful objects. Unfortunately, it also makes it easy to annoy people by moving them or their objects around without their permission. Please don't.

Don't teleport silently or obscurely. It is easy to write MOO commands that move you instantly from place to place. Please remember in such programs to print a clear, understandable message to all players in both the place you're leaving and the place you're going to.

Don't hog the server. The server is carefully shared among all of the connected players so that everyone gets a chance to execute their commands. This sharing is, by necessity, somewhat approximate. Please don't abuse it with tasks that run for a long time without pausing.

Don't waste object numbers. Some people, in a quest to own objects with "interesting" numbers (e.g., #17000, #18181, etc.) have written MOO programs that loop forever creating and recycling objects until the "good" numbers come up. Please don't do this.

It should be noted that different MUDs are truly different communities and have different societal agreements concerning appropriate behavior. There even exist a few MUDs where the only rule in the social contract is that there is no social contract. Such "anarchy" MUDs have appeared a few times in my experience and seem to be popular for a time before eventually fading away.

The prospects for mudding in the future

The clumsy system of public gatherings had been long since abandoned; neither Vashti nor her audience stirred from their rooms. Seated in her arm-chair, she spoke, while they in their arm-chairs heard her, fairly well, and saw her, fairly well.

– E. M. Forster (1928/1973)

A recent listing of Internet-accessible MUDs showed almost 200 active around the world, mostly in the United States and Scandinavia. A conservative guess that these MUDs average 100 active players each gives a total of 20,000 active mudders in the world today; this is almost certainly a significant undercount already and the numbers appear to be growing as more and more people gain Internet access.

In addition, at least one MUD-like area exists on the commercial CompuServe network in the United States and there are several more commercial MUDs active in the United Kingdom. Finally, there is Habitat (Morningstar & Farmer, 1991), a half-graphical, half-textual virtual reality in Japan, with well over 10,000 users.

I believe that text-based virtual realities and wide-area interactive "chat" facilities (Reid, 1992) are becoming more and more common and will continue to do so for the foreseeable future. Like CB radios and telephone party lines before them, MUDs seem to provide a necessary social outlet.

The MUD model is also being extended in new ways for new audiences. For example, I am currently involved in adapting the LambdaMOO server for use as an international teleconferencing and image database system for astronomers. Our plans include allowing scientists to give online presentations to their colleagues around the world, complete with "slides" and illustrations automatically displayed on the participants' workstations. The same approach could be used to create online meeting places for workers in other disciplines, as well as for other nonscientific communities. I do not believe that we are the only researchers planning such facilities. In the near future (a few years at most), I expect such specialized virtual realities to be commonplace, an accepted part of at least the academic community.

On another front, I am engaged with some colleagues in the design of a MUD for general use here at Xerox PARC. The idea here is to use virtual reality to help break down the geographical barriers of a large building, of people increasingly working from their homes, and of having a sister research laboratory in Cambridge, England. In this context, we intend to investigate the addition of digital voice to MUDs, with the conventions of the virtual reality providing a simple and intuitive style of connection management: If two people are in the same virtual room, then their audio channels are connected. Some virtual rooms may even overlap real-world rooms, such as those in which talks or other meetings are held.

Of course, one can expect a number of important differences in the social phenomena on MUDs in a professional setting. In particular, I would guess that anonymity might well be frowned upon in such places, though it may have some interesting special uses, for example in the area of refereeing papers.

Some of my colleagues have suggested that the term, "text-based virtual reality," is an oxymoron, that virtual reality refers only to the fancy graphical and motion-sensing environments being worked on in many places. They go on to predict that these more physically involving systems will supplant the text-based variety as soon as the special equipment becomes a bit more widely and cheaply available. I do not believe that this is the case.

Although I agree that the fancier systems are likely to become very popular for certain applications and among those who can afford them, I believe that MUDs have certain enduring advantages that will save them from obsolescence.

The equipment necessary to participate fully in a MUD is significantly cheaper, more widely available, and more generally useful than that for the fancy systems; this is likely to remain the case for a long time to come. For example, it is already possible to purchase palm-size portable computers with network connectivity and text displays, making it possible to use MUDs even while riding the bus, and so on. Is similarly flexible hardware for fancy virtual realities even on the horizon?

It is substantially easier for players to give themselves vivid, detailed, and interesting descriptions (and to do the same for the descriptions and behavior of the new objects they create) in a text-based system than in a graphics-based one. In McLuhan's (1964) terminology, this is because MUDs are a "cold" medium, whereas graphically based media are "hot"; that is, the sensorial parsimony of plain text tends to entice users into engaging their imaginations to fill in missing details whereas, comparatively speaking, the richness of stimuli in fancy virtual realities has an opposite tendency, pushing users' imaginations into a more passive role. I also find it difficult to believe that a graphics-based system will be able to compete with text for average users on the metric of believable detail per unit of effort expended; this is certainly the case now and I see little reason to believe it will change in the near future.

Finally, one of the great strengths of MUDs lies in the users' ability to customize them, to extend them, and to specialize them to the users' particular needs. The ease with which this can be done in MUDs is directly related to the fact that they are purely text based; in a graphics-based system, the overhead of creating new moderate-quality graphics would put the task beyond the inclinations of the average user. Whereas, with MUDs, it is easy to imagine an almost arbitrarily small community investing in the creation of a virtual reality that was truly customized for that community, it seems very unlikely that any but the largest communities would invest the greatly increased effort required for a fancier system.

Conclusions

Vashti was seized with the terrors of direct experience. She shrank back into her room, and the wall closed up again.

– E. M. Forster (1928/1973)

The emergence of MUDs has created a new kind of social sphere, both like and radically unlike the environments that have existed before. As they become more and more popular and more widely accessible, it appears likely that an increasingly significant proportion of the population will at least become familiar with mudding and perhaps become frequent participants in text-based virtual realities.

It thus behooves us to begin to try to understand these new societies, to make sense of these electronic places where we'll be spending increasing amounts of our time, both doing business and seeking pleasure. I would hope that social scientists will be at least intrigued by my amateur observations and perhaps inspired to more properly study MUDs and their players. In particular, as MUDs become more widespread, ever more people are likely to be susceptible to the kind of addiction I discuss in an earlier section; we must, as a society, begin to wrestle with the social and ethical issues brought out by such cases.

Those readers interested in trying out MUDs for themselves are encouraged to do so. The USENET newsgroup rec.games.mud periodically carries comprehensive lists of publicly available, Internet-accessible MUDs, including their detailed network addresses. My own MUD, LambdaMOO, can be reached via the standard Internet telnet protocol at the host lambda.parc.xerox.com (the numeric address is 13.2.116.36), port 8888. On a UNIX machine, for example, the command

```
telnet lambda.parc.xerox.com 8888
```

will suffice to make a connection. Once connected, feel free to page me; I connect under the names "Haakon" and "Lambda."

Acknowledgments

I was originally prodded into writing down my mudding experiences by Eric Roberts. In trying to get a better handle on an organization for the material, I was aided immeasurably by my conversations with Françoise Brun-Cottan; she consistently brought to my attention phenomena that I had become too familiar with to notice. Susan Irwin and David Nichols have been instrumental in helping me to understand some of the issues that might arise as MUDs become more sophisticated and widespread. The reviewers of this chapter provided several pointers to important related work that I might otherwise never have encountered. Finally, I must also give credit to the LambdaMOO players who participated in my online brainstorming session; their ideas, experiences, and perceptions provided a necessary perspective to my own understanding.

Notes

1 In fact, these two commands are so frequently used that single-character abbreviations are provided for them. The two example commands would usually be typed as follows:

"Can anyone hear me?
:smiles

2 The "MOO" in "LambdaMOO" stands for "MUD, Object-Oriented." The origin of the "Lambda" part is more obscure, based on my years of experience with the Lisp programming language.
3 Kiesler, Siegel, and McGuire (1991) investigated the effects of this kind of electronic anonymity on the decision-making and problem-solving processes in organizations; some of their observations parallel mine given here.

References

Forster, E. M. (1973). The machine stops. In B. Bova (Ed.), *The science fiction hall of fame* (Vol. IIB, pp. 248–279). New York: Avon. (Original work published 1928).

Kiesler, S., Siegel, J., & McGuire, T. (1991). Social psychological aspects of computer-mediated communication. In C. Dunlop & R. Kling (Eds.), *Computerization and controversy* (pp. 330–349). New York: Academic Press.

McLuhan, M. (1964). *Understanding media.* New York: McGraw-Hill.

Morningstar, C., & Farmer, F. R. (1991). The lessons of Lucasfilm's Habitat. In M. Benedikt (Ed.), *Cyberspace* (pp. 273–302). Cambridge, MA: MIT Press.

Raymond, E. S. (Ed.). (1991). *The new hacker's dictionary.* Cambridge, MA: MIT Press.

Reid, E. M. (1992). Electropolis: Communication and community on Internet Relay Chat. *Intertek,* 3.3, 7–13.

Van Gelder, L. (1991). The strange case of the electronic lover. In C. Dunlop & R. Kling (Eds.), *Computerization and controversy* (pp. 364–375). New York: Academic Press.

Reading 16

The changing meaning of play

Edward Castronova

[...]

Three years ago I was an ordinary economist pursuing generally ordinary economics research. Now, however, I am pushing deeper and deeper into a realm of experience that's growing faster than I can examine it, a fantastic cosmos of dragons and rayguns and beautifully crafted human bodies. It is also a universe that hosts massive flows of real human intercourse – information, commerce, war, politics, society, and culture. I am speaking, of course, of the phenomenon known as "massively multiplayer online role-playing games" (MMORPGs), places where thousands of users interact with one another in the guise of video game characters, on a persistent basis: many hours a day, every day, all year round. As such, these places are like real cities and fairy-tale cities at the same time, and some of the numbers they are producing might surprise you:

- Users drive around in these worlds using a video game character in much the same [...] way we use a car to drive around the Earth. Some characters are better than others: faster, better looking. They can be bought and sold, most often on eBay. As I write this, a Jedi-type character from a fantasy world based on *Star Wars* costs over $2,000.
- Typical users spend 20–30 hours per week inside the fantasy. Power users spend every available moment. Some 20 percent of users in a recent survey [...] claimed that their fantasy world was their "real" place of residence; the Earth was just a place you go to get food and sleep [...]
- This used to be a niche phenomenon. But synthetic worlds are appearing at the rate of Moore's Law (i.e., doubling every two years), and the current number of users is 10 million people, at a minimum [...]
- Each synthetic world has a play-money currency inside to facilitate player-to-player transactions. These currencies have begun to trade against the

From Castronova, E. (2005) *Synthetic Worlds: The Business and Culture of Online Games*, Chicago: The University of Chicago Press, pp. 1–7.

dollar in eBay's Category 1654, Internet Games. Many of them now trade at rates higher than those of real Earth currencies, including the yen and the Korean won.

- The commerce flow generated by people buying and selling money and other virtual items (that is, magic wands, spaceships, armor) amounts to at least $30 million annually in the United States, and $100 million globally [...]
- In Asia, people who have lost virtual items because of game-server insecurities and hacks have called the police and filed lawsuits. The police have made arrests; courts have heard cases; and plaintiffs have won [...]

It is hard to look at these developments without concluding that something quite bizarre must be going on, and perhaps something just as important as the subjects I used to work on as an ordinary economist. Thus while I have little doubt that I am just as ordinary as I was before, the subjects I write about have become quite extraordinary. Indeed, *this* subject, video games, is so extraordinary that it has attracted the attention of one such as yourself – a person who does not normally think of video games as anything more than child's play. [...] If you had seen what I have seen in the last few years, you would sense, as I do, that the line between games and real life has become blurred. Together we might begin to understand how much this blurring will change the nature of daily life for our children and grandchildren.

[...] [T]he synthetic worlds now emerging from the computer game industry, these playgrounds of the imagination, are becoming an important host of ordinary human affairs. There is much more than gaming going on there: conflict, governance, trade, love. The number of people who could be said to "live" out there in cyberspace is already numbering in the millions; it is growing; and we are already beginning to see subtle and not-so-subtle effects of this behavior at the societal level in real Earth countries. Even if you haven't paid much attention to multiplayer video game worlds up to now, soon enough, I think, you will. We all will.

Perhaps the easiest way to convince yourself that this hypothesis is, or is not, true would be to go visit one of these places yourself. [...] Certain names [...] come up more than a few times: *Ultima Online, EverQuest, Lineage, Second Life, Dark Age of Camelot, Star Wars Galaxies.* [...] Visit your local game store; as this book goes to press, several hundred thousand people are exploring the brand-new *World of Warcraft.* You could find the software, pay for subscriptions, and head out into these places to see what may be seen. I predict, however, that you might find this means of discovery awfully expensive in terms of time. You would be trying to study a completely different culture, one for which we have no prior literature and no guidebooks. The natural first reaction would be bewilderment, of course. It was for me. Only after hundreds of hours of immersion did I begin to have any success understanding what is happening there and what it might mean.

[...] I've found that for many audiences, mere exposure to this phenomenon as it is today is sufficient to render obvious some of the deeper consequences, for those aspects of human life and thought that the listener knows most about. Anthropologists see new cultures, entrepreneurs see new markets, lawyers see new precedents, and social and political experts see new pressures and looming crises. [...] [T]he long-run implications – and as a corollary the merit of video games and interactive media as objects of serious study and reflection – may already be apparent. We do not have to look very far into the future to see changes looming.

As a quick test, imagine someone told you that there was a technology that could reasonably be referred to as "practical virtual reality." This technology would allow just about anyone, at a modest cost, to spend as much time as they wished in some kind of alternate reality space that was built and stored on a computer. We are not talking about a Holodeck here; this place isn't "real" by any means.[1] However, it does feel real enough to the users that they can fairly easily immerse themselves in it, for hours on end, month after month, year after year, in a sort of parallel existence. Were such a practical virtual reality possible, we can have no doubt that profit-seeking enterprises would figure out a way to make it work. They would build around certain themes and construct entertaining activities, to draw people in. How many people might be drawn into such places for hours and hours on end? Imagine there were a large number of just-good-enough fantasy worlds for people to go live in, worlds with all kinds of themes, from knights in armor to athletes to space travelers to mobsters to almost-credible lovers. How many people?

The fact is, this "just-good-enough" virtual reality technology exists today. By the time you read this, we will have already moved beyond it, to "almost-seductive." And if you didn't answer "just a few" to the question that closed the preceding paragraph, you might want to take a break here [...] and ask yourself how things might soon be changing in your area of interest.

[...] [I]t is not hard to imagine that there will be major effects in many areas. [...] [T]he emergence of these practical virtual reality spaces will have significant consequences primarily because events inside and outside them cannot be isolated from one another. It is not too shocking to imagine that the real world can affect the virtual world; when it rains on a football game, the game is changed. But we are now learning that games may become so important to some people, at some times, that events inside games have effects outside of them. Should more people become involved in practical virtual reality spaces, these external effects will become quite serious on a macro level. While one could make a case for these external effects in a number of areas, especially culture, sociality, relationships, and individual emotion, I will focus more narrowly on my own areas of interest in the social sciences: economics, politics, and security. In my opinion, major changes in these areas would be quite serious indeed, well worth contingency planning. [...]

[...] Again, imagine you had mastered a technology of practical virtual reality. What would you do with it? It quite clearly could be good or bad for humanity, depending on its usage. Given that the technology does exist, and is being driven onward by a lucrative, savvy industry, we should be aware that while we may have quite a few years to think about all this, it behooves us to start thinking right now, before the time to make important decisions arrives.

What is a *synthetic world?*

So far I have been referring to the technology in question as a "practical virtual reality" tool, a way to make decently immersive virtual reality spaces practically available to just about anyone on demand. For the most part, I will refer to these places as *synthetic worlds:* crafted places inside computers that are designed to accommodate large numbers of people. [...] Chances are, if you are under 35 years old you know exactly what that means, because you have been playing in synthetic worlds since you were a kid and you know that they have moved online. If you're not part of the video game generation, you might have trouble seeing the connection. Your kids or grandkids play video games on their TVs, on desktop computers, on little handheld devices – what does that have to do, you might ask, with "virtual reality"?

Such a question makes good sense because games and handheld video devices are not part of our standard image of what virtual reality is all about. For most people, I suspect, the first thing that comes to mind when one thinks of "virtual reality" is a laboratory filled with expensive gear. You know, the bulky vision-goggles that go over your head, the web of wires and straps for your arms and legs, the funny half-chair, half-bike apparatus that you wiggle around on, the six-sided surround-sound rooms at Disneyland that make you feel like you're standing in the Amazon jungle or on the Moon. Jennifer Lopez in *The Cell* (2000): bodies suspended on wires, wrapped in a second skin that looks somewhat like ribbed beef jerky. *That's* virtual reality, right? Well, no. At least, not entirely, not any more. At one time, virtual reality was indeed a matter of basic lab research and ingenious sensory-input devices, a scientific research program that made headlines in the early 1990s. But the virtual reality I am talking about has emerged independently of that program; it grew out of the game industry, without any influence from the scientists. Game developers had been exposed to the same basic ideas of virtual reality that everyone else had – Gibson's *Neuromancer* (1984), Vernor Vinge's *True Names* (1981), and so on – but they took them in a completely different direction. The difference was this: the science program focused on sensory-input hardware, while the gamers focused on mentally and emotionally engaging software. As you can imagine, a person can become "immersed" either way: either the sensory inputs are so good that you actually think the crafted environment you're in is genuine, or, you become so involved mentally and emotionally in the synthetic world that you stop paying attention to the fact that it is only synthetic. It turns out that the way humans are made, the software-based approach seems to have had much more success. It certainly is more popular, and also cheaper for users and developers. And so, as we head into the twenty-first century, the dominant paradigm for virtual reality is not hardware but software, and that means that any device, even a crude one, that can engage a person in the happenings it portrays, is a little virtual reality tool. When children play at their little handhelds and when executives fiddle around with the games on their smartphones, there's immersion going on, a virtual reality brought about by games rather than devices.

Now, the contrast between the scientific and the gaming approach to virtual reality is important [...], but it's also something of a tangent, mostly because the interesting thing about these two fields is how little they have to do with one another. There's a man-bites-dog story here: virtual reality lost much of its status as an exciting technology over the past decade, and while it is now re-emerging with considerable force, what's strange is that it is not emerging from the ruins of the old paradigm. Rather, it is growing up in a completely different place. [...]

For those who did not grow up with video games and are not all that familiar with previous efforts to construct virtual reality, the basic idea behind the video game as a practical virtual reality tool is this: If the game is online, a user can log into it from any computer on the Earth. The screen turns into a window through which an alternative Earth, a synthetic world, can be seen. This other place (another planet, a historical domain, or any other plane of existence) can have mountains, stars, and fire in it; it can have gravity, or no gravity, or reverse gravity; it might have trees and grass, but also chickens and dragons, or chicken-headed dragons or dragon-headed chickens; it might have houses and taverns and castles, or spaceships, or tiki bars; and it might have people. Some of the people you would see might be software-controlled, but others would be controlled by real humans, such as yourself. In fact, there might be a mirror there, and if you press the right buttons and maneuver your viewscreen in the right way, you would see yourself, present, in that place. The window by which your computer is depicting the world is, in fact, the surface of somebody's eye, and that somebody is *you*.

More accurately, you have been given a synthetic body in the synthetic world, and your computer is rendering the world as it would be perceived by the ocular sensory device that your synthetic body possesses. If you see someone else in the world, and she is pointing her visual sensing device at you, well, the two of you are looking at one another through your computer screens. She may be in Hong Kong, and you may be in New York, but you are still occupying the same segment of cyberspace and you have just made eye contact. Of course, her appearance there may not match the looks of her body on Earth, but neither does yours. She may even be a he, not a she, or something else again. But she/he/it is a person, like you, and you can have a relationship with her that is just like any other relationship you might have with another person. The only difference is that this relationship is being mediated by a body that is one step removed from the Earth body, and therefore occurs in a place that is one step removed from the Earth.

I said above that synthetic worlds are becoming important because events inside them can have effects outside them. This flow of influence from inside to outside is generated by a very simple core mechanism that is easy to see in the vignette above. As soon as it goes online and begins to receive visitors, a synthetic world begins to host ordinary human affairs. However fantastical the place may be – whether visitors are represented as mobsters, dragons, or crumb cakes – it still and always is playing host to ordinary human beings, with their ordinary ways of interacting with one another. The physical environment is entirely crafted and can be anything we want it to be, but the human social environment that emerges within that physical environment is no different from any other human social environment. And because no one can permanently separate events in one sphere of their life from all the other spheres, that part of human life taking place in synthetic worlds will have effects everywhere. At the same time, the things that happen there will not be run-of-the-mill things. We will no longer be in Kansas, and many of the rules will be different. Thus not only will there be spillover effects; the effects, such as they are, will seem weird.

In short, synthetic worlds put ordinary humanity in a very strange place, producing forces that deserve hardheaded attention, in my view. All things that matter to ordinary people – their loves, their crusades, their morals, and their material assets – may now have a home in a place other than Earth. That place operates under different rules. As Lawrence Lessig (1999) describes it, the unusual thing about cyberspace is that we can be both here and there at the same time, and the place that is "there" can be constructed, essentially, however we might like. Thus, all of our interests are the same as they ever were, but the environment in which we pursue them has become untethered from the Earth environment with which we have become so comfortable.

[...]

Note

1 In the TV program *Star Trek: The Next Generation*, the Holodeck was a room on the *Enterprise* spaceship that could be programmed to create environments and people that were completely indistinguishable from real places and people.

References

Gibson, W. 1984. *Neuromancer*. New York: Ace Books.
Lessig, Lawrence. 1999. *Code and Other Laws of Cyberspace*. New York: Basic Books.
Vinge, Vernor. 1981/2001. *True Names*. In Vernor Vinge, *True Names and the Opening of the Cyberspace Frontier*, ed. James Frenkel. New York: Tor Books.

Players

Richard Bartle

[...]

Fundamentally, immersion is the sense that a player has of being in a virtual world. The more *immersive* a virtual world, the greater its ability to immerse its players. Some virtual worlds (particularly non-game ones) deliberately aim for low immersion, so as not to distract from their purpose; most, however, aim to be as immersive as possible.

Although players can experience many degrees of immersion, there are conceptual or emotional barriers along the way that players must pass if they are to proceed further. Immersion can therefore most usefully be described in terms of a series of levels:

- Player
- Avatar
- Character
- Persona

The human being sitting at the computer, interacting with the virtual world, is a *player*. The player will be controlling an object within the virtual world that is associated with them. The way the player regards that object is a measure of their immersion. If they consider it simply to be a computer construction with which they don't identify (as they might, say, a document in a word processor), then they are not immersed.

Most players of virtual worlds easily identify with the object they control. At the very least, they regard the object as their *representative* in the virtual world. For them, the object is their *avatar* – a puppet that they control and the conduit through which they act. Players will refer to their avatars in the third person, but may flesh them out with a few personality quirks. "Alice has a thing about cats, so

From Bartle, R. A. (2003) *Designing Virtual Worlds*, Indianapolis, IN: New Riders (a division of Pearson Education), pp. 154–157.

she won't go near them." On the whole, though, avatars are mere conveniences – ways to effect change in a virtual world.

The next stage is for players to stop thinking of the object they control as their representative, but rather as their *representation*. The object is a tokenization of the player. This is the *character* level, at which the majority of players are found. A character is an extension of a player's self, a whole personality that the player dons when they enter the virtual world. Players may maintain several characters, each a distinct and rounded personality, which the player treats as a friend. Characters are referred to by name; although a player might say, "I lost my sword last night," what they mean is more like, "Thorina lost her sword when I was playing her last night."

Avatars are dolls, characters are simulacra, but neither are people. The final level of immersion – the one which makes virtual worlds wholly different to anything else – is that of the *persona*.

A persona is a player, in a world. That's *in* it. Any separate distinction of character is gone – the player *is* the character. You're not role-playing a being, you *are* that being; you're not assuming an identity, you *are* that identity; you're not projecting a self, you *are* that self. If you're killed in a fight, you don't feel that your character has died, you feel that *you* have died.[1] There's no level of indirection, no filtering, no question: *You* are *there*.

This is something that many people examining virtual worlds from the outside fail to understand. Avatars and characters are just steps along the way. Looking at characters to try to develop an understanding of why virtual worlds are so appealing is pointless except in the case of die-hard role-players. Sometimes full immersion is likened to an altered state of consciousness[2], this is much closer to the truth, but still misses the mark (you can daydream while in a virtual world without leaving it).

It's about identity. When player and character merge to become a persona, *that's* immersion; *that's* what people get from virtual worlds that they can't get from anywhere else; *that's* when they stop playing the world and start living it.

[...]

Notes

1 Not that anyone could ever verify that this is what having died actually feels like, of course.

2 Bromberg, Heather. *Are MUDs Communities? Identity, Belonging and Consciousness in Virtual Worlds*. Rob Shields (editor), *Cultures of Internet: Virtual Spaces. Real Histories, Living Bodies*. London, Sage, 1996.

Everyday Second Life

Tom Boellstorff

[...]

A man spends his days as a tiny chipmunk, elf, or voluptuous woman. Another lives as a child and two other persons agree to be his virtual parents. Two "real"-life sisters living hundreds of miles apart meet every day to play games together or shop for new shoes for their avatars. The person making the shoes has quit his "real"-life job because he is making over five thousand U.S. dollars a month from the sale of virtual clothing. A group of Christians pray together at a church; nearby another group of persons engages in a virtual orgy, complete with ejaculating genitalia. Not far away a newsstand provides copies of a virtual newspaper with ten reporters on staff; it includes advertisements for a "real"-world car company, a virtual university offering classes, a fishing tournament, and a spaceflight museum with replicas of rockets and satellites.

This list of occurrences does not begin to scratch the surface of the myriad ways those who spent time in Second Life interacted with each other and the virtual world. During the time of my fieldwork, the level of "real"-world news coverage of Second Life increased dramatically, often focusing on aspects of the virtual world seen as sensational (for instance, that over US$1,000,000 of economic activity was occurring daily, or that a "real"-world musician was performing inworld). But events seen as exceptional are of limited value; they take place in the context of broader norms that at first glance may seem uninteresting, but are the true key to understanding culture. For this reason it will prove helpful to introduce Second Life not by means of some infamous incident, but through a portrait of what an uneventful afternoon might have looked like during the time of my fieldwork.[1] I do not intend this portrait to be representative of everyone's experience, just one example of what life in Second Life could be like during my fieldwork. Readers with experience in virtual worlds may find the description obvious, but I would ask such readers to consider what kinds of cultural assumptions are encapsulated within these apparently banal details of everyday Second Life.

From Boellstorff, T. (2008) *Coming of Age in Second Life: an Anthropologist Explores the Virtually Human*, Princeton, NJ: Princeton University Press, pp. 8–15. Reprinted by permission of Princeton University Press.

Figure 18.1 Standing at home (image by author)

Imagine yourself suddenly teleported into Second Life, alone in your home. You already have a Second Life account and thus an "avatar," which we will call Sammy Jones. On a computer – at home, at an office, or on your laptop at a café – you start the Second Life program just as you would an email program, word processor, or web browser. After logging on with your avatar name and password, you see your avatar, who never needs to eat or sleep, standing in your home (Figure 18.1). You built this house out of "primitives" (or "prims"), as objects in Second Life are known. You did so after practicing with Second Life's building tools in an area known as a "sandbox," where you can build for free but everything you build is deleted after a few hours (Figure 18.2). The piece of land upon which your house sits is 1,024 square virtual meters in size; you paid a virtual real estate agent about thirty dollars for it, conducting the transaction in linden dollars or "lindens." For the right to own land you paid Linden Lab, the company that owns Second Life, $9.95 a month for a "premium account" and an additional $5 a month for the ability to own up to 1,024 square meters of land: this is known as a "land use fee" or "tier fee."

Using your mouse and keyboard you walk around your house, adorned with furniture, paintings, and rugs. You purchased some of these furnishings from stores in Second Life; others you made yourself. Deciding you are tired of the white rug in your living room, you open your "inventory," which appears on your screen as a "window" filled with folders containing items within them (Figure 18.3).[2] You drag an icon named "green rug" from your inventory window and as if by

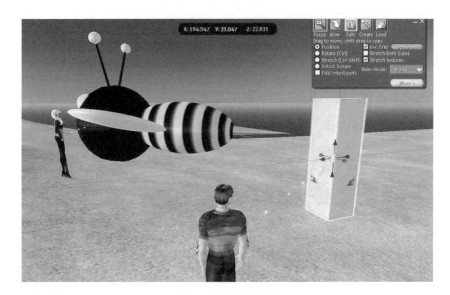

Figure 18.2 Building in a sandbox (image by author)

Figure 18.3 Perusing the "inventory" window (image by author)

magic, it materializes in your living room. You then right-click on the white rug: a "pie menu" appears with commands arranged in a circle. You choose "take" and the white rug disappears from your home; at the same time an icon named "white rug" appears in your inventory.

Now you walk out your front door and pressing the "F" key on your keyboard, you begin to fly. Gaining altitude and speed, you see a landscape of green hills receding into the distance; as you move forward, buildings, trees, and other objects appear before you (Figure 18.4). Persons in Second Life typically say objects are "rezzing" into existence, a verb that dates back to *Tron* (1982), one of the first movies to use computer-generated graphics and to represent a virtual world. The reason it takes a few seconds for objects to "rez" is that the Second Life program on your computer is a "thin client" providing only the basic interface (Kushner 2004:53): almost all of the data about the objects making up Second Life is transmitted to your computer over the Internet. In a sense, of course, the objects and the data about them are the same thing. Almost all of these objects are, like your house, not created by Linden Lab: Second Life is based upon the idea of user-created content (Ondrejka 2004a). Linden Lab maintains the basic platform for Second Life: a landscape with land, water, trees, and sky; a set of building tools; and a means to control, modify, and communicate between avatars. Nearly everything else is the result of persons or groups of people spending millions of hours every month in acts of creation. Much of this creation is for personal or informal use, but since people in Second Life can earn "real" money in the virtual

Figure 18.4 Flying across the landscape (image by author)

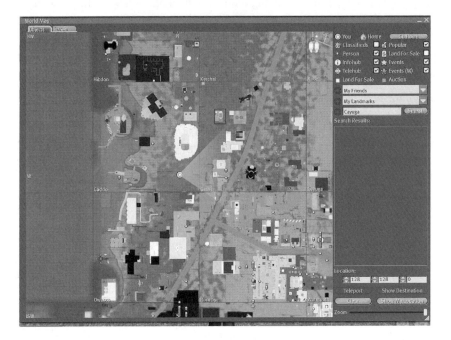

Figure 18.5 Looking at the world map, local area (image by author)

world and retain intellectual property rights over anything they create, individual entrepreneurs and even corporations create objects for sale.

Continuing to fly away from your home you see three people – more precisely, three avatars – rezzing into view. You knew they would be here because you pressed "control-M" to open a window with your "world map" and noticed three green dots on the square of land your avatar was about to enter (Figure 18.5). This square of land, 264 meters on a side, is known as a "sim" (short for "simulator"). Four sims are typically stored on one actual-world computer server; as your avatar enters a sim your computer receives information about the sim via the Internet. These servers retain all of the information about the sim's landscape as well as created objects or buildings, so that the virtual world persists when individuals turn their computers off.

The three avatars you now approach are being controlled by people who, like you, are currently logged onto Second Life: they could be next door to your physical location, a hundred miles away, or on another continent; there could even be two people controlling a single avatar together as they sit in front of a shared computer. During the time of my fieldwork it was only possible to speak audibly using third-party software and this was rarely used. However, once you are within thirty virtual meters of these three avatars they will be able to "hear" what you "say": if you type something into your chat window, the text you type will appear on their computer screens when you press the "return" key. By clicking on an avatar with your mouse you can obtain a "profile," which tells you something about the person – a short paragraph they have written about themselves, a list of their favorite places in Second Life, the groups to which they belong. All of this information refers to a "screen name"; rarely do you discover someone's "real" name. As you look through your computer screen at the back of your avatar's head and these other avatars, the persons controlling them are looking at you through their own computer screens and can click on your profile.

"How are you doing?" you type to these three persons. "Good," replies one of them, named Judy Fireside. "We are just thinking about going to the Cool Club for their 80s Dance Club Hour." You continue talking for a few minutes before deciding that you want to say something specifically to Judy Fireside, so you click on her avatar and choose "send IM" from the pie menu that appears. This opens up a window that allows you to type an "instant message" or "IM" solely to Judy. For several minutes you carry on two conversations at once – you are part of a group of four people chatting with each other, and also one of two people carrying on an instant-message conversation, perhaps commenting on what one of the other two people is saying. It is like being able to talk and whisper at the same time. You realize you want to stay in touch with Judy Fireside, so you right-click on her once again and choose "add friend" from the pie menu. This causes a message to appear on Judy's computer screen saying "Sammy Jones is offering friendship." She chooses "yes." Judy will no longer be an anonymous green dot on the world map or the "mini-map" that can be used to show your local area; you will be able to find her location and receive notification whenever she logs on or off.

Now you decide you want to go shopping for a shirt for your avatar. You say goodbye to Judy and the other two people to whom you were speaking. Opening the world map once again, you see the sim where your avatar is located and a couple others nearby. You zoom out on the map until you see Second Life in its entirety: over two thousand sims (at this point) laid out into a series of continents floating on a blue sea, known as the "mainland," and thousands of additional sims separate from the continents, known as "islands" (Figure 18.6). Over ten thousand green dots cover the mainland and islands, each representing the location of a person currently logged on to Second Life. Some dots are isolated; perhaps someone is building a house, strolling through a mall, or just sitting in a forest. You see pairs of dots: two friends catching up with each other, perhaps, or a couple having sex, or a real estate agent showing a plot of land to someone. You also see clusters of as many as seventy dots: perhaps a popular dance club, a casino, even a philosophy discussion.

Where was that favorite shirt store again? You type "control-F" on your computer and a window called "Find" appears on your screen, with tabs for locating people, places, and events. Selecting the "Places" tab you type "shirt": several hundred stores selling shirts appear in the window and you recognize one as the store you had in mind. You hit the button marked "teleport" on the Find window and after a few seconds of blackness you are half a continent away with a store

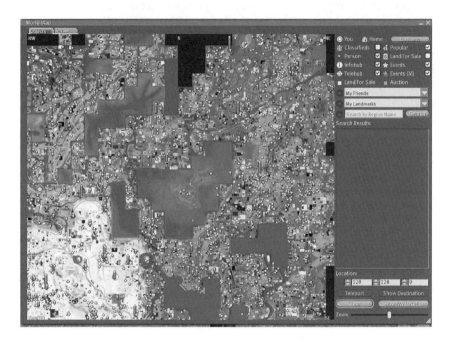

Figure 18.6 Looking at the world map, wider view (image by author)

rezzing around you. On the wall are squares with images of shirts and prices for each: 70 lindens, 150 lindens, 95 lindens. You see a shirt you like and right-click on the square with its image, choosing "buy" from the pie menu that appears. Seventy lindens (about twenty-five cents during the period of my fieldwork) is deducted from your Second Life account, and the shirt is moved into your inventory. You open your inventory window, find the shirt, and choose the command "wear"; after a few seconds your avatar is wearing the new shirt. Then you notice that a store next to this one, designed to look like a medieval castle, is selling "textures," which can be added to the surface of prims. You have been meaning to add a deck to your house and as you stroll through this second store one of its owners, his avatar sitting on a stone staircase, asks "can I help you?" You say that you are looking for a plank texture and the owner shows you a set of wood textures on sale for 300 lindens. They look great, so you purchase the textures like you purchased your shirt a few minutes ago.

The new textures safely in your inventory, you teleport home, walk outside your house, and choose the "create" command. A box appears in front of you on the ground. You choose "edit" and turn the box into a square ten meters wide, long, and tall – normally the maximum allowable size for a single prim – then flatten it to half a meter thick. The number of prims you have to work with depends on the size of your land: you have about 450 prims available on your plot, with only 300 currently used, so there is no harm in adding a bit more to your deck. You move the square flat prim just created up against the back of your house, and then create two more prims in the shape of poles to hold up the deck. In this virtual world a deck would stay up without poles, but like most people you create structures that accord visually with the laws of physics, more or less. Now you open your inventory and select one of the recently purchased wooden plank textures, dragging it onto your newly created deck and poles.

You are moving your deck a bit to the right so that it lines up with your home's back door when the instant message window pops up on your screen. It is Judy Fireside, asking "whatcha doing?" You tell Judy to come see the new deck and she teleports over with a friend, George Walker. Before long you are all deep in conversation and George is telling you and Judy about how his "real" mother has been ill lately. "But enough about that," George says: "a friend of mine is having a wedding. I just im-ed her and she said that you and Judy can come!" You and Judy both say you would be happy to attend. [. . .]

Notes

1 This method has been used effectively by other researchers (e.g., Castronova 2005:29–44). For introductions to Second Life, see the "Unofficial Complete Fool's Guide to Second Life" (http://www.sldrama.com/index.php?page=2, accessed September 29, 2006); Guest 2007; Rymaszewski et al. 2007; and B. White 2007.
2 The Second Life platform began as a program for the Microsoft Windows operating system; during the time of my fieldwork, versions for the Apple and Linux operating systems were added. Regardless of the operating system used, the interface allowed for "windows" with information (inventory, instant messages, maps, and so on) to float over the main screen.

References

Castronova, Edward. 2005. *Synthetic Worlds: The Business and Culture of Online Games.* Chicago: University of Chicago Press.

Guest, Tim. 2007. *Second Lives.* London: Hutchinson.

Kushner, David. 2003. *Masters of Doom: How Two Guys Created an Empire and Transformed Pop Culture.* New York: Random House.

Ondrejka (Linden), Cory R. 2004a. "Escaping the Gilded Cage: User Created Content and Building the Metaverse." Available at: http://papers.ssrn.com/sol3/papers.cfm?abstract_id=538362 (accessed December 1, 2004).

Rymaszewski, Michael, Wagner James Au, Mark Wallace, Catherine Winters, Cory Ondrejka, and Benjamin Batstone-Cunningham. 2007. *Second Life: The Official Guide.* Hoboken, NJ: John Wiley and Sons.

White, Brian A. 2007. *Second Life: A Guide to Your Virtual World.* Indianapolis: Que Publishing.

Part VII

Web 2.0

Introduction to Part VII

Part VII focuses on 'Web 2.0' and how communication technologies and applications are changing. We consider the effects this has on our approach to, and engagement with, online communities.

The term 'Web 2.0' is one that is widely used to refer to the way in which the Web, and more specifically the use of the Web, has been evolving. There has been some disagreement about what Web 2.0 means. Some think it is a marketing buzzword surrounded by hype. But, increasingly it is accepted as a meaningful term that describes the progression of the Web away from static content to a dynamic platform enabling content to be created by anyone, and encouraging collaboration and community.

Web 2.0 is associated with concepts such as 'user-generated content': media content that is created by end-users. People are no longer just reading or consuming web content but they are participating in, and contributing to, its creation. Web 2.0 proponents such as Charles Leadbeater (2008) discuss how the Web could enable 'mass creativity' and 'mass innovation' so that the creation and development of new ideas becomes a mass collaboration activity. Many supporters of Web 2.0 herald this emerging use of the Web as revolutionising the way in which work is carried out, information shared and content created. Some counter arguments to these utopian ideologies focus on the problems of replacing filtered, reviewed and edited content, which is created by experts, with content which is created by 'amateurs' and which may be unsubstantiated, inaccurate or biased. In addition, some critics express concerns regarding the negative impact on traditional industries involved in the dissemination of knowledge, news and the arts that comes from enabling anyone to publish media content.

Web 2.0 is explored in Part VII through the use of three very different readings. The readings are not only different in their style and the technical language they use, but they are also different in terms of the authors' perspectives and attitudes. Hopefully they will help to clarify what Web 2.0 is, or claims to be.

The first reading is by Tim O'Reilly, the founder of the company O'Reilly Media (O'Reilly, 2005). O'Reilly Media publishes books and websites, and produces conferences, on computer technology topics. O'Reilly Media is generally accredited with defining and promoting the term Web 2.0 and it is therefore useful to read the O'Reilly perspective. The reading consists of the introduction and first two sections of an article first published on the O'Reilly Media website. It identifies the activities that are associated with Web 2.0, making reference to various web-based companies and applications that were already established when the reading was first published in 2005.

The next two readings present opposing views of the way in which Web 2.0 is changing our social interactions. The first of these is a chapter called 'Publish, then filter' from the book *Here Comes Everybody: The Power of Organizing without Organizations* (Shirky, 2008). The book is written by Clay Shirky, who is a proponent of online collaboration. The reading takes an optimistic attitude towards the impact of Web 2.0 on society, and provides an overview of Web 2.0 activities and concepts, such as social networking and user-generated content. (Social networking will be considered in more detail in Part VIII.)

The third and final reading is an extract from the 2007 book *The Cult of the Amateur* by Andrew Keen, a renowned critic of Web 2.0 (Keen, 2007). The reading provides a counter argument to the ideologies expressed by Shirky. It focuses on the negative impacts on society due to the growing amount of user generated content that is available online, and as the distinction between author and audience becomes increasingly vague.

Part VII presents different points of view on Web 2.0. Commentators are divided about the impact that Web 2.0 philosophies are having on society. It is important that those using Web 2.0 technologies to create and publish content, to find information or to interact online are aware of both sides of the debate.

References

Keen, A. (2007) *The Cult of the Amateur*, London: Nicholas Brealey, pp. 1–9.

Leadbeater, C. (2008) *We-Think: Mass Innovation, not Mass Production*, London: Profile Books Ltd.

O'Reilly (2005) 'What is Web 2.0? Design patterns and business models for the next generation of software', http://www.oreillynet.com/pub/a/oreilly/tim/news/2005/09/30/what-is-web-20.html [up to the end of Section 2]. Accessed 29 January 2009.

Shirky, C. (2008), *Here Comes Everybody: The Power of Organizing without Organizations*, New York: The Penguin Press, Chapter 4, pp. 81–108.

What is Web 2.0?

Design patterns and business models for the next generation of software

Tim O'Reilly

The bursting of the dot-com bubble in the fall of 2001 marked a turning point for the web. Many people concluded that the web was overhyped, when in fact bubbles and consequent shakeouts appear to be a common feature of all technological revolutions. Shakeouts typically mark the point at which an ascendant technology is ready to take its place at center stage. The pretenders are given the bum's rush, the real success stories show their strength, and there begins to be an understanding of what separates one from the other.

The concept of "Web 2.0" began with a conference brainstorming session between O'Reilly and MediaLive International. Dale Dougherty, web pioneer and O'Reilly VP, noted that far from having "crashed", the web was more important than ever, with exciting new applications and sites popping up with surprising regularity. What's more, the companies that had survived the collapse seemed to have some things in common. Could it be that the dot-com collapse marked some kind of turning point for the web, such that a call to action such as "Web 2.0" might make sense? We agreed that it did, and so the Web 2.0 Conference was born.

In the year and a half since, the term "Web 2.0" has clearly taken hold, with more than 9.5 million citations in Google. But there's still a huge amount of disagreement about just what Web 2.0 means, with some people decrying it as a meaningless marketing buzzword, and others accepting it as the new conventional wisdom.

This article is an attempt to clarify just what we mean by Web 2.0.

In our initial brainstorming, we formulated our sense of Web 2.0 by example:

Web 1.0		**Web 2.0**
DoubleClick	$\longrightarrow$	Google AdSense
Ofoto	$\longrightarrow$	Flickr
Akamai	$\longrightarrow$	BitTorrent
mp3.com	$\longrightarrow$	Napster
Britannica Online	$\longrightarrow$	Wikipedia
personal websites	$\longrightarrow$	blogging
evite	$\longrightarrow$	upcoming.org and EVDB
domain name speculation	$\longrightarrow$	search engine optimization
page views	$\longrightarrow$	cost per click
screen scraping	$\longrightarrow$	web services
publishing	$\longrightarrow$	participation
content management systems	$\longrightarrow$	wikis
directories (taxonomy)	$\longrightarrow$	tagging ("folksonomy")
stickiness	$\longrightarrow$	syndication

The list went on and on. But what was it that made us identify one application or approach as "Web 1.0" and another as "Web 2.0"? (The question is particularly urgent because the Web 2.0 meme has become so widespread that companies are now pasting it on as a marketing buzzword, with no real understanding of just what it means. The question is particularly difficult because many of those buzzword-addicted startups are definitely *not* Web 2.0, while some of the applications we identified as Web 2.0, like Napster and BitTorrent, are not even properly web applications!) We began trying to tease out the principles that are demonstrated in one way or another by the success stories of Web 1.0 and by the most interesting of the new applications.

I   The Web as platform

Like many important concepts, Web 2.0 doesn't have a hard boundary, but rather, a gravitational core. You can visualize Web 2.0 as a set of principles and practices that tie together a veritable solar system of sites that demonstrate some or all of those principles, at a varying distance from that core.

For example, at the first Web 2.0 conference, in October 2004, John Battelle and I listed a preliminary set of principles in our opening talk. The first of those principles was "The web as platform." Yet that was also a rallying cry of Web 1.0 darling Netscape, which went down in flames after a heated battle with Microsoft. What's more, two of our initial Web 1.0 exemplars, DoubleClick and Akamai, were both pioneers in treating the web as a platform. People don't often think of it as "web services", but in fact, ad serving was the first widely deployed web service, and the first widely deployed "mashup" (to use another term that has

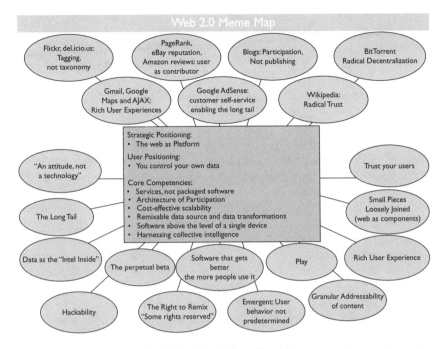

Figure 19.1 A "meme map" of Web 2.0 that was developed at a brainstorming session during FOO Camp, a conference at O'Reilly Media. It's very much a work in progress, but shows the many ideas that radiate out from the Web 2.0 core

gained currency of late). Every banner ad is served as a seamless cooperation between two websites, delivering an integrated page to a reader on yet another computer. Akamai also treats the network as the platform, and at a deeper level of the stack, building a transparent caching and content delivery network that eases bandwidth congestion.

Nonetheless, these pioneers provided useful contrasts because later entrants have taken their solution to the same problem even further, understanding something deeper about the nature of the new platform. Both DoubleClick and Akamai were Web 2.0 pioneers, yet we can also see how it's possible to realize more of the possibilities by embracing additional Web 2.0 design patterns.

Let's drill down for a moment into each of these three cases, teasing out some of the essential elements of difference.

Netscape vs. Google

If Netscape was the standard bearer for Web 1.0, Google is most certainly the standard bearer for Web 2.0, if only because their respective IPOs [initial public offering] were defining events for each era. So let's start with a comparison of these two companies and their positioning.

Netscape framed "the web as platform" in terms of the old software paradigm: their flagship product was the web browser, a desktop application, and their strategy was to use their dominance in the browser market to establish a market for high-priced server products. Control over standards for displaying content and applications in the browser would, in theory, give Netscape the kind of market power enjoyed by Microsoft in the PC market. Much like the "horseless carriage" framed the automobile as an extension of the familiar, Netscape promoted a "webtop" to replace the desktop, and planned to populate that webtop with information updates and applets pushed to the webtop by information providers who would purchase Netscape servers.

In the end, both web browsers and web servers turned out to be commodities, and value moved "up the stack" to services delivered over the web platform.

Google, by contrast, began its life as a native web application, never sold or packaged, but delivered as a service, with customers paying, directly or indirectly, for the use of that service. None of the trappings of the old software industry are present. No scheduled software releases, just continuous improvement. No licensing or sale, just usage. No porting to different platforms so that customers can run the software on their own equipment, just a massively scalable collection of commodity PCs running open source operating systems plus homegrown applications and utilities that no one outside the company ever gets to see.

At bottom, Google requires a competency that Netscape never needed: database management. Google isn't just a collection of software tools, it's a specialized database. Without the data, the tools are useless; without the software, the data is unmanageable. Software licensing and control over APIs – the lever of power in the previous era – is irrelevant because the software never need be distributed but only performed, and also because without the ability to collect and manage the data, the software is of little use. In fact, *the value of the software is proportional to the scale and dynamism of the data it helps to manage.*

Google's service is not a server – though it is delivered by a massive collection of internet servers – nor a browser – though it is experienced by the user within the browser. Nor does its flagship search service even host the content that it enables users to find. Much like a phone call, which happens not just on the phones at either end of the call, but on the network in between, Google happens in the space between browser and search engine and destination content server, as an enabler or middleman between the user and his or her online experience.

While both Netscape and Google could be described as software companies, it's clear that Netscape belonged to the same software world as Lotus, Microsoft, Oracle, SAP, and other companies that got their start in the 1980's software revolution, while Google's fellows are other internet applications like eBay, Amazon, Napster, and yes, DoubleClick and Akamai.

DoubleClick vs. Overture and AdSense

Like Google, DoubleClick is a true child of the internet era. It harnesses software as a service, has a core competency in data management, and, as noted above, was a pioneer in web services long before web services even had a name. However, DoubleClick was ultimately limited by its business model. It bought into the '90s notion that the web was about publishing, not participation; that advertisers, not consumers, ought to call the shots; that size mattered, and that the internet was increasingly being dominated by the top websites as measured by MediaMetrix and other web ad scoring companies.

As a result, DoubleClick proudly cites on its website "over 2000 successful implementations" of its software. Yahoo! Search Marketing (formerly Overture) and Google AdSense, by contrast, already serve hundreds of thousands of advertisers apiece.

Overture and Google's success came from an understanding of what Chris Anderson refers to as "the long tail," the collective power of the small sites that make up the bulk of the web's content. DoubleClick's offerings require a formal sales contract, limiting their market to the few thousand largest websites. Overture and Google figured out how to enable ad placement on virtually any web page. What's more, they eschewed publisher/ad-agency friendly advertising formats such as banner ads and popups in favor of minimally intrusive, context-sensitive, consumer-friendly text advertising.

The Web 2.0 lesson: *leverage customer-self service and algorithmic data management to reach out to the entire web, to the edges and not just the center, to the long tail and not just the head.*

Not surprisingly, other web 2.0 success stories demonstrate this same behavior. eBay enables occasional transactions of only a few dollars between single individuals, acting as an automated intermediary. Napster (though shut down for legal reasons) built its network not by building a centralized song database, but by architecting a system in such a way that every downloader also became a server, and thus grew the network.

Akamai vs. BitTorrent

Like DoubleClick, Akamai is optimized to do business with the head, not the tail, with the center, not the edges. While it serves the benefit of the individuals at the edge of the web by smoothing their access to the high-demand sites at the center, it collects its revenue from those central sites.

BitTorrent, like other pioneers in the P2P movement, takes a radical approach to internet decentralization. Every client is also a server; files are broken up into fragments that can be served from multiple locations, transparently harnessing the network of downloaders to provide both bandwidth and data to other users. The more popular the file, in fact, the faster it can be served, as there are more users providing bandwidth and fragments of the complete file.

BitTorrent thus demonstrates a key Web 2.0 principle: *the service automatically gets better the more people use it.* While Akamai must add servers to improve service, every BitTorrent consumer brings his own resources to the party. There's an implicit "architecture of participation", a built-in ethic of cooperation, in which the service acts primarily as an intelligent broker, connecting the edges to each other and harnessing the power of the users themselves.

2   Harnessing collective intelligence

The central principle behind the success of the giants born in the Web 1.0 era who have survived to lead the Web 2.0 era appears to be this, that they have embraced the power of the web to harness collective intelligence:

- Hyperlinking is the foundation of the web. As users add new content, and new sites, it is bound in to the structure of the web by other users discovering the content and linking to it. Much as synapses form in the brain, with associations becoming stronger through repetition or intensity, the web of connections grows organically as an output of the collective activity of all web users.

- Yahoo!, the first great internet success story, was born as a catalog, or directory of links, an aggregation of the best work of thousands, then millions of web users. While Yahoo! has since moved into the business of creating many types of content, its role as a portal to the collective work of the net's users remains the core of its value.

- Google's breakthrough in search, which quickly made it the undisputed search market leader, was PageRank, a method of using the link structure of the web rather than just the characteristics of documents to provide better search results.

- eBay's product is the collective activity of all its users; like the web itself, eBay grows organically in response to user activity, and the company's role is as an enabler of a context in which that user activity can happen. What's more, eBay's competitive advantage comes almost entirely from the critical mass of buyers and sellers, which makes any new entrant offering similar services significantly less attractive.

- Amazon sells the same products as competitors such as Barnesandnoble.com, and they receive the same product descriptions, cover images, and editorial content from their vendors. But Amazon has made a science of user engagement. They have an order of magnitude more user reviews, invitations to participate in varied ways on virtually every page – and even more importantly, they use user activity to produce better search results. While a Barnesandnoble.com search is likely to lead with the company's own products, or sponsored results, Amazon always leads with "most popular", a real-time computation based not only on sales but other factors that

Amazon insiders call the "flow" around products. With an order of magnitude more user participation, it's no surprise that Amazon's sales also outpace competitors.

Now, innovative companies that pick up on this insight and perhaps extend it even further, are making their mark on the web:

- Wikipedia, an online encyclopedia based on the unlikely notion that an entry can be added by any web user, and edited by any other, is a radical experiment in trust, applying Eric Raymond's dictum (originally coined in the context of open source software) that "with enough eyeballs, all bugs are shallow," to content creation. Wikipedia is already in the top 100 websites, and many think it will be in the top ten before long. This is a profound change in the dynamics of content creation!
- Sites like del.icio.us and Flickr, two companies that have received a great deal of attention of late, have pioneered a concept that some people call "folksonomy" (in contrast to taxonomy), a style of collaborative categorization of sites using freely chosen keywords, often referred to as tags. Tagging allows for the kind of multiple, overlapping associations that the brain itself uses, rather than rigid categories. In the canonical example, a Flickr photo of a puppy might be tagged both "puppy" and "cute" – allowing for retrieval along natural axes generated user activity.
- Collaborative spam filtering products like Cloudmark aggregate the individual decisions of email users about what is and is not spam, outperforming systems that rely on analysis of the messages themselves.
- It is a truism that the greatest internet success stories don't advertise their products. Their adoption is driven by "viral marketing" – that is, recommendations propagating directly from one user to another. You can almost make the case that if a site or product relies on advertising to get the word out, it isn't Web 2.0.
- Even much of the infrastructure of the web – including the Linux, Apache, MySQL, and Perl, PHP, or Python code involved in most web servers – relies on the peer-production methods of open source, in themselves an instance of collective, net-enabled intelligence. There are more than 100,000 open source software projects listed on SourceForge.net. Anyone can add a project, anyone can download and use the code, and new projects migrate from the edges to the center as a result of users putting them to work, an organic software adoption process relying almost entirely on viral marketing.

The lesson: *Network effects from user contributions are the key to market dominance in the Web 2.0 era.*

Blogging and the wisdom of crowds

One of the most highly touted features of the Web 2.0 era is the rise of blogging. Personal home pages have been around since the early days of the web, and the personal diary and daily opinion column around much longer than that, so just what is the fuss all about?

At its most basic, a blog is just a personal home page in diary format. But as Rich Skrenta notes, the chronological organization of a blog "seems like a trivial difference, but it drives an entirely different delivery, advertising and value chain."

One of the things that has made a difference is a technology called RSS. RSS is the most significant advance in the fundamental architecture of the web since early hackers realized that CGI could be used to create database-backed websites. RSS allows someone to link not just to a page, but to subscribe to it, with notification every time that page changes. Skrenta calls this "the incremental web." Others call it the "live web".

Now, of course, "dynamic websites" (i.e., database-backed sites with dynamically generated content) replaced static web pages well over ten years ago. What's dynamic about the live web are not just the pages, but the links. A link to a weblog is expected to point to a perennially changing page, with "permalinks" for any individual entry, and notification for each change. An RSS feed is thus a much stronger link than, say a bookmark or a link to a single page.

RSS also means that the web browser is not the only means of viewing a web page. While some RSS aggregators, such as Bloglines, are web-based, others are desktop clients, and still others allow users of portable devices to subscribe to constantly updated content.

RSS is now being used to push not just notices of new blog entries, but also all kinds of data updates, including stock quotes, weather data, and photo availability. This use is actually a return to one of its roots: RSS was born in 1997 out of the confluence of Dave Winer's "Really Simple Syndication" technology, used to push out blog updates, and Netscape's "Rich Site Summary", which allowed users to create custom Netscape home pages with regularly updated data flows. Netscape lost interest, and the technology was carried forward by blogging pioneer Userland, Winer's company. In the current crop of applications, we see, though, the heritage of both parents.

But RSS is only part of what makes a weblog different from an ordinary web page. Tom Coates remarks on the significance of the permalink:

> It may seem like a trivial piece of functionality now, but it was effectively the device that turned weblogs from an ease-of-publishing phenomenon into a conversational mess of overlapping communities. For the first time it became relatively easy to gesture directly at a highly specific post on someone else's site and talk about it. Discussion emerged. Chat emerged. And – as a result – friendships emerged or became more entrenched. The permalink was the first – and most successful – attempt to build bridges between weblogs.

In many ways, the combination of RSS and permalinks adds many of the features of NNTP, the Network News Protocol of the Usenet, onto HTTP, the web protocol. The "blogosphere" can be thought of as a new, peer-to-peer equivalent to Usenet and bulletin-boards, the conversational watering holes of the early internet. Not only can people subscribe to each other's sites, and easily link to individual comments on a page, but also, via a mechanism known as trackbacks, they can see when anyone else links to their pages, and can respond, either with reciprocal links, or by adding comments.

Interestingly, two-way links were the goal of early hypertext systems like Xanadu. Hypertext purists have celebrated trackbacks as a step towards two way links. But note that trackbacks are not properly two-way – rather, they are really (potentially) symmetrical one-way links that create the effect of two way links. The difference may seem subtle, but in practice it is enormous. Social networking systems like Friendster, Orkut, and LinkedIn, which require acknowledgment by the recipient in order to establish a connection, lack the same scalability as the web. As noted by Caterina Fake, co-founder of the Flickr photo sharing service, attention is only coincidentally reciprocal. (Flickr thus allows users to set watch lists – any user can subscribe to any other user's photostream via RSS. The object of attention is notified, but does not have to approve the connection.)

If an essential part of Web 2.0 is harnessing collective intelligence, turning the web into a kind of global brain, the blogosphere is the equivalent of constant mental chatter in the forebrain, the voice we hear in all of our heads. It may not reflect the deep structure of the brain, which is often unconscious, but is instead the equivalent of conscious thought. And as a reflection of conscious thought and attention, the blogosphere has begun to have a powerful effect.

First, because search engines use link structure to help predict useful pages, bloggers, as the most prolific and timely linkers, have a disproportionate role in shaping search engine results. Second, because the blogging community is so highly self-referential, bloggers paying attention to other bloggers magnifies their visibility and power. The "echo chamber" that critics decry is also an amplifier.

If it were merely an amplifier, blogging would be uninteresting. But like Wikipedia, blogging harnesses collective intelligence as a kind of filter. What James Suriowecki calls "the wisdom of crowds" comes into play, and much as PageRank produces better results than analysis of any individual document, the collective attention of the blogosphere selects for value.

While mainstream media may see individual blogs as competitors, what is really unnerving is that the competition is with the blogosphere as a whole. This is not just a competition between sites, but a competition between business models. The world of Web 2.0 is also the world of what Dan Gillmor calls "we, the media," a world in which "the former audience", not a few people in a back room, decides what's important. [...]

Box 19.1   A platform beats an application every time

In each of its past confrontations with rivals, Microsoft has successfully played the platform card, trumping even the most dominant applications. Windows allowed Microsoft to displace Lotus 1-2-3 with Excel, WordPerfect with Word, and Netscape Navigator with Internet Explorer.

This time, though, the clash isn't between a platform and an application, but between two platforms, each with a radically different business model: On the one side, a single software provider, whose massive installed base and tightly integrated operating system and APIs give control over the programming paradigm; on the other, a system without an owner, tied together by a set of protocols, open standards and agreements for cooperation.

Windows represents the pinnacle of proprietary control via software APIs. Netscape tried to wrest control from Microsoft using the same techniques that Microsoft itself had used against other rivals, and failed. But Apache, which held to the open standards of the web, has prospered. The battle is no longer unequal, a platform versus a single application, but platform versus platform, with the question being which platform, and more profoundly, which architecture, and which business model, is better suited to the opportunity ahead.

Windows was a brilliant solution to the problems of the early PC era. It leveled the playing field for application developers, solving a host of problems that had previously bedeviled the industry. But a single monolithic approach, controlled by a single vendor, is no longer a solution, it's a problem. Communications-oriented systems, as the internet-as-platform most certainly is, require interoperability. Unless a vendor can control both ends of every interaction, the possibilities of user lock-in via software APIs are limited.

Any Web 2.0 vendor that seeks to lock in its application gains by controlling the platform will, by definition, no longer be playing to the strengths of the platform.

This is not to say that there are not opportunities for lock-in and competitive advantage, but we believe they are not to be found via control over software APIs and protocols. There is a new game afoot. The companies that succeed in the Web 2.0 era will be those that understand the rules of that game, rather than trying to go back to the rules of the PC software era.

Box 19.2 The architecture of participation

Some systems are designed to encourage participation. In his paper, "The Cornucopia of the Commons," Dan Bricklin noted that there are three ways to build a large database. The first, demonstrated by Yahoo!, is to pay people to do it. The second, inspired by lessons from the open source community, is to get volunteers to perform the same task. The Open Directory Project, an open source Yahoo! competitor, is the result. But Napster demonstrated a third way. Because Napster set its defaults to automatically serve any music that was downloaded, every user automatically helped to build the value of the shared database. This same approach has been followed by all other P2P file sharing services.

One of the key lessons of the Web 2.0 era is this: *Users add value.* But only a small percentage of users will go to the trouble of adding value to your application via explicit means. Therefore, Web 2.0 companies *set inclusive defaults for aggregating user data and building value as a side-effect of ordinary use of the application.* As noted above, they build systems that get better the more people use them.

Mitch Kapor once noted that "architecture is politics." Participation is intrinsic to Napster, part of its fundamental architecture.

This architectural insight may also be more central to the success of open source software than the more frequently cited appeal to volunteerism. The architecture of the internet, and the World Wide Web, as well as of open source software projects like Linux, Apache, and Perl, is such that users pursuing their own "selfish" interests build collective value as an automatic byproduct. Each of these projects has a small core, well-defined extension mechanisms, and an approach that lets any well-behaved component be added by anyone, growing the outer layers of what Larry Wall, the creator of Perl, refers to as "the onion." In other words, these technologies demonstrate network effects, simply through the way that they have been designed.

These projects can be seen to have a natural architecture of participation. But as Amazon demonstrates, by consistent effort (as well as economic incentives such as the Associates program), it is possible to overlay such an architecture on a system that would not normally seem to possess it.

Publish, then filter

Clay Shirky

Abstract   The media landscape is transformed, because personal communication and publishing, previously separate functions, now shade into one another. One result is to break the older pattern of professional filtering of the good from the mediocre before publication; now such filtering is increasingly social, and happens after the fact.

Here, on a random Tuesday afternoon in May, is some of what is on offer from the world's mass of amateurs.

At LiveJournal, Kelly says:

> yesterdayyyyy, after the storm of the freaking century, i went to the mall with deanna, dixon and chris. we ran into everyone in the world there, got food, and eventually picked out clothes for dixon. found katie and ryan and forced katie to come back to my house with me and dixon. then deanna came a little after, then jimmy pezz, and then lynn. good times, good times. today, i woke up to my dog barking like a maniac and someone knocking on my window. i was so freaked out, but then jackii told me it was jack so i was just like whatever and went back to sleep. i have no idea what im doing today but partyyy tonighttt

At YouTube texasgirly1979's twenty-six-second video of a pit bull nudging some baby chicks with his nose has been viewed 1,173,489 times.

At MySpace a user going by Loyonon posts a message on Julie's page:

> Julieeeeeeeeee I can't believe I missed you last night!!! Trac talked to you and said you were TRASHED off your ASS! Damn, I missed it. lol ["laughing out loud"]

From Shirky, C. (2008). *Here Comes Everybody: The Power of Organizing without Organizations*, New York: The Penguin Press.

At Flickr user Frecklescorp has uploaded a picture of a woman at a fancy dress party, playing a ukulele.

At Xanga user Angel_An_Of_Lips says:

> Hey everyI srry i havent been on a while i have been caught up in a lot of things like softball and volleyball my new dog and im goin to Tenn. on thursday so i wont be on here for bout a week but i promise i will get on and show pic. and michigan was so funnnn~! welp we got a jack russel terrier and this is wut it looks like!! . . . . isnt he sooo cute . . . . i no!!! welp thats all i got to say oh oh yah i got my hair cut it is in my pic. cool uhh . . . ~!

And that, of course, is a drop in the bucket. Surveying this vast collection of personal postings, in-joke photographs, and poorly shot video, it's easy to conclude that, while the old world of scarcity may have had some disadvantages, it spared us the worst of amateur production. Surely it is as bad to gorge on junk as to starve?

The catchall label for this material is "user-generated content." That phrase, though, is something of a misnomer. When you create a document on your computer, your document fits some generic version of the phrase, but that isn't really what user-generated content refers to. Similarly, when Stephen King composes a novel on his computer, that isn't user-generated content either, even though Mr. King is a user of software just as surely as anyone else. User-generated content isn't just the output of ordinary people with access to creative tools like word processors and drawing programs; it requires access to *re*-creative tools as well, tools like Flickr and Wikipedia and weblogs that provide those same people with the ability to distribute their creations to others. This is why the file on your computer doesn't count as user-generated content – it doesn't find its way to an audience. It is also why Mr. King's novel-in-progress doesn't count – he is paid to get an audience. User-generated content is a group phenomenon, and an amateur one. When people talk about user-generated content, they are describing the ways that users create and share media with one another, with no professionals anywhere in sight. Seen this way, the idea of user-generated content is actually not just a personal theory of creative capabilities but a social theory of media relations.

MySpace, the wildly successful social networking site, has tens of millions of users. We know this because the management of MySpace (and of its parent company, News Corp) tells the public how many users they have at every opportunity. But most users don't experience MySpace at the scale of tens of millions. Most users interact with only a few others – the median number of friends on MySpace is two, while the average number of "friends" is fifty-five. (That latter figure is in quotes because the average is skewed upward by individuals who list themselves as "friends" of popular bands or of the site's founder, Tom.) Even this average of fifty-five friends, skewed upward as it is, demonstrates the imbalance: the site has had more than a hundred million accounts created, but most people link to a few dozen others at most. No one (except News Corp) can easily address the site's assembled millions; most conversation goes on in much smaller groups, albeit interconnected ones. This pattern is general to services that rely on social networking, like Facebook, LiveJournal, and Xanga. It is even true of the weblog world in general – dozens of weblogs have an audience of a million or more, and millions have an audience of a dozen or less.

It's easy to see this as a kind of failure. Who would want to be a publisher with only a dozen readers? It's also easy to see why the audience for most user-generated content is so small, filled as it is with narrow, spelling-challenged observations about going to the mall and picking out clothes for Dixon. And it's easy to deride this sort of thing as self-absorbed publishing – why would anyone put such drivel out in public?

It's simple. They're not talking to you.

We misread these seemingly inane posts because we're so unused to seeing written material in public that isn't intended for us. The people posting messages to one another in small groups are doing a different kind of communicating than people posting messages for hundreds or thousands of people to read. More is different, but less is different too. An audience isn't just a big community; it can be more anonymous, with many fewer ties among users. A community isn't just a small audience either; it has a social density that audiences lack. The bloggers and social network users operating in small groups are part of a community, and they are enjoying something analogous to the privacy of the mall. On any given day you could go to the food court in a mall and find a group of teenagers hanging out and talking to one another. They are in public, and you could certainly sit at the next table over and listen in on them if you wanted to. And what would they be saying to one another? They'd be saying, "I can't believe I missed you last night!!! Trac talked to you and said you were TRASHED off your ASS!" They'd be doing something similar to what they are doing on LiveJournal or Xanga, in other words, but if you were listening in on their conversation at the mall, as opposed to reading their post, it would be clear that you were the weird one.

Most user-generated content isn't "content" at all, in the sense of being created for general consumption, any more than a phone call between you and a relative is "family-generated content." Most of what gets created on any given day is just the ordinary stuff of life – gossip, little updates, thinking out loud – but now it's done in the same medium as professionally produced material. Similarly, people won't prefer professionally produced content in situations where community matters: I have a terrible singing voice, but my children would be offended if I played a well-sung version of "Happy Birthday" on the stereo, as opposed to singing it myself, badly. Saying something to a few people we know used to be quite distinct from saying something to many people we don't know. The distinction between communications and broadcast media was always a function of technology rather than a deep truth about human nature. Prior to the internet, when we talked about media, we were talking about two different things: broadcast media and communications media. Broadcast media, such as radio and television but also newspapers and movies (the term refers to a message being broadly delivered from a central place, whatever the medium), are designed to put messages out for all to see (or in some cases, for all buyers or subscribers to see). Broadcast media are shaped, conceptually, like a megaphone, amplifying a one-way message from one sender to many receivers. Communications media, from telegrams to phone calls to faxes, are designed to facilitate two-way conversations. Conceptually, communications media are like a tube; the message put into one end is intended for a particular recipient at the other end.

Communications media was between one sender and one recipient. This is a one-to-one pattern – I talk and you listen, then you talk and I listen. Broadcast media was between one sender and many recipients, and the recipients couldn't talk back. This is a one-to-many pattern – I talk, and talk, and talk, and all you can do is choose to listen or tune out. The pattern we *didn't* have until recently was many-to-many, where communications tools enabled group conversation. E-mail was the first really simple and global tool for this pattern (though many others, like text messaging and IM, have since been invented).

Now that our communications technology is changing, the distinctions among those patterns of communication are evaporating; what was once a sharp break between two styles of communicating is becoming a smooth transition. Most user-generated content is created as communication in small groups, but since we're so unused to communications media and broadcast media being mixed together, we think that everyone is now broadcasting. This is a mistake. If we listened in on other people's phone calls, we'd know to expect small talk, inside jokes, and the like, but people's phone calls aren't out in the open. One of the driving forces behind much user-generated content is that conversation is no longer limited to social cul-de-sacs like the phone.

The distinction between broadcast and communications, which is to say between one-to-many and one-to-one tools, used to be so clear that we could distinguish between a personal and impersonal message just by the type of medium used. Someone writing you a letter might say "I love you," and someone on TV might say "I love you," but you would have no trouble understanding which of those messages was really addressed to you. We place considerable value on messages that are addressed to us personally, and we are good at distinguishing between messages meant for us individually (like love letters) and those meant for people like us (like those coming from late-night preachers and pitchmen). An entire industry, direct mail, sprang up around trying to trick people into believing that mass messages were really specifically addressed to them personally. Millions of dollars have been spent on developing and testing ways of making bulk advertisements look like personal mail, including addressing the recipient by name and printing what looks like handwritten memos from the nominal sender. My annoyance at getting mail exhorting someone named Caly Shinky to "Act now!" comes from recognizing this trick while seeing it fail. Home shopping television shows use a related trick, instructing their phone sales representatives to be friendly to the callers and to compliment them on their good taste in selecting whatever it is they are buying, because they know that at least some of the motivation to buy comes from a desire to alleviate the loneliness of watching television. Though this friendliness makes each call take longer on average, it also makes the viewer happy, even though the original motivation to call came from watching people on TV – people who cannot, by definition, care about you personally.

Some user-generated content, of course, is quite consciously addressed to the public. Popular weblogs like Boing Boing (net culture), the Huffington Post (left-wing U.S. politics), and Power Line (right-wing U.S. politics) are all recognizably media outlets, with huge audiences instead of small clusters of friends. But between the small readership of the volleyball-playing Angel_An_Of_Lips on Xanga and the audience of over a million for Boing Boing, there is no obvious point where a blog (or indeed any user-created material) stops functioning like a diary for friends and starts functioning like a media outlet. Alisara Chirapongse (aka gnarlykitty) wrote about things of interest to her and her fellow Thai fashionistas, and then, during the coup, she briefly became a global voice. Community now shades into audience; it's as if your phone could turn into a radio station at the turn of a knob.

The real world affords us many ways of keeping public, private, and secret utterances separate from one another, starting with the fact that groups have until recently largely been limited to meeting in the real world, and things you say in the real world are heard only by the people you are talking to and only while you are talking to them. Online, by contrast, the default mode for many forms of communication is instant, global, and nearly permanent. In this world the private register suffers – those of us who grew up with a strong separation between communication and broadcast media have a hard time seeing something posted to a weblog as being in a private register, even when the content is obviously an in-joke or ordinary gossip, because we assume that if something is out where we can find it, it must have been written for us.

The fact that people are all talking to one another in these small clusters also explains why bloggers with a dozen readers don't have a small audience: they don't have an audience at all, they just have friends. In fact, as blogging was getting popular at the beginning of this decade, the blogging software with the most loyal users was none other than LiveJournal, which had more clusters of friends blogging for one another than any other blogging tool. If blogging were primarily about getting a big audience, LiveJournal should have suffered the most from disappointed users abandoning the service, but the opposite was the case. Writing things for your friends to read and reading what your friends write creates a different kind of pleasure than writing for an audience. Before the internet went mainstream, it took considerable effort to say something that would be heard by a significant number of people, so we regard any publicly available material as being offered directly to us. Now that the cost of posting things in a global medium has collapsed, much of what gets posted on any given day is in public but not for the public.

Fame happens

It's also possible to make the opposite mistake: not that conversational utterances are publishing, but that all publications are now part of a conversation. This view is common, though, and is based on the obvious notion that the Web is different from broadcast media like TV because the Web can support real interaction among users.

In this view, the effects of television are mainly caused by its technological limits. Television has millions of inbound arrows – viewers watching the screen – and no outbound arrows at all. You can see Oprah; Oprah can't see you. On the Web, by contrast, the arrows of attention are all potentially reciprocal; anyone can point to anyone else, regardless of geography, infrastructure, or other limits. If Oprah had a weblog, you could link to her, and she could link to you. This potential seems as if it should allow everyone to interact with everyone else, undoing the one-way nature of television. But calling that potential interactivity would be like calling a newspaper interactive because it publishes letters to the editor.

The Web makes interactivity technologically possible, but what technology giveth, social factors taketh away. In the case of the famous, any potential interactivity is squashed, because fame isn't an attitude, and it isn't technological artifact. Fame is simply an imbalance between inbound and outbound attention, more arrows pointing in than out. Two things have to happen for someone to be famous, neither of them related to technology. The first is scale: he or she has to have some minimum amount of attention, an audience in the thousands or more. (This is why the internet version of the Warhol quote – "In the future everyone will be famous to fifteen people" – is appealing but wrong.) Second, he or she has to be unable to reciprocate. We know this pattern from television; audiences for the most popular shows are huge, and reciprocal attention is technologically impossible. We believed (often because we wanted to believe) that technical limits caused this imbalance in attention. When weblogs and other forms of interactive media began to spread, they enabled direct, unfiltered conversation among all parties and removed the structural imbalances of fame. This removal of the technological limits has exposed a second set of social ones.

Though the possibility of two-way links is profoundly good, it is not a cure-all. On the Web interactivity has no technological limits, but it does still have strong cognitive limits: no matter who you are, you can only read so many weblogs, can trade e-mail with only so many people, and so on. Oprah has e-mail, but her address would become useless the minute it became public. These social constraints mean that even when a medium is two-way, its most popular practitioners will be forced into a one-way pattern. Whether Oprah *wants* to talk to each and every member of her audience is irrelevant: Oprah *can't* talk to even a fraction of a percent of her audience, ever, because she is famous, which means she is the recipient of more attention than she can return in any medium. These social constraints didn't much matter at small scale. In the early days of weblogs (prior to 2002, roughly) there was a remarkable and loose-jointed conversation among webloggers of all stripes, and those with a reasonable posting tempo could count themselves one of the party. In those days weblogging was mainly an interactive pursuit, and it happened so naturally that it was easy to imagine that interactivity was a basic part of the bargain.

Then things got urban, with millions of bloggers and readers. At this point social limits kicked in. If you have a weblog, and a thousand other webloggers point to you, you cannot read what they are saying, much less react. More is different: cities are not just large towns, and a big audience is not just a small one cloned many times. The limits on interaction that come with scale are hard to detect, because every visible aspect of the system stays the same. Nothing about the software or the users changes, but the increased population still alters the circumstances beyond your control. In this situation, no matter how assiduously someone wants to interact with their readers, the growing audience will ultimately defeat that possibility. Someone blogging alongside a handful of friends can read everything those friends write and can respond to any comments their friends make – the scale is small enough to allow for a real conversation. Someone writing for thousands of people, though, or millions, has to start choosing who to respond to and who to ignore, and over time, ignore becomes the default choice. They have, in a word, become famous.

Glenn Reynolds, a homegrown hero of the weblog world, reports over a million unique viewers a month for Instapundit.com, a circulation that would put him comfortably in the top twenty daily papers in the United States. You can see how interactivity is defeated by an audience of this size – spending even a minute a month interacting with just ten thousand of his readers (only one percent of his total audience) would take forty hours a week. This is what "interactivity" looks like at this scale – no interaction at all with almost all of the audience, and infrequent and minuscule interaction with the rest, and it has implications for media of all types. Weblogs won't destroy the one-way mirror of fame, and "interactive TV" is an oxymoron, because gathering an audience at TV scale defeats anything more interactive than voting for someone on *American Idol*.

The surprise held out by social tools like weblogs is that scale alone, even in a medium that allows for two-way connections, is enough to create and sustain the imbalance of fame. The mere technological possibility of reply isn't enough to overcome the human limits on attention. Charles Lindbergh couldn't bear to let anyone else answer his fan mail, promising himself he would get around to it eventually (which, of course, he never did). Egalitarianism is possible only in small social systems. Once a medium gets past a certain size, fame is a forced move. Early reports of the death of traditional media portrayed the Web as a kind of anti-TV – two-way where TV is one-way, interactive where TV is passive, and (implicitly) good where TV is bad. Now we know that the Web is not a perfect antidote to the problems of mass media, because some of those problems are human and are not amenable to technological fixes. This is bad news for that school of media criticism that has assumed that the authorities are keeping the masses down. In the weblog world there are no authorities, only masses, and yet the accumulated weight of attention continues to create the kind of imbalances we associate with traditional media.

The famous are different from you and me, because they cannot return or even acknowledge the attention they get, and technology cannot change that. If we want large systems where attention is unconstrained, fame will be an inevitable by-product, and as our systems get larger, its effects will become more pronounced, not less. A version of this is happening with e-mail – because it is easier to ask a question than to answer it, we get the curious effect of a group of people all able to overwhelm one another by asking, cumulatively, more questions than they can cumulatively answer. As Merlin Mann, a software usability expert, describes the pattern:

> Email is such a funny thing. People hand you these single little messages that are no heavier than a river pebble. But it doesn't take long until you have acquired a pile of pebbles that's taller than you and heavier than you could ever hope to move, even if you wanted to do it over a few dozen trips. But for the person who took the time to hand you their pebble, it seems outrageous that you can't handle that one tiny thing. "What 'pile'? It's just a pebble!"

E-mail, and particularly the ability to create group conversations effortlessly without needing the permission of the recipients, is providing a way for an increasing number of us to experience the downside of fame, which is being unable to reciprocate in the way our friends and colleagues would like us to.

The limiting effect of scale on interaction is bad news for people hoping for the dawning of an egalitarian age ushered in by our social tools. We can hope that fame will become more dynamic, and that the elevation to fame will be more bottom-up, but we can no longer hope for a world where everyone can interact with everyone else. Whatever the technology, our social constraints will mean that the famous of the world will always be with us. The people with too much inbound attention live in a different environment from everyone else; to paraphrase F. Scott Fitzgerald, the attention-rich are different from you and me, in ways that are not encapsulated by the media they use, and in ways that won't go away even when new media arrive.

For the last fifty years the two most important communications media in most people's lives were the telephone and television: different media with different functions. It turns out that the difference between conversational tools and broadcast tools was arbitrary, but the difference between conversing and broadcasting is real. Even in a medium that allowed for perfect interactivity for all participants (something we have a reasonable approximation of today), the limits of human cognition will mean that scale alone will kill conversation. In such a medium, even without any professional bottlenecks or forced passivity, fame happens.

Filtering as a tool for communities of practice

Comparisons between the neatness of traditional media and the messiness of social media often overlook the fact that the comparison isn't just between systems of production but between systems of filtering as well. You can see how critical filtering tools are to the traditional landscape if you imagine taking a good-sized bookstore, picking it up, and shaking its contents out onto a football field. Somewhere in the resulting pile of books lie the works of Aristotle, Newton, and Auden, but if you wade in and start picking up books at random, you're much likelier to get *Love's Tender Fury* and *Chicken Soup for the Hoosier Soul*. We're so used to the way a bookstore is laid out that we don't notice how much prior knowledge we need to have about its layout and categories for it to be even minimally useful. As the investor Esther Dyson says, "When we call something intuitive, we often mean familiar."

The hidden contours of the filtering problem shaped much of what is familiar about older forms of media. Television shows, for instance, come in units of half an hour, not because the creators of television discovered that that is the aesthetically ideal unit of time, but because audiences had to remember when their favorite shows were on. A show that starts at 7:51 and goes on until 8:47 is at a considerable disadvantage to a show that starts at 8:00 and goes till 9:00, and that disadvantage is entirely cognitive – the odd times are simply harder to remember. (It's hard to have appointment TV if you can't recall when the appointment is.) The length and time slots of television had nothing to do with video as a medium and everything to do with the need to aid the viewer's memory. Similarly, everything from *TV Guide* to the rise of content-specific channels on cable like MTV and the Cartoon Network were responses to the problem of helping viewers find their way to interesting material.

Traditional media have a few built-in constraints that make the filtering problem relatively simple. Most important, publishing and broadcasting cost money. Any cost creates some sort of barrier, and the high cost of most traditional media creates high barriers. As a result, there is an upper limit to the number of books, or television shows, or movies that can exist. Simply to remain viable, anyone producing traditional media has to decide what to produce and what not to; the good work has to be sorted from the mediocre in advance of publication. Since the basic economics of publishing puts a cap on the overall volume of content, it also forces every publisher or producer to filter the material in advance.

Though the filtering of the good from the mediocre starts as an economic imperative, the public enjoys the value of that filtering as well, because we have historically relied on the publisher's judgment to help ensure minimum standards of quality. Where publishing is hard and expensive, every instance of the written word comes with an implicit promise: someone besides the writer thought this was worth reading. Every book and magazine article and newspaper (as well as every published photo and every bit of broadcast speech or song or bit of video) had to pass through some editorial judgment. You can see this kind of filtering at work whenever someone is referred to as a "published author." The label is a way of assuring people that some external filter has been applied to the work. (The converse of this effect explains our skepticism about self-published books and the label reserved for publishers who print such books – the vanity press.)

The old ways of filtering were neither universal nor ideal; they were simply good for the technology of the day, and reasonably effective. We were used to them, and now we have to get used to other ways of solving the same problem. Mass amateurization has created a filtering problem vastly larger than we had with traditional media, so much larger, in fact, that many of the old solutions are simply broken. The brute economic logic of allowing anyone to create anything and make it available to anyone creates such a staggering volume of new material, every day, that no group of professionals will be adequate to filter the material. Mass amateurization of publishing makes mass amateurization of filtering a forced move. Filter-then-publish, whatever its advantages, rested on a scarcity of media that is a thing of the past. The expansion of social media means that the only working system is publish-then-filter.

We have lost the clean distinctions between communications media and broadcast media. As social media like MySpace now scale effortlessly between a community of a few and an audience of a few million, the old habit of treating communications tools like the phone differently from broadcast tools like television no longer makes sense. The two patterns shade into each other, and now small group communications and large broadcast outlets all exist as part of a single interconnected ecosystem. This change is the principal source of "user-generated content." Users – people – have always talked to one another, incessantly and at great length. It's just that the user-to-user messages were kept separate from older media, like TV and newspapers.

The activities of the amateur creators are self-reinforcing. If people can share their work in an environment where they can also converse with one another, they will begin talking about the things they have shared. As the author and activist Cory Doctorow puts it, "Conversation is king. Content is just something to talk about." The conversation that forms around shared photos, videos, weblog posts, and the like is often about how to do it better next time – how to be a better photographer or a better writer or a better programmer. The goal of getting better at something is different from the goal of being good at it; there is a pleasure in improving your abilities even if that doesn't translate into absolute perfection. (As William S. Burroughs, the Beat author, once put it, "If a thing is worth doing, it's worth doing badly.") On Flickr, many users create "high dynamic range" photos (HDR), where three exposures of the same shot are combined. The resulting photos are often quite striking, as they have a bigger range of contrast – the brights are brighter and the darks are darker – than any of the individual source photos. Prior to photo-sharing services, anyone looking at such a photo could wonder aloud, "How did they do that?" With photo sharing, every picture is a potential site for social interaction, and viewers can and do ask the question directly, "How did you do that?," with a real hope of getting an answer. The conversations attached to these photos are often long and detailed, offering tutorials and advice on the best tools and techniques for creating HDR photos. This form of communication is what the sociologist Etienne Wenger calls a community of practice, a group of people who converse about some shared task in order to get better at it.

John Seely Brown and Paul Duguid, in their book *The Social Life of Information*, put the dilemma this way: "What if HP [Hewlett-Packard] knew what HP knows?" They had observed that the sum of the individual minds at HP had much more information than the company had access to, even though it was allowed to direct the efforts of those employees. Brown and Duguid documented ways in which employees do better at sharing information with one another directly than when they go through official channels. They noticed that supposedly autonomous Xerox repair people were gathering at a local breakfast spot and trading tips about certain kinds of repairs, thus educating one another in the lore not covered by the manuals. Without any official support, the repair people had formed a community of practice. Seeing this phenomenon, Brown convinced Xerox to give the repair staff walkie-talkies, so they could continue that sort of communication during the day.

By lowering transaction costs, social tools provide a platform for communities of practice. The walkie-talkies make asking and answering "How did you do that?" questions easy. They would seem to transfer the burden from the asker to the answerer, but they also raise the answerer's status in the community. By providing an opportunity for the visible display of expertise or talent, the public asking of questions creates a motivation to answer in public as well, and that answer, once perfected, persists even if both the original asker and the answerer lose interest. Communities of practice are inherently cooperative, and are beautifully supported by social tools, because that is exactly the kind of community whose members can recruit one another or allow themselves to be found by interested searchers. They can thrive and even grow to enormous size without advertising their existence in public. On Flickr alone there are thousands of groups dedicated to exploring and perfecting certain kinds of photos: landscape and portraiture, of course, but also photos featuring the color red, or those composed of a square photo perfectly framing a circle, or photos of tiny animals clinging to human fingers.

There are thousands of examples of communities of practice. The Web company Yahoo! hosts thousands of mailing lists, many of them devoted to advancing the practice of everything from Creole cooking to designing radio-controlled sailboats. Gaia Online is a community for teenage fans of anime and manga, the Japanese animation and cartoon forms; their discussion groups include long threads devoted to critiquing one another's work and tutorials on the arcana of the form, like how to draw girls with really big eyes. Albino Blacksheep is a community for programmers working on interactive games and animation. All these groups offer the kind of advice, feedback, and encouragement that characterizes communities of practice. These communities can be huge – Gaia Online has millions of users. For most of the history of the internet, online groups were smaller than traditional audiences – big-city newspapers and national TV shows reached more people than communal offerings. Now, though, with a billion people online and more on the way, it's easy and cheap to get the attention of a million people or, more important, to help those people get one another's attention. In traditional media we know the names of most of the newspapers that have more than a million readers, because they have to appeal to such a general audience, but sites like Albino Blacksheep and Gaia Online occupy the odd and new category of meganiches – nichelike in their appeal to a very particular audience, but with a number of participants previously available only to mainstream media.

Every webpage is a latent community. Each page collects the attention of people interested in its contents, and those people might well be interested in conversing with one another, too. In almost all cases the community will remain latent, either because the potential ties are too weak (any two users of Google are not likely to have much else in common) or because the people looking at the page are separated by too wide a gulf of time, and so on. But things like the comments section on Flickr allow those people who do want to activate otherwise-latent groups to at least try it. The basic question "How did you do that?" seems like a simple request for a transfer of information, but when it takes place out in public, it is also a spur to such communities of practice, bridging the former gap between publishing and conversation.

Though some people participate in communities of practice for the positive effects on their employability, within the community they operate with different, nonfinancial motives. Love has profound effects on small groups of people – it helps explain why we treat our family and friends as we do – but its scope is local and limited. We feed our friends, care for our children, and delight in the company of loved ones, all for reasons and in ways that are impossible to explain using the language of getting and spending. But large-scale and long-term effort require that someone draw a salary. Even philanthropy exhibits this property; the givers can be motivated by a desire to do the right thing, but the recipient, whether the Red Cross or the Metropolitan Opera, has to have a large staff to direct those donations toward the desired effect. Life teaches us that motivations other than getting paid aren't enough to add up to serious work.

And now we have to unlearn that lesson, because it is less true with each passing year. People now have access to myriad tools that let them share writing, images, video – any form of expressive content, in fact – and use that sharing as an anchor for community and cooperation. The twentieth century, with the spread of radio and television, was the broadcast century. The normal pattern for media was that they were created by a small group of professionals and then delivered to a large group of consumers. But media, in the word's literal sense as the middle layer between people, have always been a three-part affair. People like to consume media, of course, but they also like to produce it ("Look what I made!") and they like to share it ("Look what I found!"). Because we now have media that support both making and sharing, as well as consuming, those capabilities are reappearing, after a century mainly given over to consumption. We are used to a world where little things happen for love and big things happen for money. Love motivates people to bake a cake and money motivates people to make an encyclopedia. Now, though, we can do big things for love.

Revolution and coevolution

There's a story in my family about my parents' first date. My father, wanting to impress my mother, decided to take her to a drive-in movie. Lacking anything to drive in to the drive-in, however, he had to borrow his father's car. Once they were at the movie, my mother, wanting to impress my father, ordered the most sophisticated drink available, which was a root beer float. Now my mother hates root beer, always has, and after imbibing it, she proceeded to throw up on the floor of my grandfather's car. My father had to drive her home, missing the movie he'd driven fifteen miles and paid a dollar to see. Then he had to clean the car and return it with an explanation and an apology. (There was, fortunately for me, a second date.)

Now, what part of that story is about the internal combustion engine? None of it, in any obvious way, but all of it, in another way. No engine, no cars. No cars, no using cars for dates. (The effect of automobiles on romance would be hard to overstate.) No dates in cars, no drive-in movies. And so on. Our life is so permeated with the automotive that we understand immediately how my father must have felt when my grandfather let him borrow the car, and how carefully he must have cleaned it before returning it, without thinking about internal combustion at all.

This pattern of coevolution of technology and society is true of communications tools as well. Here's a tech history question: which went mainstream first, the fax or the Web? People over thirty-five have a hard time understanding why you'd even ask – the fax machine obviously predates the Web for general adoption. Here's another: which went mainstream first, the radio or the telephone? The same people often have to think about this question, even though the practical demonstration of radio came almost two decades after that of the telephone, a larger gap than separated the fax and the Web. We have to think about radio and television because for everyone alive today, those two technologies have always existed. And for college students today, that is true of the fax and the Web. Communications tools don't get socially interesting until they get technologically boring. The invention of a tool doesn't create change; it has to have been around long enough that most of society is using it. It's when a technology becomes normal, then ubiquitous, and finally so pervasive as to be invisible, that the really profound changes happen, and for young people today, our new social tools have passed normal and are heading to ubiquitous, and invisible is coming.

We are living in the middle of the largest increase in expressive capability in the history of the human race. More people can communicate more things to more people than has ever been possible in the past, and the size and speed of this increase, from under one million participants to over one billion in a generation, makes the change unprecedented, even considered against the background of previous revolutions in communications tools. The truly dramatic changes in such tools can be counted on the fingers of one hand: the printing press and movable type (considered as one long period of innovation); the telegraph and telephone; recorded content (music, then movies); and finally the harnessing of radio signals (for broadcasting radio and TV). None of these examples was a simple improvement, which is to say a better way of doing what a society already did. Instead, each was a real break with the continuity of the past, because any radical change in our ability to communicate with one another changes society. A culture with printing presses is a different *kind* of culture from one that doesn't have them.

There was a persistent imbalance in these earlier changes, however. The telephone, the technological revolution that put the most expressive power in the hands of the individual, didn't create an audience; telephones were designed for conversation. Meanwhile the printing press and recorded and broadcast media created huge audiences but left control of the media in the hands of a small group of professionals. As mobile phones and the internet both spread and merge, we now have a platform that creates both expressive power and audience size. Every new user is a potential creator and consumer, and an audience whose members can cooperate directly with one another, many to many, is a former audience. Even if what the audience creates is nothing more than a few text messages or e-mails, those messages can be addressed not just to individuals but to groups, and they can be copied and forwarded endlessly.

Our social tools are not an improvement to modern society; they are a challenge to it. New technology makes new things possible: put another way, when new technology appears, previously impossible things start occurring. If enough of those impossible things are important and happen in a bundle, quickly, the change becomes a revolution.

The hallmark of revolution is that the goals of the revolutionaries cannot be contained by the institutional structure of the existing society. As a result, either the revolutionaries are put down, or some of those institutions are altered, replaced, or destroyed. We are plainly witnessing a restructuring of the media businesses, but their suffering isn't unique, it's prophetic. All businesses are media businesses, because whatever else they do, all businesses rely on the managing of information for two audiences – employees and the world. The increase in the power of both individuals and groups, outside traditional organizational structures, is unprecedented. Many institutions we rely on today will not survive this change without significant alteration, and the more an institution or industry relies on information as its core product, the greater and more complete the change will be. The linking of symmetrical participation and amateur production makes this period of change remarkable. Symmetrical participation means that once people have the capacity to receive information, they have the capability to send it as well. Owning a television does not give you the ability to make TV shows, but owning a computer means that you can create as well as receive many kinds of content, from the written word through sound and images. Amateur production, the result of all this new capability, means that the category of "consumer" is now a temporary behavior rather than a permanent identity.

Notes

Page 237: **social networking site** After the 2002 success of Friendster, the first widely adopted social networking service, many more were created. Judith Meskill created a list of over three hundred (!) social networking services by 2005, and many more have been created since then. That list, though no longer updated, is at socialsoftware.weblogsinc.com/2005/02/14/home-of-the-social-networking-services-meta-list/.

Two interesting pieces on social networking are: danah boyd's "Identity Production in a Networked Culture: Why Youth Heart MySpace" (transcript of her AAAS talk from 2006 at www.danah.org/papers/AAAS2006.html), describing the forces that led to the success of those services among teens; and an untitled weblog post by Danny O'Brien (www.oblomovka.com/entries/2003/10/13) describing the tensions among public, private, and secret modes of conversation in social media.

Page 243: **Email is such a funny thing** Merlin Mann offered that description of email at "The Strange Allure (and False Hope) of Email Bankruptcy" (www.43folders.com/2007/05/30/email-bankruptcy-2/).

Page 245: **"Conversation is king. Content is just something to talk about."** Cory Doctorow offered that observation in a blog post on BoingBoing.net entitled "Disney Exec: Piracy Is Just a Business Model" (www.boingboing.net/2006/10/10/disney-exec-piracy-i.html).

Page 246: **community of practice** Etienne Wenger first published on this subject in *Communities of Practice: Learning, Meaning and Identity*, Cambridge University Press (1998), and writes more on it (and about social learning generally) at www.ewenger.com.

The cult of the amateur

Andrew Keen

If I didn't know better, I'd think it was 1999 all over again. The boom has returned to Silicon Valley, and the mad utopians are once again running wild. I bumped into one such evangelist at a recent San Francisco mixer.

Over glasses of fruity local Chardonnay, we swapped notes about our newest new things. He told me his current gig involved a new software for publishing music, text, and video on the Internet.

"It's MySpace meets YouTube meets Wikipedia meets Google," he said. "On steroids."

In reply, I explained I was working on a polemic about the destructive impact of the digital revolution on our culture, economy, and values.

"It's ignorance meets egoism meets bad taste meets mob rule," I said, unable to resist a smile. "On steroids."

He smiled uneasily in return. "So it's Huxley meets the digital age," he said. "You're rewriting Huxley for the twenty-first century." He raised his wine glass in my honor. "To *Brave New World 2.0!*"

We clinked wine glasses. But I knew we were toasting the wrong Huxley. Rather than Aldous, the inspiration behind this book comes from his grandfather, T. H. Huxley, the nineteenth-century evolutionary biologist and author of the "infinite monkey theorem." Huxley's theory says that if you provide infinite monkeys with infinite typewriters, some monkey somewhere will eventually create a masterpiece – a play by Shakespeare, a Platonic dialogue, or an economic treatise by Adam Smith.[1]

In the pre-Internet age, T. H. Huxley's scenario of infinite monkeys empowered with infinite technology seemed more like a mathematical jest than a dystopian vision. But what had once appeared as a joke now seems to foretell the consequences of a flattening of culture that is blurring the lines between traditional audience and author, creator and consumer, expert and amateur. This is no laughing matter.

Today's technology hooks all those monkeys up with all those typewriters. Except in our Web 2.0 world, the typewriters aren't quite typewriters, but rather

From Keen, A. (2007), *The Cult of the Amateur*, Nicolas Brealey Publishing (UK/Commonwealth) Random House (US/Canada), pp. 1–9.

networked personal computers, and the monkeys aren't quite monkeys, but rather Internet users. And instead of creating masterpieces, these millions and millions of exuberant monkeys – many with no more talent in the creative arts than our primate cousins – are creating an endless digital forest of mediocrity. For today's amateur monkeys can use their networked computers to publish everything from uninformed political commentary, to unseemly home videos, to embarrassingly amateurish music, to unreadable poems, reviews, essays, and novels.

At the heart of this infinite monkey experiment in self-publishing is the Internet diary, the ubiquitous blog. Blogging has become such a mania that a new blog is being created every second of every minute of every hour of every day. We are blogging with monkeylike shamelessness about our private lives, our sex lives, our dream lives, our lack of lives, our Second Lives. At the time of writing there are fifty-three million blogs on the Internet, and this number is doubling every six months. In the time it took you to read this paragraph, ten new blogs were launched.

If we keep up this pace, there will be over five hundred million blogs by 2010, collectively corrupting and confusing popular opinion about everything from politics, to commerce, to arts and culture. Blogs have become so dizzyingly infinite that they've undermined our sense of what is true and what is false, what is real and what is imaginary. These days, kids can't tell the difference between credible news by objective professional journalists and what they read on joeshmoe. blogspot.com. For these Generation Y utopians, every posting is just another person's version of the truth; every fiction is just another person's version of the facts.

Then there is Wikipedia, an online encyclopedia where anyone with opposable thumbs and a fifth-grade education can publish anything on any topic from AC/DC to Zoroastrianism. Since Wikipedia's birth, more than fifteen thousand contributors have created nearly three million entries in over a hundred different languages – none of them edited or vetted for accuracy. With hundreds of thousands of visitors a day, Wikipedia has become the third most visited site for information and current events; a more trusted source for news than the CNN or BBC Web sites, even though Wikipedia has no reporters, no editorial staff, and no experience in news-gathering. It's the blind leading the blind – infinite monkeys providing infinite information for infinite readers, perpetuating the cycle of misinformation and ignorance.

On Wikipedia, everyone with an agenda can rewrite an entry to their liking – and contributors frequently do. *Forbes* recently reported, for example, a story of anonymous McDonald's and Wal-Mart employees furtively using Wikipedia entries as a medium for deceptively spreading corporate propaganda. On the McDonald's entry, a link to Eric Schlosser's *Fast Food Nation* conveniently disappeared; on Wal-Mart's somebody eliminated a line about underpaid employees making less than 20 percent of the competition.[2]

But the Internet's infinite monkey experiment is not limited to the written word. T. H. Huxley's nineteenth-century typewriter has evolved into not only the computer, but also the camcorder, turning the Internet into a vast library for user-generated video content. One site, YouTube, is a portal of amateur videos that, at the time of writing, was the world's fastest-growing site,[3] attracting sixty-five thousand new videos daily and boasting sixty million clips being watched each day; that adds up to over twenty-five million new videos a year,[4] and some twenty-five billion hits. In the fall of 2006, this overnight sensation was bought by Google for over a billion and a half dollars.

YouTube eclipses even the blogs in the inanity and absurdity of its content. Nothing seems too prosaic or narcissistic for these videographer monkeys. The site is an infinite gallery of amateur movies showing poor fools dancing, singing, eating, washing, shopping, driving, cleaning, sleeping, or just staring into their computers. In August 2006, one hugely popular video called "The Easter Bunny Hates You" showed a man in a bunny suit harassing and attacking people on the streets; according to *Forbes* magazine, this video was viewed more than three million times in two weeks. A few other favorite subjects include a young woman watching another YouTube user who is watching yet another user – a virtual hall of mirrors that eventually leads to a woman making a peanut butter and jelly sandwich in front of the television; a Malaysian dancer in absurdly short skirts grooving to Ricky Martin and Britney Spears; a dog chasing its tail; an Englishwoman instructing her viewers how to eat a chocolate and marmalade cookie; and, in a highly appropriate addition to the YouTube library, a video of dancing stuffed monkeys.

What's more disturbing than the fact that millions of us willingly tune in to such nonsense each day is that some Web sites are making monkeys out of us without our even knowing it. By entering words into Google's search engine, we are actually creating something called "collective intelligence," the sum wisdom of all Google users. The logic of Google's search engine, what technologists call its algorithm, reflects the "wisdom" of the crowd. In other words, the more people click on a link that results from a search, the more likely that link will come up in subsequent searches. The search engine is an aggregation of the ninety million questions we collectively ask Google each day; in other words, it just tells us what we already know.

This same "wisdom" of the crowd is manifested on editor-free news-aggregation sites such as Digg and Reddit. The ordering of the headlines on these sites reflects what other users have been reading rather than the expert judgment of news editors. As I write, there is a brutal war going on in Lebanon between Israel and Hezbollah. But the Reddit user wouldn't know this because there is nothing about Israel, Lebanon, or Hezbollah on the site's top twenty "hot" stories. Instead, subscribers can read about a flat-chested English actress, the walking habits of elephants, a spoof of the latest Mac commercial, and underground tunnels in Japan. Reddit is a mirror of our most banal interests. It makes a mockery of traditional news media and turns current events into a childish game of Trivial Pursuit.

The *New York Times* reports that 50 percent of all bloggers blog for the sole purpose of reporting and sharing experiences about their personal lives. The tagline for YouTube is "Broadcast Yourself." And broadcast ourselves we do, with all the shameless self-admiration of the mythical Narcissus. As traditional mainstream media is replaced by a personalized one, the Internet has become a mirror to ourselves. Rather than using it to seek news, information, or culture, we use it to actually BE the news, the information, the culture.

This infinite desire for personal attention is driving the hottest part of the new Internet economy – social-networking sites like MySpace, Facebook, and Bebo. As shrines for the cult of self-broadcasting, these sites have become tabula rasas of our individual desires and identities. They claim to be all about "social networking" with others, but in reality they exist so that we can advertise ourselves: everything from our favorite books and movies, to photos from our summer vacations, to "testimonials" praising our more winsome qualities or recapping our latest drunken exploits. It's hardly surprising that the increasingly tasteless nature of such self-advertisements has led to an infestation of anonymous sexual predators and pedophiles.

But our cultural standards and moral values are not all that are at stake. Gravest of all, the very traditional institutions that have helped to foster and create our news, our music, our literature, our television shows, and our movies are under assault as well. Newspapers and news-magazines, one of the most reliable sources of information about the world we live in, are flailing, thanks to the proliferation of free blogs and sites like Craigslist that offer free classifieds, undermining paid ad placements. In the first quarter of 2006, profits plummeted dramatically at all the major newspaper companies – down 69 percent at the New York Times Company, 28 percent at the Tribune Company, and 11 percent at Gannett, the nation's largest newspaper company. Circulation is down, too. At the *San Francisco Chronicle*, ironically one of the newspapers of record for Silicon Valley, readership was down a dizzying 16 percent in the middle two quarters of 2005 alone.[5] And in 2007, Time, Inc., laid off almost 300 people, primarily from editorial, from such magazines as *Time, People*, and *Sports Illustrated*.

Those of us who still read the newspaper and magazines know that people are buying less music, too. Thanks to the rampant digital piracy spawned by file-sharing technology, sales of recorded music dropped over 20 percent between 2000 and 2006.[6]

In parallel with the rise of YouTube, Hollywood is experiencing its own financial troubles. Domestic box office sales now represent less than 20 percent of Hollywood's revenue and, with the leveling off of DVD sales and the rampant global piracy, the industry is desperately searching for a new business model that will enable it to profitably distribute movies on the Internet. According to *The New Yorker* film critic David Denby, many studio executives in Hollywood are now in a "panic" over declining revenue. One bleak consequence is cuts. Disney, for example, announced 650 job cuts in 2006, and an almost 50 percent drop in the number of animated movies produced annually.[7]

Old media is facing extinction. But if so, what will take its place? Apparently, it will be Silicon Valley's hot new search engines, social media sites, and video portals. Every new page on MySpace, every new blog post, every new YouTube video adds up to another potential source of advertising revenue lost to mainstream media. Thus, Rupert Murdoch's canny – or desperate – decision in July 2005 to buy MySpace for five hundred and eighty million dollars. Thus, the $1.65 billion sale of YouTube and the explosion of venture capital funding YouTube copycat sites. And, thus, the seemingly unstoppable growth at Google where, in the second quarter of 2006, revenue surged to almost two and a half billion dollars.

What happens, you might ask, when ignorance meets egoism meets bad taste meets mob rule?

The monkeys take over. Say good-bye to today's experts and cultural gatekeepers – our reporters, news anchors, editors, music companies, and Hollywood movie studios. In today's cult of the amateur,[8] the monkeys are running the show. With their infinite typewriters, they are authoring the future. And we may not like how it reads.

Notes

1 For more about Huxley's theory, see Jorge Luis Borges' 1939 essay "The Total Library."
2 Evan Hessel, "Shillipedia," *Forbes*, June 19, 2006.
3 http://mashable.com/2006/07/22/youtube-is-worlds-fastest-growing-website/
4 Scott Wooley, "Video Fixation," *Forbes*, October 16, 2006.
5 Audit Bureau of Circulations, September 2005, reports. BBC News, January 23, 2006. (http://news.bbc.co.uk/2/hi/entertainment/4639066.stm.)
6 Jeff Howe, "No Suit Required," *Wired*, September 2006.
7 Frank Ahrens, "Disney to Reorganize Its Lagging Movie Studios," *Washington Post*, July 20, 2006.
8 The term "cult of the amateur" was first coined by Nicholas Carr in his essay "The Amorality of Web 2.0," roughtype.com, October 3, 2005.

Part VIII

Social networking

Introduction to Part VIII

Social networks are the social structures that represent the connections, and strength of connections, between people. Part VIII focuses on how these structures have been impacted by changing patterns in online interaction and in particular by the growth of social network sites.

Social networking involves creating and maintaining connections and relationships with the people we know. These processes are a fundamental part of everyday life. The interactions we experience with the people we know, or meet, contribute to our well-being, learning, and personal and professional development. They therefore need to be informative, supportive and diverse.

Around 1997, social network sites began to emerge on the Internet. These sites provide online spaces where people can express and manage their social networks. On sites such as MySpace and Facebook, people create a descriptive profile of themselves, add photos, and connect to people they know, or find, on the site. The people to whom a user is connected are displayed as part of their profile information. The knowledge of who a person is connected to provides indirect information about that person. It also enables new connections to be established, through 'friends of friends', with a certain degree of trust already in place (Donath and boyd, 2004). Communication among those that have agreed to be connected is facilitated through a multitude of methods, both asynchronous and synchronous. Messages can be exchanged privately between two or more people or displayed publicly for all connected users to see.

Social network sites have become a mainstream and popular method for communication and collaboration for many people. The single reading in this part considers their evolution over the first decade of their existence. The reading is by danah boyd and Nicole Ellison and was originally published in 2007 in the Journal of Computer Mediated Communication (boyd and Ellison, 2007). It provides a detailed description of social network sites and the features that they incorporate, including their history and a timeline indicating the major milestones since the first sites appeared up until the journal was published. The reading originally served as an introduction to a special themed issue of the journal. It therefore refers to, and introduces, some of the papers included in later sections of that issue.

Around the time the reading by boyd and Ellison was first published, there was a lot of activity in the development of social network sites. Many people were using social network sites for the first time and some of the more long-standing users were beginning to shape the features and applications, and influence how they were used. Sites focused around different interests, such as photo or video sharing or creating business contacts, were well established at that time and are still attracting new users. As well as feature-rich social networking platforms, a role has now evolved for much lighter services referred to as 'micro-blogging'. Originally popularised by Twitter (one of the fastest growing social network sites at the beginning of 2009), these services allow users to write short messages or updates that are immediately displayed on their profile page. These updates are then sent to other users who have signed up to be 'followers' of that person (although links need not be two-way). Updates can be received through various channels, including client applications and SMS (text message).

Probably due to the unprecedented popularity of social network sites, there has been much speculation, in the media and on the Web, regarding their longevity. Some people think that their popularity is already declining and will continue to do so. There are also concerns about the safety of social network sites. Many of these debates focus on the privacy issues associated with publishing fragments of personal information online and the very real threat of these fragments being collated to commit identity fraud. There are also concerns regarding the lack of technical controls to validate users' ages or identities, thus creating a particular threat to children using the sites to find new friends.

Part VIII considers how online tools have developed to support the social aspect of communication and collaboration. Social network sites have become popular and have allowed users to reach, and maintain contact with, a wide network of people. Some sites are feature rich and support images, videos, custom-designed applications and various methods for message exchange. Others are simpler and focus on the exchange of short text based messages. Social network sites are continually evolving and new developments are taking place.

References

Donath, J. and boyd, d. (2004) 'Public displays of connection', *BT Technology Journal*, 22(4), pp. 71–82.

boyd, d.m. and Ellison, N.B. (2007) 'Social network sites: definition, history and scholarship', *Journal of Computer-Mediated Communication*, 13(1), Article 11.

Social network sites

Definition, history, and scholarship

danah m. boyd and Nicole B. Ellison

Abstract   Social network sites (SNSs) are increasingly attracting the attention of academic and industry researchers intrigued by their affordances and reach. This special theme section of the Journal of Computer-Mediated Communication brings together scholarship on these emergent phenomena. In this introductory article, we describe features of SNSs and propose a comprehensive definition. We then present one perspective on the history of such sites, discussing key changes and developments. After briefly summarizing existing scholarship concerning SNSs, we discuss the articles in this special section and conclude with considerations for future research.

Introduction

Since their introduction, social network sites (SNSs) such as MySpace, Facebook, Cyworld, and Bebo have attracted millions of users, many of whom have integrated these sites into their daily practices. As of this writing, there are hundreds of SNSs, with various technological affordances, supporting a wide range of interests and practices. While their key technological features are fairly consistent, the cultures that emerge around SNSs are varied. Most sites support the maintenance of pre-existing social networks, but others help strangers connect based on shared interests, political views, or activities. Some sites cater to diverse audiences, while others attract people based on common language or shared racial, sexual, religious, or nationality-based identities. Sites also vary in the extent to which they incorporate new information and communication tools, such as mobile connectivity, blogging, and photo/video-sharing.

Scholars from disparate fields have examined SNSs in order to understand the practices, implications, culture, and meaning of the sites, as well as users' engagement with them. This special theme section of the *Journal of Computer-Mediated Communication* brings together a unique collection of articles that analyze a

boyd, d. m. and Ellison, N. B. (2008), 'Social network sites: Definition, history, and scholarship', *Journal of Computer–Mediated Communication*, 13(1), Article 11.

wide spectrum of social network sites using various methodological techniques, theoretical traditions, and analytic approaches. By collecting these articles in this issue, our goal is to showcase some of the interdisciplinary scholarship around these sites.

The purpose of this introduction is to provide a conceptual, historical, and scholarly context for the articles in this collection. We begin by defining what constitutes a social network site and then present one perspective on the historical development of SNSs, drawing from personal interviews and public accounts of sites and their changes over time. Following this, we review recent scholarship on SNSs and attempt to contextualize and highlight key works. We conclude with a description of the articles included in this special section and suggestions for future research.

Social network sites: a definition

We define social network sites as web-based services that allow individuals to (1) construct a public or semi-public profile within a bounded system, (2) articulate a list of other users with whom they share a connection, and (3) view and traverse their list of connections and those made by others within the system. The nature and nomenclature of these connections may vary from site to site.

While we use the term "social network site" to describe this phenomenon, the term "social networking sites" also appears in public discourse, and the two terms are often used interchangeably. We chose not to employ the term "networking" for two reasons: emphasis and scope. "Networking" emphasizes relationship initiation, often between strangers. While networking is possible on these sites, it is not the primary practice on many of them, nor is it what differentiates them from other forms of computer-mediated communication (CMC).

What makes social network sites unique is not that they allow individuals to meet strangers, but rather that they enable users to articulate and make visible their social networks. This can result in connections between individuals that would not otherwise be made, but that is often not the goal, and these meetings are frequently between "latent ties" (Haythornthwaite, 2005) who share some offline connection. On many of the large SNSs, participants are not necessarily "networking" or looking to meet new people; instead, they are primarily communicating with people who are already a part of their extended social network. To emphasize this articulated social network as a critical organizing feature of these sites, we label them "social network sites."

While SNSs have implemented a wide variety of technical features, their backbone consists of visible profiles that display an articulated list of Friends[1] who are also users of the system. Profiles are unique pages where one can "type oneself into being" (Sundén, 2003, p. 3). After joining an SNS, an individual is asked to fill out forms containing a series of questions. The profile is generated using the answers to these questions, which typically include descriptors such as age, location, interests, and an "about me" section. Most sites also encourage users to

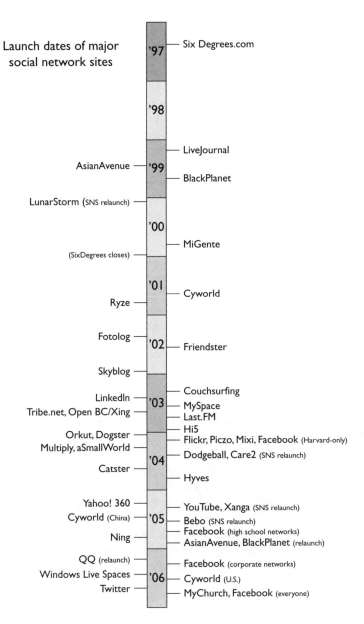

Launch dates of major social network sites

'97		Six Degrees.com
'98		
'99	AsianAvenue	LiveJournal
		BlackPlanet
'00	LunarStorm (SNS relaunch)	MiGente
	(SixDegrees closes)	
'01	Ryze	Cyworld
'02	Fotolog	Friendster
	Skyblog	
'03	LinkedIn	Couchsurfing
	Tribe.net, Open BC/Xing	MySpace
		Last.FM
'04	Orkut, Dogster	Hi5
	Multiply, aSmallWorld	Flickr, Piczo, Mixi, Facebook (Harvard-only)
		Dodgeball, Care2 (SNS relaunch)
	Catster	Hyves
'05	Yahoo! 360	YouTube, Xanga (SNS relaunch)
	Cyworld (China)	Bebo (SNS relaunch)
	Ning	Facebook (high school networks)
		AsianAvenue, BlackPlanet (relaunch)
'06	QQ (relaunch)	Facebook (corporate networks)
	Windows Live Spaces	Cyworld (U.S.)
	Twitter	MyChurch, Facebook (everyone)

Figure 22.1 Timeline of the launch dates of many major SNSs and dates when community sites re-launched with SNS features

upload a profile photo. Some sites allow users to enhance their profiles by adding multimedia content or modifying their profile's look and feel. Others, such as Facebook, allow users to add modules ("Applications") that enhance their profile.

The visibility of a profile varies by site and according to user discretion. By default, profiles on Friendster and Tribe.net are crawled by search engines, making them visible to anyone, regardless of whether or not the viewer has an account. Alternatively, LinkedIn controls what a viewer may see based on whether she or he has a paid account. Sites like MySpace allow users to choose whether they want their profile to be public or "Friends only." Facebook takes a different approach – by default, users who are part of the same "network" can view each other's profiles, unless a profile owner has decided to deny permission to those in their network. Structural variations around visibility and access are one of the primary ways that SNSs differentiate themselves from each other.

After joining a social network site, users are prompted to identify others in the system with whom they have a relationship. The label for these relationships differs depending on the site – popular terms include "Friends," "Contacts," and "Fans." Most SNSs require bi-directional confirmation for Friendship, but some do not. These one-directional ties are sometimes labeled as "Fans" or "Followers," but many sites call these Friends as well. The term "Friends" can be misleading, because the connection does not necessarily mean friendship in the everyday vernacular sense, and the reasons people connect are varied (boyd, 2006a).

The public display of connections is a crucial component of SNSs. The Friends list contains links to each Friend's profile, enabling viewers to traverse the network graph by clicking through the Friends lists. On most sites, the list of Friends is visible to anyone who is permitted to view the profile, although there are exceptions. For instance, some MySpace users have hacked their profiles to hide the Friends display, and LinkedIn allows users to opt out of displaying their network.

Most SNSs also provide a mechanism for users to leave messages on their Friends' profiles. This feature typically involves leaving "comments," although sites employ various labels for this feature. In addition, SNSs often have a private messaging feature similar to webmail. While both private messages and comments are popular on most of the major SNSs, they are not universally available.

Not all social network sites began as such. QQ started as a Chinese instant messaging service, LunarStorm as a community site, Cyworld as a Korean discussion forum tool, and Skyrock (formerly Skyblog) was a French blogging service before adding SNS features. Classmates.com, a directory of school affiliates launched in 1995, began supporting articulated lists of Friends after SNSs became popular. AsianAvenue, MiGente, and BlackPlanet were early popular ethnic community sites with limited Friends functionality before re-launching in 2005–2006 with SNS features and structure.

Beyond profiles, Friends, comments, and private messaging, SNSs vary greatly in their features and user base. Some have photo-sharing or video-sharing capabilities; others have built-in blogging and instant messaging technology. There are mobile-specific SNSs (e.g., Dodgeball), but some web-based SNSs also support limited mobile interactions (e.g., Facebook, MySpace, and Cyworld). Many SNSs target people from specific geographical regions or linguistic groups, although this does not always determine the site's constituency. Orkut, for example, was launched in the United States with an English-only interface, but Portuguese-speaking Brazilians quickly became the dominant user group (Kopytoff, 2004). Some sites are designed with specific ethnic, religious, sexual orientation, political, or other identity-driven categories in mind. There are even SNSs for dogs (Dogster) and cats (Catster), although their owners must manage their profiles.

While SNSs are often designed to be widely accessible, many attract homogeneous populations initially, so it is not uncommon to find groups using sites to segregate themselves by nationality, age, educational level, or other factors that typically segment society (Hargittai, this issue), even if that was not the intention of the designers.

A history of social network sites

The early years

According to the definition above, the first recognizable social network site launched in 1997. SixDegrees.com allowed users to create profiles, list their Friends and, beginning in 1998, surf the Friends lists. Each of these features existed in some form before SixDegrees, of course. Profiles existed on most major dating sites and many community sites. AIM and ICQ buddy lists supported lists of Friends, although those Friends were not visible to others. Classmates.com allowed people to affiliate with their high school or college and surf the network for others who were also affiliated, but users could not create profiles or list Friends until years later. SixDegrees was the first to combine these features.

SixDegrees promoted itself as a tool to help people connect with and send messages to others. While SixDegrees attracted millions of users, it failed to become a sustainable business and, in 2000, the service closed. Looking back, its founder believes that SixDegrees was simply ahead of its time (A. Weinreich, personal communication, July 11, 2007). While people were already flocking to the Internet, most did not have extended networks of friends who were online. Early adopters complained that there was little to do after accepting Friend requests, and most users were not interested in meeting strangers.

From 1997 to 2001, a number of community tools began supporting various combinations of profiles and publicly articulated Friends. AsianAvenue, BlackPlanet, and MiGente allowed users to create personal, professional, and dating profiles – users could identify Friends on their personal profiles without seeking approval for those connections (O. Wasow, personal communication, August 16, 2007). Likewise, shortly after its launch in 1999, LiveJournal listed one-directional connections on user pages. LiveJournal's creator suspects that he fashioned these Friends after instant messaging buddy lists (B. Fitzpatrick, personal communication, June 15, 2007) – on LiveJournal, people mark others as Friends to follow their journals and manage privacy settings. The Korean virtual worlds site Cyworld was started in 1999 and added SNS features in 2001, independent of these other sites (see Kim & Yun, this issue). Likewise, when the Swedish web community LunarStorm refashioned itself as an SNS in 2000, it contained Friends lists, guestbooks, and diary pages (D. Skog, personal communication, September 24, 2007).

The next wave of SNSs began when Ryze.com was launched in 2001 to help people leverage their business networks. Ryze's founder reports that he first introduced the site to his friends – primarily members of the San Francisco business and technology community, including the entrepreneurs and investors behind many future SNSs (A. Scott, personal communication, June 14, 2007). In particular, the people behind Ryze, Tribe.net, LinkedIn, and Friendster were tightly entwined personally and professionally. They believed that they could support each other without competing (Festa, 2003). In the end, Ryze never acquired mass popularity, Tribe.net grew to attract a passionate niche user base, LinkedIn became a powerful business service, and Friendster became the most significant, if only as "one of the biggest disappointments in Internet history" (Chafkin, 2007, p. 1).

Like any brief history of a major phenomenon, ours is necessarily incomplete. In the following section we discuss Friendster, MySpace, and Facebook, three key SNSs that shaped the business, cultural, and research landscape.

The rise (and fall) of Friendster

Friendster launched in 2002 as a social complement to Ryze. It was designed to compete with Match.com, a profitable online dating site (Cohen, 2003). While most dating sites focused on introducing people to strangers with similar interests, Friendster was designed to help friends-of-friends meet, based on the assumption that friends-of-friends would make better romantic partners than would strangers (J. Abrams, personal communication, March 27, 2003). Friendster gained traction among three groups of early adopters who shaped the site – bloggers, attendees of the Burning Man arts festival, and gay men (boyd, 2004) – and grew to 300,000 users through word of mouth before traditional press coverage began in May 2003 (O'Shea, 2003).

As Friendster's popularity surged, the site encountered technical and social difficulties (boyd, 2006b). Friendster's servers and databases were ill-equipped to handle its rapid growth, and the site faltered regularly, frustrating users who replaced email with Friendster. Because organic growth had been critical to creating a coherent community, the onslaught of new users who learned about the site from media coverage upset the cultural balance. Furthermore, exponential growth meant a collapse in social contexts: Users had to face their bosses and former classmates alongside their close friends. To complicate matters, Friendster began restricting the activities of its most passionate users.

The initial design of Friendster restricted users from viewing profiles of people who were more than four degrees away (friends-of-friends-of-friends-of-friends). In order to view additional profiles, users began adding acquaintances and interesting-looking strangers to expand their reach. Some began massively collecting Friends, an activity that was implicitly encouraged through a "most popular" feature. The ultimate collectors were fake profiles representing iconic fictional characters: celebrities, concepts, and other such entities. These "Fakesters" outraged the company, who banished fake profiles and eliminated the "most popular" feature (boyd, in press-b). While few people actually created Fakesters, many more enjoyed surfing Fakesters for entertainment or using functional Fakesters (e.g., "Brown University") to find people they knew.

The active deletion of Fakesters (and genuine users who chose non-realistic photos) signaled to some that the company did not share users' interests. Many early adopters left because of the combination of technical difficulties, social collisions, and a rupture of trust between users and the site (boyd, 2006b). However, at the same time that it was fading in the U.S., its popularity skyrocketed in the Philippines, Singapore, Malaysia, and Indonesia (Goldberg, 2007).

SNSs hit the mainstream

From 2003 onward, many new SNSs were launched, prompting social software analyst Clay Shirky (2003) to coin the term YASNS: "Yet Another Social Networking Service." Most took the form of profile-centric sites, trying to replicate the early success of Friendster or target specific demographics. While socially-organized SNSs solicit broad audiences, professional sites such as LinkedIn, Visible Path, and Xing (formerly openBC) focus on business people. "Passion-centric" SNSs like Dogster (T. Rheingold, personal communication, August 2, 2007) help strangers connect based on shared interests. Care2 helps activists meet, Couchsurfing connects travelers to people with couches, and MyChurch joins Christian churches and their members. Furthermore, as the social media and user-generated content phenomena grew, websites focused on media sharing began implementing SNS features and becoming SNSs themselves. Examples include Flickr (photo sharing), Last.FM (music listening habits), and YouTube (video sharing).

With the plethora of venture-backed startups launching in Silicon Valley, few people paid attention to SNSs that gained popularity elsewhere, even those built by major corporations. For example, Google's Orkut failed to build a sustainable U.S. user base, but a "Brazilian invasion" (Fragoso, 2006) made Orkut the national SNS of Brazil. Microsoft's Windows Live Spaces (a.k.a. MSN Spaces) also launched to lukewarm U.S. reception but became extremely popular elsewhere.

Few analysts or journalists noticed when MySpace launched in Santa Monica, California, hundreds of miles from Silicon Valley. MySpace was begun in

2003 to compete with sites like Friendster, Xanga, and AsianAvenue, according to co-founder Tom Anderson (personal communication, August 2, 2007); the founders wanted to attract estranged Friendster users (T. Anderson, personal communication, February 2, 2006). After rumors emerged that Friendster would adopt a fee-based system, users posted Friendster messages encouraging people to join alternate SNSs, including Tribe.net and MySpace (T. Anderson, personal communication, August 2, 2007). Because of this, MySpace was able to grow rapidly by capitalizing on Friendster's alienation of its early adopters. One particularly notable group that encouraged others to switch were indie-rock bands who were expelled from Friendster for failing to comply with profile regulations.

While MySpace was not launched with bands in mind, they were welcomed. Indie-rock bands from the Los Angeles region began creating profiles, and local promoters used MySpace to advertise VIP passes for popular clubs. Intrigued, MySpace contacted local musicians to see how they could support them (T. Anderson, personal communication, September 28, 2006). Bands were not the sole source of MySpace growth, but the symbiotic relationship between bands and fans helped MySpace expand beyond former Friendster users. The bands-and-fans dynamic was mutually beneficial: Bands wanted to be able to contact fans, while fans desired attention from their favorite bands and used Friend connections to signal identity and affiliation.

Futhermore, MySpace differentiated itself by regularly adding features based on user demand (boyd, 2006b) and by allowing users to personalize their pages. This "feature" emerged because MySpace did not restrict users from adding HTML into the forms that framed their profiles; a copy/paste code culture emerged on the web to support users in generating unique MySpace backgrounds and layouts (Perkel, in press).

Teenagers began joining MySpace *en masse* in 2004. Unlike older users, most teens were never on Friendster – some joined because they wanted to connect with their favorite bands; others were introduced to the site through older family members. As teens began signing up, they encouraged their friends to join. Rather than rejecting underage users, MySpace changed its user policy to allow minors. As the site grew, three distinct populations began to form: musicians/artists, teenagers, and the post-college urban social crowd. By and large, the latter two groups did not interact with one another except through bands. Because of the lack of mainstream press coverage during 2004, few others noticed the site's growing popularity.

Then, in July 2005, News Corporation purchased MySpace for $580 million (BBC, 2005), attracting massive media attention. Afterwards, safety issues plagued MySpace. The site was implicated in a series of sexual interactions between adults and minors, prompting legal action (Consumer Affairs, 2006). A moral panic concerning sexual predators quickly spread (Bahney, 2006), although research suggests that the concerns were exaggerated.[2]

A global phenomenon

While MySpace attracted the majority of media attention in the U.S. and abroad, SNSs were proliferating and growing in popularity worldwide. Friendster gained traction in the Pacific Islands, Orkut became the premier SNS in Brazil before growing rapidly in India (Madhavan, 2007), Mixi attained widespread adoption in Japan, LunarStorm took off in Sweden, Dutch users embraced Hyves, Grono captured Poland, Hi5 was adopted in smaller countries in Latin America, South America, and Europe, and Bebo became very popular in the United Kingdom, New Zealand, and Australia. Additionally, previously popular communication and community services began implementing SNS features. The Chinese QQ instant messaging service instantly became the largest SNS worldwide when it added profiles and made friends visible (McLeod, 2006), while the forum tool Cyworld cornered the Korean market by introducing homepages and buddies (Ewers, 2006).

Blogging services with complete SNS features also became popular. In the U.S., blogging tools with SNS features, such as Xanga, LiveJournal, and Vox, attracted broad audiences. Skyrock reigns in France, and Windows Live Spaces dominates numerous markets worldwide, including in Mexico, Italy, and Spain. Although SNSs like QQ, Orkut, and Live Spaces are just as large as, if not larger than, MySpace, they receive little coverage in U.S. and English-speaking media, making it difficult to track their trajectories.

Expanding niche communities

Alongside these open services, other SNSs launched to support niche demographics before expanding to a broader audience. Unlike previous SNSs, Facebook was designed to support distinct college networks only. Facebook began in early 2004 as a Harvard-only SNS (Cassidy, 2006). To join, a user had to have a harvard.edu email address. As Facebook began supporting other schools, those users were also required to have university email addresses associated with those institutions, a requirement that kept the site relatively closed and contributed to users' perceptions of the site as an intimate, private community.

Beginning in September 2005, Facebook expanded to include high school students, professionals inside corporate networks, and, eventually, everyone. The change to open signup did not mean that new users could easily access users in closed networks – gaining access to corporate networks still required the appropriate.com address, while gaining access to high school networks required administrator approval. (As of this writing, only membership in regional networks requires no permission.) Unlike other SNSs, Facebook users are unable to make their full profiles public to all users. Another feature that differentiates Facebook is the ability for outside developers to build "Applications" which allow users to personalize their profiles and perform other tasks, such as compare movie preferences and chart travel histories.

While most SNSs focus on growing broadly and exponentially, others explicitly seek narrower audiences. Some, like aSmallWorld and BeautifulPeople, intentionally restrict access to appear selective and elite. Others – activity-centered sites like Couchsurfing, identity-driven sites like BlackPlanet, and affiliation-focused sites like MyChurch – are limited by their target demographic and thus tend to be smaller. Finally, anyone who wishes to create a niche social network site can do so on Ning, a platform and hosting service that encourages users to create their own SNSs.

Currently, there are no reliable data regarding how many people use SNSs, although marketing research indicates that SNSs are growing in popularity worldwide (comScore, 2007). This growth has prompted many corporations to invest time and money in creating, purchasing, promoting, and advertising SNSs. At the same time, other companies are blocking their employees from accessing the sites. Additionally, the U.S. military banned soldiers from accessing MySpace (Frosch, 2007) and the Canadian government prohibited employees from Facebook (Benzie, 2007), while the U.S. Congress has proposed legislation to ban youth from accessing SNSs in schools and libraries (H.R. 5319, 2006; S. 49, 2007).

The rise of SNSs indicates a shift in the organization of online communities. While websites dedicated to communities of interest still exist and prosper, SNSs are primarily organized around people, not interests. Early public online communities such as Usenet and public discussion forums were structured by topics or according to topical hierarchies, but social network sites are structured as personal (or "egocentric") networks, with the individual at the center of their own community. This more accurately mirrors unmediated social structures, where "the world is composed of networks, not groups" (Wellman, 1988, p. 37). The introduction of SNS features has introduced a new organizational framework for online communities, and with it, a vibrant new research context.

Previous scholarship

Scholarship concerning SNSs is emerging from diverse disciplinary and methodological traditions, addresses a range of topics, and builds on a large body of CMC research. The goal of this section is to survey research that is directly concerned with social network sites, and in so doing, to set the stage for the articles in this special issue. To date, the bulk of SNS research has focused on impression management and friendship performance, networks and network structure, online/offline connections, and privacy issues.

Impression management and friendship performance

Like other online contexts in which individuals are consciously able to construct an online representation of self – such as online dating profiles and MUDS – SNSs constitute an important research context for scholars investigating processes of impression management, self-presentation, and friendship performance. In one of the earliest academic articles on SNSs, boyd (2004) examined Friendster as a locus of publicly articulated social networks that allowed users to negotiate presentations of self and connect with others. Donath and boyd (2004) extended this to suggest that "public displays of connection" serve as important identity signals that help people navigate the networked social world, in that an extended network may serve to validate identity information presented in profiles.

While most sites encourage users to construct accurate representations of themselves, participants do this to varying degrees. Marwick (2005) found that users on three different SNSs had complex strategies for negotiating the rigidity of a prescribed "authentic" profile, while boyd (in press-b) examined the phenomenon of "Fakesters" and argued that profiles could never be "real." The extent to which portraits are authentic or playful varies across sites; both social and technological forces shape user practices. Skog (2005) found that the status feature on LunarStorm strongly influenced how people behaved and what they choose to reveal – profiles there indicate one's status as measured by activity (e.g., sending messages) and indicators of authenticity (e.g., using a "real" photo instead of a drawing).

Another aspect of self-presentation is the articulation of friendship links, which serve as identity markers for the profile owner. Impression management is one of the reasons given by Friendster users for choosing particular friends (Donath & boyd, 2004). Recognizing this, Zinman and Donath (2007) noted that MySpace spammers leverage people's willingness to connect to interesting people to find targets for their spam.

In their examination of LiveJournal "friendship," Fono and Raynes-Goldie (2006) described users' understandings regarding public displays of connections and how the Friending function can operate as a catalyst for social drama. In listing user motivations for Friending, boyd (2006a) points out that "Friends" on SNSs are not the same as "friends" in the everyday sense; instead, Friends provide context by offering users an imagined audience to guide behavioral norms. Other work in this area has examined the use of Friendster Testimonials as self-presentational devices (boyd & Heer, 2006) and the extent to which the attractiveness of one's Friends (as indicated by Facebook's "Wall" feature) impacts impression formation (Walther, Van Der Heide, Kim, & Westerman, in press).

Networks and network structure

Social network sites also provide rich sources of naturalistic behavioral data. Profile and linkage data from SNSs can be gathered either through the use of automated collection techniques or through datasets provided directly from the company, enabling network analysis researchers to explore large-scale patterns of friending, usage, and other visible indicators (Hogan, in press), and continuing an analysis trend that started with examinations of blogs and other websites. For instance, Golder, Wilkinson, and Huberman (2007) examined an anonymized dataset consisting of 362 million messages exchanged by over four million Face-book users for insight into Friending and messaging activities. Lampe, Ellison, and Steinfield (2007) explored the relationship between profile elements and num-ber of Facebook friends, finding that profile fields that reduce transaction costs and are harder to falsify are most likely to be associated with larger number of friendship links. These kinds of data also lend themselves well to analysis through network visualization (Adamic, Buyukkokten, & Adar, 2003; Heer & boyd, 2005; Paolillo & Wright, 2005).

SNS researchers have also studied the network structure of Friendship. Ana-lyzing the roles people played in the growth of Flickr and Yahoo! 360's networks, Kumar, Novak, and Tomkins (2006) argued that there are passive members, inviters, and linkers "who fully participate in the social evolution of the network" (p. 1). Scholarship concerning LiveJournal's network has included a Friendship classification scheme (Hsu, Lancaster, Paradesi, & Weniger, 2007), an analysis of the role of language in the topology of Friendship (Herring et al., 2007), research into the importance of geography in Friending (Liben-Nowell, Novak, Kumar, Raghavan, and Tomkins, 2005), and studies on what motivates people to join par-ticular communities (Backstrom, Huttenlocher, Kleinberg, & Lan, 2006). Based on Orkut data, Spertus, Sahami, and Buyukkokten (2005) identified a topology of users through their membership in certain communities; they suggest that sites can use this to recommend additional communities of interest to users. Finally, Liu, Maes, and Davenport (2006) argued that Friend connections are not the only network structure worth investigating. They examined the ways in which the performance of tastes (favorite music, books, film, etc.) constitutes an alternate network structure, which they call a "taste fabric."

Bridging online and offline social networks

Although exceptions exist, the available research suggests that most SNSs pri-marily support pre-existing social relations. Ellison, Steinfield, and Lampe (2007) suggest that Facebook is used to maintain existing offline relationships or solidify offline connections, as opposed to meeting new people. These relationships may be weak ties, but typically there is some common offline element among indi-viduals who friend one another, such as a shared class at school. This is one of the chief dimensions that differentiate SNSs from earlier forms of public CMC such as newsgroups (Ellison et al., 2007). Research in this vein has investigated how online interactions interface with offline ones. For instance, Lampe, Ellison, and Steinfield (2006) found that Facebook users engage in "searching" for people with whom they have an offline connection more than they "browse" for complete strangers to meet. Likewise, Pew research found that 91% of U.S. teens who use SNSs do so to connect with friends (Lenhart & Madden, 2007).

Given that SNSs enable individuals to connect with one another, it is not surprising that they have become deeply embedded in users' lives. In Korea, Cyworld has become an integral part of everyday life – Choi (2006) found that

85% of that study's respondents "listed the maintenance and reinforcement of pre-existing social networks as their main motive for Cyworld use" (p. 181). Likewise, boyd (2008) argues that MySpace and Facebook enable U.S. youth to socialize with their friends even when they are unable to gather in unmediated situations; she argues that SNSs are "networked publics" that support sociability, just as unmediated public spaces do.

Privacy

Popular press coverage of SNSs has emphasized potential privacy concerns, primarily concerning the safety of younger users (George, 2006; Kornblum & Marklein, 2006). Researchers have investigated the potential threats to privacy associated with SNSs. In one of the first academic studies of privacy and SNSs, Gross and Acquisti (2005) analyzed 4,000 Carnegie Mellon University Facebook profiles and outlined the potential threats to privacy contained in the personal information included on the site by students, such as the potential ability to reconstruct users' social security numbers using information often found in profiles, such as hometown and date of birth.

Acquisti and Gross (2006) argue that there is often a disconnect between students' desire to protect privacy and their behaviors, a theme that is also explored in Stutzman's (2006) survey of Facebook users and Barnes's (2006) description of the "privacy paradox" that occurs when teens are not aware of the public nature of the Internet. In analyzing trust on social network sites, Dwyer, Hiltz, and Passerini (2007) argued that trust and usage goals may affect what people are willing to share – Facebook users expressed greater trust in Facebook than MySpace users did in MySpace and thus were more willing to share information on the site.

In another study examining security issues and SNSs, Jagatic, Johnson, Jakobsson, and Menczer (2007) used freely accessible profile data from SNSs to craft a "phishing" scheme that appeared to originate from a friend on the network; their targets were much more likely to give away information to this "friend" than to a perceived stranger. Survey data offer a more optimistic perspective on the issue, suggesting that teens are aware of potential privacy threats online and that many are proactive about taking steps to minimize certain potential risks. Pew found that 55% of online teens have profiles, 66% of whom report that their profile is not visible to all Internet users (Lenhart & Madden, 2007). Of the teens with completely open profiles, 46% reported including at least some false information.

Privacy is also implicated in users' ability to control impressions and manage social contexts. Boyd (in press-a) asserted that Facebook's introduction of the "News Feed" feature disrupted students' sense of control, even though data exposed through the feed were previously accessible. Preibusch, Hoser, Gürses, and Berendt (2007) argued that the privacy options offered by SNSs do not provide users with the flexibility they need to handle conflicts with Friends who have different conceptions of privacy; they suggest a framework for privacy in SNSs that they believe would help resolve these conflicts.

SNSs are also challenging legal conceptions of privacy. Hodge (2006) argued that the fourth amendment to the U.S. Constitution and legal decisions concerning privacy are not equipped to address social network sites. For example, do police officers have the right to access content posted to Facebook without a warrant? The legality of this hinges on users' expectation of privacy and whether or not Facebook profiles are considered public or private.

Other research

In addition to the themes identified above, a growing body of scholarship addresses other aspects of SNSs, their users, and the practices they enable. For example, scholarship on the ways in which race and ethnicity (Byrne, in press; Gajjala, 2007), religion (Nyland & Near, 2007), gender (Geidner, Flook, & Bell, 2007; Hjorth & Kim, 2005), and sexuality connect to, are affected by, and are enacted in social network sites raise interesting questions about how identity is shaped within these sites. Fragoso (2006) examined the role of national identity in SNS use through an investigation into the "Brazilian invasion" of Orkut and the resulting culture clash between Brazilians and Americans on the site. Other scholars are beginning to do cross-cultural comparisons of SNS use – Hjorth and Yuji (in press) compare Japanese usage of Mixi and Korean usage of Cyworld, while Herring et al. (2007) examine the practices of users who bridge different languages on LiveJournal – but more work in this area is needed.

Scholars are documenting the implications of SNS use with respect to schools, universities, and libraries. For example, scholarship has examined how students feel about having professors on Facebook (Hewitt & Forte, 2006) and how faculty participation affects student-professor relations (Mazer, Murphy, & Simonds, 2007). Charnigo and Barnett-Ellis (2007) found that librarians are overwhelmingly aware of Facebook and are against proposed U.S. legislation that would ban minors from accessing SNSs at libraries, but that most see SNSs as outside the purview of librarianship. Finally, challenging the view that there is nothing educational about SNSs, Perkel (in press) analyzed copy/paste practices on MySpace as a form of literacy involving social and technical skills.

This overview is not comprehensive due to space limitations and because much work on SNSs is still in the process of being published. Additionally, we have not included literature in languages other than English (e.g., Recuero, 2005 on social capital and Orkut), due to our own linguistic limitations.

Overview of this special theme section

The articles in this section address a variety of social network sites – BlackPlanet, Cyworld, Dodgeball, Facebook, MySpace, and YouTube – from multiple theoretical and methodological angles, building on previous studies of SNSs and broader theoretical traditions within CMC research, including relationship maintenance and issues of identity, performance, privacy, self-presentation, and civic engagement.

These pieces collectively provide insight into some of the ways in which online and offline experiences are deeply entwined. Using a relational dialectics approach, Kyung-Hee Kim and Haejin Yun analyze how Cyworld supports both interpersonal relations and self-relation for Korean users. They trace the subtle ways in which deeply engrained cultural beliefs and activities are integrated into online communication and behaviors on Cyworld – the online context reinforces certain aspects of users' cultural expectations about relationship maintenance (e.g., the concept of reciprocity), while the unique affordances of Cyworld enable participants to overcome offline constraints. Dara Byrne uses content analysis to examine civic engagement in forums on BlackPlanet and finds that online discussions are still plagued with the problems offline activists have long encountered. Drawing on interview and observation data, Lee Humphreys investigates early adopters' practices involving Dodgeball, a mobile social network service. She looks at the ways in which networked communication is reshaping offline social geography.

Other articles in this collection illustrate how innovative research methods can elucidate patterns of behavior that would be indistinguishable otherwise. For instance, Hugo Liu examines participants' performance of tastes and interests by analyzing and modeling the preferences listed on over 127,000 MySpace profiles, resulting in unique "taste maps." Likewise, through survey data collected at a college with diverse students in the U.S., Eszter Hargittai illuminates usage patterns that would otherwise be masked. She finds that adoption of particular services correlates with individuals' race and parental education level.

Existing theory is deployed, challenged, and extended by the approaches adopted in the articles in this section. Judith Donath extends signaling theory to explain different tactics SNS users adopt to reduce social costs while managing trust and identity. She argues that the construction and maintenance of relations on SNSs is akin to "social grooming." Patricia Lange complicates traditional dichotomies between "public" and "private" by analyzing how YouTube participants blur these lines in their video-sharing practices.

The articles in this collection highlight the significance of social network sites in the lives of users and as a topic of research. Collectively, they show how networked practices mirror, support, and alter known everyday practices, especially with respect to how people present (and hide) aspects of themselves and connect with others. The fact that participation on social network sites leaves online traces offers unprecedented opportunities for researchers. The scholarship in this special theme section takes advantage of this affordance, resulting in work that helps explain practices online and offline, as well as those that blend the two environments.

Future research

The work described above and included in this special theme section contributes to an on-going dialogue about the importance of social network sites, both for practitioners and researchers. Vast, uncharted waters still remain to be explored.

Methodologically, SNS researchers' ability to make causal claims is limited by a lack of experimental or longitudinal studies. Although the situation is rapidly changing, scholars still have a limited understanding of who is and who is not using these sites, why, and for what purposes, especially outside the U.S. Such questions will require large-scale quantitative and qualitative research. Richer, ethnographic research on populations more difficult to access (including non-users) would further aid scholars' ability to understand the long-term implications of these tools. We hope that the work described here and included in this collection will help build a foundation for future investigations of these and other important issues surrounding social network sites.

Acknowledgments

We are grateful to the external reviewers who volunteered their time and expertise to review papers and contribute valuable feedback and to those practitioners and analysts who provided information to help shape the history section. Thank you also to Susan Herring, whose patience and support appeared infinite.

About the authors

danah m. boyd is a Ph.D. candidate in the School of Information at the University of California-Berkeley and a Fellow at the Harvard University Berkman Center for Internet and Society. Her research focuses on how people negotiate mediated contexts like social network sites for sociable purposes.

Address: 102 South Hall, Berkeley, CA 94720–4600, USA.

Nicole B. Ellison is an assistant professor in the Department of Telecommunication, Information Studies, and Media at Michigan State University. Her research explores issues of self-presentation, relationship development, and identity in online environments such as weblogs, online dating sites, and social network sites.

Address: 403 Communication Arts and Sciences, East Lansing, MI 48824, USA.

Notes

1 To differentiate the articulated list of Friends on SNSs from the colloquial term "friends," we capitalize the former.
2 Although one out of seven teenagers received unwanted sexual solicitations online, only 9% came from people over the age of 25 (Wolak, Mitchell, & Finkelhor, 2006). Research suggests that popular narratives around sexual predators on SNSs are misleading – cases of unsuspecting teens being lured by sexual predators are rare (Finkelhor, Ybarra, Lenhart, boyd, & Lordan, 2007). Furthermore, only .08% of students surveyed by the National School Boards Association (2007) met someone in person from an online encounter without permission from a parent.

References

Acquisti, A., & Gross, R. (2006). Imagined communities: Awareness, information sharing, and privacy on the Facebook. In P. Golle & G. Danezis (Eds.), *Proceedings of 6th Workshop on Privacy Enhancing Technologies* (pp. 36–58). Cambridge, UK: Robinson College.

Adamic, L. A., Büyükkökten, O., & Adar, E. (2003). A social network caught in the Web. *First Monday*, 8(6). Retrieved July 30, 2007 from http://www.firstmonday. org/issues/issue8_6/adamic/index.html.

Backstrom, L., Huttenlocher, D., Kleinberg, J., & Lan, X. (2006). Group formation in large social networks: Membership, growth, and evolution. *Proceedings of 12th International Conference on Knowledge Discovery in Data Mining* (pp. 44–54). New York: ACM Press.

Bahney, A. (2006, March 9). Don't talk to invisible strangers. *New York Times*. Retrieved July 21, 2007 from http://www.nytimes.com/2006/03/09/fashion/thursdaystyles/ 09parents.html.

Barnes, S. (2006). A privacy paradox: Social networking in the United States. *First Monday*, 11(9). Retrieved September 8, 2007 from http://www.firstmonday.org/ issues/issue11_9/barnes/index.html.

BBC. (2005, July 19). *News Corp in $580m Internet buy*. Retrieved July 21, 2007 from http://news.bbc.co.uk/2/hi/business/4695495.stm.

Benzie, R. (2007, May 3). Facebook banned for Ontario staffers. *The Star*. Retrieved July 21, 2007 from http://www.thestar.com/News/article/210014.

boyd, d. (2004). Friendster and publicly articulated social networks. *Proceedings of ACM Conference on Human Factors in Computing Systems* (pp. 1279–1282). New York: ACM Press.

boyd, d. (2006a). Friends, Friendsters, and MySpace Top 8: Writing community into being on social network sites. *First Monday*, 11(12). Retrieved July 21, 2007 from http://www.firstmonday.org/issues/issue11_12/boyd/

boyd, d. (2006b, March 21). Friendster lost steam. Is MySpace just a fad? *Apophenia Blog*. Retrieved July 21, 2007 from http://www.danah.org/papers/ FriendsterMy SpaceEssay.html.

boyd, d. (in press-a). Facebook's privacy trainwreck: Exposure, invasion, and social convergence. *Convergence*, **14**(1).

boyd, d. (in press-b). None of this is real. In J. Karaganis (Ed.), *Structures of Participation*. New York: Social Science Research Council.

boyd, d. (2008). Why youth (heart) social network sites: The role of networked publics in teenage social life. In D. Buckingham (Ed.), *Youth, Identity, and Digital Media* (pp. 119–142). Cambridge, MA: MIT Press.

boyd, d., & Heer, J. (2006). Profiles as conversation: Networked identity performance on Friendster. *Proceedings of Thirty-Ninth Hawai'i International Conference on System Sciences*. Los Alamitos, CA: IEEE Press.

Byrne, D. (in press). The future of (the) 'race': Identity, discourse and the rise of computer-mediated public spheres. In A. Everett (Ed.), *MacArthur Foundation Book Series on Digital Learning: Race and Ethnicity Volume* (pp. 15–38). Cambridge, MA: MIT Press.

Cassidy, J. (2006, May 15). Me media: How hanging out on the Internet became big business. *The New Yorker*, **82**(13), 50.

Chafkin, M. (2007, June). How to kill a great idea! *Inc. Magazine*. Retrieved August 27, 2007 from http://www.inc.com/magazine/20070601/features-how-to-kill-a-great-idea.html.

Charnigo, L., & Barnett-Ellis, P. (2007). Checking out Facebook.com: The impact of a digital trend on academic libraries. *Information Technology and Libraries*, **26**(1), 23.

Choi, J. H. (2006). Living in *Cyworld*: Contextualising Cy-Ties in South Korea. In A. Bruns & J. Jacobs (Eds.), *Use of Blogs (Digital Formations)* (pp. 173–186). New York: Peter Lang.

Cohen, R. (2003, July 5). Livewire: Web sites try to make internet dating less creepy. *Reuters*. Retrieved July 5, 2003 from http://asia.reuters.com/newsArticle.jhtml?type=internetNews&storyID=3041934.

comScore. (2007). Social networking goes global. Reston, VA. Retrieved September 9, 2007 from http://www.comscore.com/press/release.asp?press=1555.

Consumer Affairs. (2006, February 5). Connecticut opens MySpace.com probe. *Consumer Affairs*. Retrieved July 21, 2007 from http://www.consumeraffairs.com/news04/2006/02/myspace.html.

Donath, J., & boyd, d. (2004). Public displays of connection. *BT Technology Journal*, 22(4), 71–82.

Dwyer, C., Hiltz, S. R., & Passerini, K. (2007). Trust and privacy concern within social networking sites: A comparison of Facebook and MySpace. *Proceedings of AMCIS 2007*, Keystone, CO. Retrieved September 21, 2007 from http://csis.pace.edu/~dwyer/research/DwyerAMCIS2007.pdf.

Ellison, N., Steinfield, C., & Lampe, C. (2007). The benefits of Facebook "friends": Exploring the relationship between college students' use of online social networks and social capital. *Journal of Computer-Mediated Communication*, **12**(3), article 1. Retrieved July 30, 2007 from http://jcmc.indiana.edu/vol12/issue4/ellison.html.

Ewers, J. (2006, November 9). Cyworld: Bigger than YouTube? *U.S. News & World Report*. Retrieved July 30, 2007 from *LexisNexis*.

Festa, P. (2003, November 11). Investors snub Friendster in patent grab. *CNet News*. Retrieved August 26, 2007 from http://news.com.com/2100-1032_3-5106136.html.

Finkelhor, D., Ybarra, M., Lenhart, A., boyd, d., & Lordan, T. (2007, May 3). Just the facts about online youth victimization: Researchers present the facts and debunk myths. *Internet Caucus Advisory Committee Event*. Retrieved July 21, 2007 from http://www.netcaucus.org/events/2007/youth/20070503transcript.pdf.

Fono, D., & Raynes-Goldie, K. (2006). Hyperfriendship and beyond: Friends and social norms on LiveJournal. In M. Consalvo & C. Haythornthwaite (Eds.), *Internet Research Annual Volume 4: Selected Papers from the AOIR Conference* (pp. 91–103). New York: Peter Lang.

Fragoso, S. (2006). WTF a crazy Brazilian invasion. In F. Sudweeks & H. Hrachovec (Eds.), *Proceedings of CATaC 2006* (pp. 255–274). Murdoch, Australia: Murdoch University.

Frosch, D. (2007, May 15). Pentagon blocks 13 web sites from military computers. *New York Times*. Retrieved July 21, 2007 from http://www.nytimes.com/2007/05/15/washington/15block.html.

Gajjala, R. (2007). Shifting frames: Race, ethnicity, and intercultural communication in online social networking and virtual work. In M. B. Hinner (Ed.), *The Role of*

Communication in Business Transactions and Relationships (pp. 257–276). New York: Peter Lang.

Geidner, N. W., Flook, C. A., & Bell, M. W. (2007, April). *Masculinity and online social networks: Male self-identification on Facebook.com.* Paper presented at Eastern Communication Association 98th Annual Meeting, Providence, RI.

George, A. (2006, September 18). Living online: The end of privacy? *New Scientist*, 2569. Retrieved August 29, 2007 from http://www.newscientist.com/channel/tech/mg19125691.700-living-online-the-end-of-privacy.html.

Goldberg, S. (2007, May 13). Analysis: Friendster is doing just fine. *Digital Media Wire*. Retrieved July 30, 2007 from http://www.dmwmedia.com/news/2007/05/14/analysis-friendster-is-doing-just-fine.

Golder, S. A., Wilkinson, D., & Huberman, B. A. (2007, June). Rhythms of social interaction: Messaging within a massive online network. In C. Steinfield, B. Pentland, M. Ackerman, & N. Contractor (Eds.), *Proceedings of Third International Conference on Communities and Technologies* (pp. 41–66). London: Springer.

Gross, R., & Acquisti, A. (2005). Information revelation and privacy in online social networks. *Proceedings of WPES'05* (pp. 71–80). Alexandria, VA: ACM.

Haythornthwaite, C. (2005). Social networks and Internet connectivity effects. *Information, Communication, & Society*, **8**(2), 125–147.

Heer, J., & boyd, d. (2005). Vizster: Visualizing online social networks. *Proceedings of Symposium on Information Visualization* (pp. 33–40). Minneapolis, MN: IEEE Press.

Herring, S. C., Paolillo, J. C., Ramos Vielba, I., Kouper, I., Wright, E., Stoerger, S., Scheidt, L. A., & Clark, B. (2007). Language networks on LiveJournal. *Proceedings of the Fortieth Hawai'i International Conference on System Sciences*. Los Alamitos, CA: IEEE Press.

Hewitt, A., & Forte, A. (2006, November). *Crossing boundaries: Identity management and student/faculty relationships on the Facebook.* Poster presented at CSCW, Banff, Alberta.

Hjorth, L., & Kim, H. (2005). Being there and being here: Gendered customising of mobile 3G practices through a case study in Seoul. *Convergence*, **11**(2), 49–55.

Hjorth, L., & Yuji, M. (in press). Logging on locality: A cross-cultural case study of virtual communities Mixi (Japan) and Mini-hompy (Korea). In B. Smaill (Ed.), *Youth and Media in the Asia Pacific*. Cambridge, UK: Cambridge University Press.

Hodge, M. J. (2006). The Fourth Amendment and privacy issues on the "new" Internet: Facebook.com and MySpace.com. *Southern Illinois University Law Journal*, 31, 95–122.

Hogan, B. (in press). Analyzing social networks via the Internet. In N. Fielding, R. Lee, & G. Blank (Eds.), *Sage Handbook of Online Research Methods*. Thousand Oaks, CA: Sage.

H. R. 5319. (2006, May 9). *Deleting Online Predators Act of 2006*. H.R. 5319, 109th Congress. Retrieved July 21, 2007 from http://www.govtrack.us/congress/billtext.xpd?bill=h109-5319.

Hsu, W. H., Lancaster, J., Paradesi, M. S. R., & Weninger, T. (2007). Structural link analysis from user profiles and friends networks: A feature construction approach. *Proceedings of ICWSM-2007* (pp. 75–80). Boulder, CO.

Jagatic, T., Johnson, N., Jakobsson, M., & Menczer, F. (2007). Social phishing. *Communications of the ACM*, **5**(10), 94–100.

Kopytoff, V. (2004, November 29). Google's orkut puzzles experts. San Francisco Chronicle. Retrieved July 30, 2007 from http://www.sfgate.com/cgi-bin/article.cgi?f=/ c/a/2004/11/29/BUGU9A0BH441.DTL.

Kornblum, J., & Marklein, M. B. (2006, March 8). What you say online could haunt you. USA Today. Retrieved August 29, 2007 from http://www.usatoday. com/tech/news/internetprivacy/2006-03-08-facebook-myspace_x.htm.

Kumar, R., Novak, J., & Tomkins, A. (2006). Structure and evolution of online social networks. *Proceedings of 12th International Conference on Knowledge Discovery in Data Mining* (pp. 611–617). New York: ACM Press.

Lampe, C., Ellison, N., & Steinfield, C. (2006). A Face(book) in the crowd: Social searching vs. social browsing. *Proceedings of CSCW-2006* (pp. 167–170). New York: ACM Press.

Lampe, C., Ellison, N., & Steinfeld, C. (2007). A familiar Face(book): Profile elements as signals in an online social network. *Proceedings of Conference on Human Factors in Computing Systems* (pp. 435–444). New York: ACM Press.

Lenhart, A., & Madden, M. (2007, April 18). Teens, privacy, & online social networks. *Pew Internet and American Life Project Report*. Retrieved July 30, 2007 from http://www.pewinternet.org/pdfs/PIP_Teens_Privacy_SNS_Report_Final.pdf.

Liben-Nowell, D., Novak, J., Kumar, R., Raghavan, P., & Tomkins, A. (2005) Geographic routing in social networks. *Proceedings of National Academy of Sciences*, **102**(33) 11,623–11,628.

Liu, H., Maes, P., & Davenport, G. (2006). Unraveling the taste fabric of social networks. *International Journal on Semantic Web and Information Systems*, **2**(1), 42–71.

Madhavan, N. (2007, July 6). India gets more Net Cool. *Hindustan Times*. Retrieved July 30, 2007 from http://www.hindustantimes.com/StoryPage/StoryPage. aspx?id=f2565bb8-663e-48c1-94ee-d99567577bdd.

Marwick, A. (2005, October). *"I'm a lot more interesting than a Friendster profile:" Identity presentation, authenticity, and power in social networking services.* Paper presented at Internet Research 6.0, Chicago, IL.

Mazer, J. P., Murphy, R. E., & Simonds, C. J. (2007). I'll see you on "Facebook:" The effects of computer-mediated teacher self-disclosure on student motivation, affective learning, and classroom climate. *Communication Education*, **56**(1), 1–17.

McLeod, D. (2006, October 6). QQ Attracting eyeballs. *Financial Mail (South Africa)*, p. 36. Retrieved July 30, 2007 from *LexisNexis*.

National School Boards Association. (2007, July). *Creating and connecting: Research and guidelines on online social – and educational – networking.* Alexandria, VA. Retrieved September 23, 2007 from http://www.nsba.org/site/docs/41400/41340.pdf.

Nyland, R., & Near, C. (2007, February). *Jesus is my friend: Religiosity as a mediating factor in Internet social networking use.* Paper presented at AEJMC Midwinter Conference, Reno, NV.

O'Shea, W. (2003, July 4–10). Six Degrees of sexual frustration: Connecting the dates with Friendster.com. *Village Voice*. Retrieved July 21, 2007 from http://www.villagevoice.com/news/0323,oshea, 44576, 1.html.

Paolillo, J. C., & Wright, E. (2005). Social network analysis on the semantic web: Techniques and challenges for visualizing FOAF. In V. Geroimenko & C. Chen (Eds.), *Visualizing the Semantic Web* (pp. 229–242). Berlin: Springer.

Perkel, D. (in press). Copy and paste literacy? Literacy practices in the production of a MySpace profile. In K. Drotner, H. S. Jensen, & K. Schroeder (Eds.), *Informal Learning and Digital Media: Constructions, Contexts, Consequences.* Newcastle, UK: Cambridge Scholars Press.

Preibusch, S., Hoser, B., Gürses, S., & Berendt, B. (2007, June). Ubiquitous social networks – opportunities and challenges for privacy-aware user modelling. *Proceedings of Workshop on Data Mining for User Modeling. Corfu, Greece.* Retrieved October 20, 2007 from http://vasarely.wiwi.hu-berlin.de/DM.UM07/Proceedings/05-Preibusch.pdf.

Recuero, R. (2005). O capital social em redes sociais na Internet. *Revista FAMECOS,* **28**, 88–106. Retrieved September 13, 2007 from http://www.pucrs.br/famecos/pos/revfamecos/28/raquelrecuero.pdf.

S. 49. (2007, January 4). *Protecting Children in the 21st Century Act.* S. 49, 110th Congress. Retrieved July 30, 2007 from http://thomas.loc.gov/cgi-bin/query/F?c110:1:./temp/~c110dJQpcy:e445:

Shirky, C. (2003, May 13). People on page: YASNS... *Corante's Many-to-Many.* Retrieved July 21, 2007 from http://many.corante.com/archives/2003/05/12/people_on_page_yasns.php.

Skog, D. (2005). Social interaction in virtual communities: The significance of technology. *International Journal of Web Based Communities,* **1**(4), 464–474.

Spertus, E., Sahami, M., & Buyukkokten, O. (2005). Evaluating similarity measures: A large-scale study in the orkut social network. *Proceedings of 11th International Conference on Knowledge Discovery in Data Mining* (pp. 678–684). New York: ACM Press.

Stutzman, F. (2006). An evaluation of identity-sharing behavior in social network communities. *Journal of the International Digital Media and Arts Association,* **3**(1), 10–18.

Sundén, J. (2003). *Material Virtualities.* New York: Peter Lang.

Walther, J. B., Van Der Heide, B., Kim, S. Y., & Westerman, D. (in press). The role of friends' appearance and behavior on evaluations of individuals on Facebook: Are we known by the company we keep? *Human Communication Research.*

Wellman, B. (1988). Structural analysis: From method and metaphor to theory and substance. In B. Wellman & S. D. Berkowitz (Eds.), *Social Structures: A Network Approach* (pp. 19–61). Cambridge, UK: Cambridge University Press.

Wolak, J., Mitchell, K., & Finkelhor, D. (2006). Online victimization of youth: Five years later. *Report from Crimes Against Children Research Center, University of New Hampshire.* Retrieved July 21, 2007 from http://www.unh.edu/ccrc/pdf/CV138.pdf.

Zinman, A., & Donath, J. (2007, August). *Is Britney Spears spam?* Paper presented at the Fourth Conference on Email and Anti-Spam, Mountain View, CA.

Index

Page numbers in *italics* denotes a table/diagram